"In today's media-rich environment, pr
of a nation's foreign policy, particularly
and institutions are involved in construc‌ ‌ ‌ ‌ ‌‌‌‌‌‌auves, and Miskimmon, O'Loughlin, and Roselle present perceptive analysis of how this process works. Strategic Narratives is invaluable reading for those wanting to
understand modern diplomacy."

—Philip Seib, University of Southern California

"This fascinating book is both theoretically and empirically rich. The authors
demonstrate how strategic narratives are used to persuade and interpret, how
they may be contested or formed as uncontested, and how they shape the
interactions of diverse actors in the international environment. They illustrate these dynamics in relation to cases as diverse as the 'Rise of China'
narrative in the U.S., the 'David and Goliath' narrative in Israel, and the anti-
whaling narratives of activists in the 1960s. A must read for students and
practitioners who want to understand public diplomacy in the media age."

—K.M. Fierke, University of St. Andrews

Strategic Narratives

Communication is central to how we understand international affairs. Political leaders, diplomats, and citizens recognize that communication shapes global politics. This has only been amplified in a new media environment characterized by Internet access to information, social media, and the transformation of who can communicate and how. Soft power, public diplomacy 2.0, network power—scholars and policymakers are concerned with understanding what is happening.

This book is the first to develop a systematic framework to understand how political actors seek to shape order through narrative projection in this new environment. To explain the changing world order—the rise of the BRICS, the dilemmas of climate change, poverty, and terrorism, the intractability of conflict—the authors explore how actors form and project narratives and how third parties interpret and interact with these narratives. The concept of strategic narrative draws together the most salient of international relations concepts, including the links between power and ideas; international and domestic; and state and nonstate actors. The book is anchored around four themes: order, actors, uncertainty, and contestation. Through these, *Strategic Narratives* shows both the possibilities and the limits of communication and power, and makes an important contribution to theorizing and studying empirically contemporary international relations.

Alister Miskimmon is head of the Department of Politics and International Relations at Royal Holloway, University of London. His research interests include strategic narratives, security studies, European integration, and German foreign policy.

Ben O'Loughlin is professor of International Relations and codirector of the New Political Communication Unit at Royal Holloway, University of London. He is coeditor of the journal *Media, War & Conflict*. He is specialist adviser to the UK House of Lords Select Committee on Soft Power and the UK's Influence.

Laura Roselle is professor of political science at Elon University and visiting professor of public policy at Duke University. She is president of the Information Technology and Politics section of the American Political Science Association (2012–2013), and is coeditor of the journal *Media, War & Conflict*.

Routledge Studies in Global Information, Politics, and Society

**Edited by Kenneth Rogerson, Duke University; and
Laura Roselle, Elon University**

International communication encompasses everything from one-to-one cross-cultural interactions to the global reach of a broad range of information and communications technologies and processes. *Routledge Studies in Global Information, Politics, and Society* celebrates—and embraces—this depth and breadth. To completely understand communication, it must be studied in concert with many factors, since, most often, it is the foundational principle on which other subjects rest. This series provides a publishing space for scholarship in the expansive, yet intersecting, categories of communication and information processes and other disciplines.

Strategic Narratives

Communication Power and
the New World Order

**Alister Miskimmon, Ben O'Loughlin,
and Laura Roselle**

NEW YORK AND LONDON

First published 2013
by Routledge
711 Third Avenue, New York, NY 10017

Simultaneously published in the UK
by Routledge
2 Park Square, Milton Park, Abingdon, Oxon OX14 4RN

*Routledge is an imprint of the Taylor & Francis Group,
an informa business*

Library of Congress Cataloging-in-Publication Data

Miskimmon, Alister.
Strategic narratives : communication power and the new world order /
    Alister Miskimmon, Ben O'Loughlin, Laura Roselle.
        pages cm. — (Routledge studies in global information, politics
and society ; 3)
    1. Communication in politics.   2. Mass media.   3. Social media.
4. International relations.   5. Social policy.   I. O'Loughlin, Ben, 1976–
II. Roselle, Laura.   III. Title.
    JA85.M54 2013
    327.101′4—dc23
    2013021539

ISBN: 978-0-415-71760-1 (hbk)
ISBN: 978-0-415-72188-2 (pbk)
ISBN: 978-1-315-87126-4 (ebk)

Typeset in Sabon
by Apex CoVantage, LLC

Printed and bound in the United States of America by Publishers Graphics,
LLC on sustainably sourced paper.

Contents

Tables

Preface

We began by thinking about power transitions. All modern transitions from one world order to the next have involved major international conflict. We started to talk about strategic narratives in 2007. News reports at the time told us of a shifting balance of power from West to East, from the US and the EU to the BRICS and "the rest". We were struck that international relations theory would tell us to expect a fundamental, systemic war, the victors deciding on the nature of the next phase of world order. We asked whether any of the great powers could create a narrative about that future order that they could all buy into. Could a compelling narrative make World War III unnecessary?

Naïve perhaps, but this was a time when leaders were spending a great deal of effort legitimizing big ideas in international relations through narratives. The war on terror presented a cast of heroes and villains, the trigger of 9/11, the battle for hearts and minds, and projections of victory only after a generational struggle. The war on terror narrative was used to justify a wholesale reordering of domestic and international politics. Then the global financial system collapsed. Politicians and media again presented publics around the world with a sequence of events around which blame could be attached and a happy ending projected, but one that would demand sacrifice, austerity, and—in this case—no wholesale policy changes. Through these narratives of security and economy, political leaders tried to shape the experience of living through these years. They used narratives strategically to create commonsense understandings of the past, present, and future, in order to garner legitimacy for particular and highly contestable policy responses.

These strategic narratives rarely succeeded. One must always assume that communication will fail; people are hard to convince. But a rapidly shifting media ecology was making it more and more difficult for leaders to control their narratives and even know whom they were addressing. International relations depend on communication, and communication was beginning to work in different ways. This book is about how leaders try to use narratives strategically in this challenging context. It is a context that promises greater speed, reach, and engagement in international communication but actually creates new anxieties, vulnerabilities, and risks at the same time. Nevertheless, political leaders have no choice but to try to create a consensus around their narrative. Given the violent precedent of past power transitions, we think they should have no choice but to try.

Acknowledgements

This book has resulted from a series of conversations with extremely help-ful, curious and very knowledgeable people over a number of years. The initial idea of strategic narrative was conceived with Andreas Antoniades, University of Sussex. With his insight and energy we ran our first work-shop on strategic narrative in New York in 2009, generously funded by the International Studies Association (ISA). This led to a working paper, "Great Power Politics and Strategic Narratives," published by the University of Sussex. Andreas was central to the progress of this project and we wish to acknowledge his part in the development of our ideas.

These ideas have been refined through a series of conferences on strate-gic narrative. The Reframing the Nation conference in London 2009 was co-convened with Marie Gillespie and the ESRC Centre for Research on Socio-Cultural Change (CRESC). Marie gave a tremendous amount of time and reflection to the project and we were delighted to discover the range of scholarly work being carried out on identity, media, and global poli-tics. Ideas were further developed through two working groups in the US and Sweden. Enormous thanks are due to the program chairs of both the Political Communication section of the American Political Science Associa-tion (APSA) 2010 convention in Washington DC and the 2010 Standing Group in IR (SGIR) convention in Stockholm. APSA's Richard Davis and the SGIR's Andreas Nölke and Antje Wiener allowed us to convene several days of scholarly discussion tackling the role of strategic narrative in different issue areas and parts of the world. We have also presented chapters at the University of Potsdam, the Norwegian Institute for Defence Studies, Oslo, Norwegian Atlantic Committee, Oslo, University of Sydney, the Australian National University, Elon University, the University of Leeds, King's Col-lege London, the University of Hamburg, the Annenberg-Oxford summer school, the University of Oxford, the Diplomatic Academy of Vienna, Royal Holloway, University of London, and at ISA, British International Studies Association (BISA), and APSA in 2011, 2012, and 2013.

Many people have contributed to the emergence of this book through commenting on written work, stimulating our thinking through discussions about the strategic narrative thesis and providing support and enthusiasm during the writing process. These include Helen Adair, Richard Anderson, Cristina Archetti, Amelia Arsenault, Michelle Bentley, Felix Berenskoetter, David Betz, Robin Brown, Bob Boynton, Andrew Chadwick, Felix Ciuta, Stephen Coleman, Nick Cull, Chiara de Franco, Charlotte Epstein, Federica Ferrari, Karin Fierke, Kathy Fitzpatrick, Sir Lawrence Freedman, Iginio Gagliardone, Bastian Giegerich, Marie Gillespie, Ben Goldsmith, James Gow, Lene Hansen, Simon Haselock, Andrew Hoskins, Jason Kirk, Michael Kuchinsky, Steven Livingston, Sarah Logan, Fritz Mayer, Allan McConnell, Ellen Mickiewicz, Marissa Moran, Sarah Oates, Donna Marie Oglesby, Monroe Price, Ken Rogerson, Vivien Schmidt, Philip Seib, David Smith, Sir Rupert Smith, Sharon Spray, Nicole Stremlau, Safia Swimelar, Cameron Thies, Antje Wiener, Colin Wight, and Jan Zielonka.

Much of Miskimmon and O'Loughlin's work has been supported by the Centre for European Politics and the New Political Communication Unit at Royal Holloway, University of London. Roselle's work has been supported by the award of a Senior Faculty Fellowship at Elon University.

We are grateful for the terrific work of Darcy Bullock and the editorial team at Routledge, Series Editor Ken Rogerson for his support of the project, and the anonymous reviewers. We would also like to thank Luuk Molthof for his assistance in the preparation of the manuscript.

Series Editor Foreword

There is difference between what narratives *are* and what narratives *do*. From the choice of specific words to put context around a moment, such as "Obamacare," to overarching stories that underscore the rationale for a series of actions, such as "weapons of mass destruction," narratives matter.

We begin this book by taking the time to understand what those narratives are. We are greatly appreciative when scholars undertake to explain why they work the way do, under what conditions they are used (and not), and when they can be manipulated and molded for personal, national and international gain.

Miskimmon, O'Loughlin, and Roselle offer exactly this type of explanation, pushing us beyond just knowing what the narratives are. Melding historical cases with contemporary events, we understand that narrative formation and development does not take place in a vacuum. On the contrary, the impact of strategic narratives may be wider than we imagined.

—Kenneth Rogerson, Series Editor

1   Introduction

Something interesting has been happening at the intersection of international relations and communication in the early twenty-first century, an ineffable sense that how international relations is done, by whom, and what it involves, are all being disrupted by new media ecologies. We argue in this book that narrative, how it is both formed and projected in a communication environment, helps explain the major dynamics in international affairs. Underlying this argument are three points. First, narratives are central to human relations; they shape our world and constrain behavior. Second, political actors attempt to use narratives strategically. Third, our communication environment fundamentally affects how narratives are communicated and flow, and with what effects. This book is about strategic narratives in the twenty-first-century media ecology.

International relations (IR) scholars have not fully incorporated the communication of narratives into broader theoretical arguments about structure, agency, and the construction of order in the international system. This work contributes to the remedy of this deficit by looking substantively, theoretically, and practically at strategic narratives. Driving this study is an attempt to understand the changing world in which we live. The end of global wars in 1918 and 1945 proved to be critical junctures, points in which actors wielded power to construct new international orders. The end of the Cold War appeared to be another juncture in which a new world order would be built. However, power has become more diffuse in the world and we propose that a changing communications environment makes it far more difficult for leading powers to justify and implement their strategic narrative so as to define the international system. Understanding dynamics of continuity and change in the world will depend on the degree of narrative alignment between powerful economic and political actors. Power transition has traditionally been understood to involve violence, replacing one order with another,[1] with new ideas triumphing over old.[2] Projecting an accepted strategic narrative of a new world order will be key to whether this current period of transition can remain largely peaceful.

In considering how the communication of narratives allows actors to manage this transition, an important starting point for our study has been

Manuel Castells' recent work *Communication Power*.[3] Castells' contribution is vital because he understands how power relationships work through communication. He investigates how the operation of power is being reconfigured by what he famously chronicled as "network society."[4] In network society, media technologies enable new networked patterns of relations in economic, social, and political life and new ways of relating to one another. By the 2000s, the chief change Castells identified was the emergence of "mass self-communication."[5] The Internet and social media meant the ability to broadcast and narrate to many was no longer the preserve of elites, but something anybody could potentially try. The implication of Castells' analysis is that communication changes how power works. New networks of communication formed in the 2000s that seemed to upset previous flows that elites had learnt to manage. This allowed new forms of social and political organization, symbolized by waves of protest and uprisings in 2011,[6] and created a sense of anxiety and vulnerability among the big powers of international relations,[7] triggering a range of attempts to find ways to control global communication, some deft and some heavy-handed. Castells' study of how political actors project narratives to achieve goals in international relations within network society is limited; he looks at the narrative used by the US administration before the 2003 Iraq War to legitimize its intervention[8] and narratives of grievance in the Arab Spring,[9] and his value lies in a single but profound theoretical move. Castells makes the connection between a changing communications environment and a change to how politics works. A focus on networks and communication does not imply we throw out the study of political institutions and material power. Instead, it points to the manner in which political institutions and material power are deeply enmeshed in networks and communication. Castells' theory of communication power gets at that ineffable sense that international relations is being disrupted by changing media ecologies.

Strategic narratives are a means for political actors to construct a shared meaning of the past, present, and future of international politics to shape the behavior of domestic and international actors. Strategic narratives are a tool for political actors to extend their influence, manage expectations, and change the discursive environment in which they operate. They are narratives about both states and the system itself, both about who we are and what kind of order we want. The point of strategic narratives is to influence the behavior of others. In the short term, Freedman writes, "Narratives are designed or nurtured with the intention of structuring the responses of others to developing events."[10] But in the long term, getting others at home and abroad to buy in to your strategic narrative can shape their interests, their identity, and their understanding of how international relations works and where it is heading. A recent influential publication written by two serving US servicemen called for a national strategic narrative to chart the uncertain future facing US foreign policy.[11] In the preface to the publication, Anne-Marie Slaughter argues[12]:

> A narrative is a story. A national strategic narrative must be a story that
> all Americans can understand and identify with in their own lives. . . .
> We seek . . . to be the nation other nations listen to, rely on and emulate
> out of respect and admiration.[13]

Slaughter's focus is on the need for an overarching national narrative. This
links with Nye's influential concept of soft power. Central to Nye's initial
formulation was a concern to forge a new US narrative of international affairs to give meaning to the post–Cold War era and help foreign policy makers navigate their way through this new order. Debate in the US centered on
Nye's contention that hard power was not enough to shape the world after
the fall of the Berlin Wall. Nye called for greater strategic engagement by the
US to address potential instability in the system and to ensure continued US
dominance after the demise of the Soviet Union.[14] Power, according to Nye,
rests on attraction as well as coercion, a theme also present in Morgenthau's
work.[15] This debate was mirrored in the European Union (EU). Leaders there
tried to understand what defined the EU's growing international standing,
despite its lack of formal hard power capabilities. Manners' concept of Normative Power Europe suggested that the emulation of the EU's normative
foundations was central to its international influence.[16] There has also been
much debate in Europe about how "to *convince* [non-Europeans] of the benefits of our model and values," shifting attention to the EU's agency to affect
others.[17] Kaldor and colleagues argue that the EU should employ a strategic
narrative of human rights to forge influence with others and to legitimize EU
foreign policy among EU citizens.[18] However, the need to turn these values
today into a narrative about the future has yet to be realized. Once, Europe
offered a narrative about moving away from recurring, brutal internal war
through ever-closer union and integration. For Europeans today born with
no sense of connection to those wars, it is not clear that narrative has meaning. However, European leaders do not at present possess a future-oriented
narrative about where Europe will be in a generation.

The idea of strategic narrative has become prominent in the fields of war,
security, and strategic communication.[19] The United Kingdom Ministry of
Defence has stated, for instance:

> In the global information environment it is very easy for competing
> narratives to also be heard. Some may be deliberately combative—our
> adversaries for example, or perhaps hostile media. Where our narrative
> meets the competing narratives is referred to as the battle of the narra-
> tives, although the reality is that this is an enduring competition rather
> than a battle with winners and losers.[20]

This interest in strategic narrative has coincided with ideas about a new
public diplomacy in the last decade. The arrival of social media offered
the promise that ordinary people could interact with political and media

organizations and with each other. The world's great powers also invested in multilingual transnational television in remarkably similar ways. China's CCTV, Al-Jazeera, the BBC, France TV, Russia Today, CNN, and Iran's Press TV all seek to provide both channels to communicate *to* audiences around the world and online platforms *for* audiences to discuss content and events amongst themselves.[21] This raised the question of whether it was now possible to engage publics at home and abroad to new degrees.[22] If you are a political leader, could you use "public diplomacy 2.0" to expose publics to your strategic narrative, convince them of the validity of your narrative, and even get them to become vehicles and proponents of it? It appeared possible to put into practice, for the first time on a genuinely international basis, normative models of public spheres and cosmopolitan dialogue. More cynically, it seemed to be possible to put these models into practice in order to realize instrumental goals, for instance to influence overseas publics to get them to put pressure on their own governments to enact certain policies.

What has not been fully understood is how these processes of communication are affecting classic questions in international relations about power, cooperation, contestation, and order. The conceptions of strategic narrative present in contemporary debates in foreign policy and public diplomacy lack a framework to follow the process through the formation, projection, and reception of a narrative or account for the interactions that follow, both domestically and internationally. Our aim is therefore not only to engage in an academic debate about the nature of influence in international relations, but also to clarify an emerging strand of policy and practice that is ill-defined at present.

We argue that narratives about international actors structure expectations about behavior in the international system; however, there are also national or state narratives that focus attention on the state itself, rather than describing its place in the international system. Thus, national identities and roles are associated with actors as well. This relates to national narratives that include characterizations of the state as actor. Work on national character or role theory, for example, fits here.[23] So too does work on American exceptionalism,[24] and work on nationalist ideology as regenerationist myth.[25] But how are these collective actors constructed and how are they constrained by narratives? What is the process by which new actors, with accompanying narratives, come to be? We argue that the communication of narratives about the structure of the international system and its accompanying actors is created strategically, within a set of specific contextual constraints. Thus strategic narratives structure the international system and expected actor behavior. This focus on strategic narratives allows us to understand how leaders "filter identity discourses"[26] even as a new international order is created.

In addition, our discussion of the importance of narratives in defining and describing actors in international system narratives suggests that political actors may then use these narratives for strategic purposes in policy making and implementation under certain circumstances. In other words, actors can also construct policies "with public justifications which enact the identity and moral purpose of the state."[27] Political actors have some (varying) level of ability to act to construct narratives even as they are constrained by them. Further, political actors do not have one identity, but many, and these are contextual. Narratives may be created strategically, but political actors cannot produce any narrative at any time. The construction of a great power narrative, for example, is shaped by domestic and international political contexts, the communication environment, and the goals of the political leadership. This points directly to the importance of understanding political contestation (to which we turn in Chapter 4) and the media ecology (covered more substantially in Chapter 5).

WHAT ARE NARRATIVES?

How do you know a narrative when you see it? Kenneth Burke, in his classic *Grammar of Motives* (1969), noted that narrative requires an actor, an action, a goal or intention, a scene, and an instrument. Conceptually, narratives are frameworks that allow humans to connect apparently unconnected phenomena around some causal transformation.[28] The endpoint of this transformation bestows meaning upon all parts of the whole as a sequence of human actions is given connection and an overall sense.[29] A narrative entails an initial situation or order, a problem that disrupts that order, and a resolution that reestablishes order, though that order may be slightly altered from the initial situation. Narrative therefore is distinguished by a particular structure through which sense is achieved. This structure is comprised of actors; events, plot, and time; and setting and space.[30] Strategic narratives are representations of a sequence of events and identities, a communicative tool through which political actors—usually elites—attempt to give determined meaning to past, present, and future in order to achieve political objectives. Critically, strategic narratives integrate interests and goals—they articulate end states and suggest how to get there.

Actors are central to the structure of narratives. Actors become characterized, based on their own self-presentation but also how others understand them, leading to the creation of an actor's reputation. Fifty years ago Hans Morgenthau wrote, "In the struggle for existence and power . . . what others think about us is as important as what we actually are."[31] Actors work to frame their own character and that of others, by selecting and highlighting some facets of their history or actions in order to promote a particular interpretation and evaluation of their character. Equally, the theme of the narrative itself—the international system, an actor, or an issue—will at any moment be framed by various actors in certain ways. These frames therefore contribute to the construction of shared meaning of certain components within a narrative, and the narrative gives a particular meaning to their connection. Thus we are concerned with both the characterization or construction of actors within narratives, and the strategic use of narratives by political actors.

Narratives also contain events, plot, and setting, and implicit with these, a sense of time—beginning, middle, and end, for example. International relations involve actors such as states or international organizations who hold long-term narratives about themselves, about issues, and about the international system. However, international relations also involves events, crises, summits, and other episodes, all of which themselves become narrated. Several analysts have used terms to describe these short-term narratives or stories of episodes.[32] ÓTuathail uses the term *story line*: "Storylines are sense-making organizational devices tying the different elements of a policy challenge together into a reasonably coherent and convincing narrative."[33] He argues that for each moment in politics, leaders follow scripts according to normal roles and situations, and that these scripts provide the "'building blocks of storylines for them to follow."[34] Price also uses the term *script* to describe an episode during the Arab uprising in spring of 2011, when local and global media were expecting a domino effect of regimes and leaders toppling. He notes that, for the day of February 1, 2011, the Egyptian President, Hosni Mubarak, did not seem to follow the script:

> When Mubarak spoke to the Egyptian public, it was widely anticipated that he would recognize the importance of the rising civil society, speak respectfully of processes of fundamental change, and gracefully announce a purposive set of practices for shuffling off the political stage. Instead, he gave a somewhat angry, defensive speech in which he emphasized ways he would continue to control the levers of power rather than summarily disappear. The reaction in the Egyptian military, the protestors in the street, and the international policy world in Europe and the United States was virtually unanimous. Mubarak blundered, he had violated expectations in some fundamental way. Within 24 hours, he found himself forced to resign.[35]

For Price, these scripts are strategic because they create consensus about how actors should function in that type of situation. We know that certain events become templates through which new events are given meaning—the color revolutions of Eastern Europe as a template for the Arab uprising in 2011, "another Vietnam" and "quagmire" as templates the US sought to avoid in Iraq after 2003.[36] These template events possessed narrativity, with a before, during, and after; and a causal transformation, in these cases regime change and military defeat respectively. Hence, the template creates an expectation or understanding of how the new event will unfold; it will follow the script. That these expectations feed back into events, shaping behavior, is evident from the shock when Mubarak did *not* follow the script. And ultimately, he was made to. However, to explain that entire process entails analyzing more than the script and whether it was followed on that day. There is a need to analyze its formation and reception, to understand why it was convincing and moved actors to behave as they did.[37]

It is that temporal dimension and sense of movement that distinguishes narrative from discourse and frames. Narratives can orient audiences to a future as leaders craft them out of discourses and frames. Discourses are the raw material of communication—bodies of knowledge about science, law, history, theology—that actors plot into narratives. We take a Foucauldian conception of discourse as a set of meanings and practices that contain rules about what is say-able and know-able and that create roles which actors fill.[38] Discourses do not feature a causal transformation that takes actors from one status quo to another, as narratives do. Actors can only form and project a narrative based upon the discourses available to them in their historical situation, so discourses have a structuring effect upon narrative action. Actors reflexively work with discourse to construct narratives with the instrumental aim to influence the opinions and behavior of others. History, analogies, metaphors, symbols, and images can trigger and/or shape narratives.

Framing refers to the act of "*selecting and highlighting some facets of events or issues, and making connections among them so as to promote a particular interpretation, evaluation, and/or solution,*" according to Robert Entman.[39] Framing is a practice undertaken by political leaders, journalists, and other elites and is particularly associated with the shaping of public opinion.[40] There is a large body of scholarly work attempting to identify the presence of particular frames in news reports or political speeches in the field of foreign policy and correlate these frames with movements in public opinion or policy[41] or even establish causal effects on attitudes through experimental research.[42] As with discourse, frames as analytical units lack the temporal and causal features narratives necessarily possess. In other words, understanding narratives help us understand why and how framing works. A news report may frame an event in a certain way, but it does not *necessarily* introduce past causes or future outcomes (though speculation is often a feature of news). However, the various components of a narrative must be framed a certain way, so framing must be taken into account.

To understand international relations it is necessary to distinguish three types of narratives: system narratives, identity narratives, and issue narratives. System narratives are about the nature of the structure of international affairs. Roberts (2006) argues that narratives help us explain how structures "emerge and are sustained, changed, and transformed over time."[43] The agency of actors is inherent to this process. As Chapter 2 outlines, identity narratives are about the identities of actors in international affairs that are in a process of constant negotiation and contestation. Issue narratives are strategic in the sense of seeking to shape the terrain on which policy discussions take place. Bially-Mattern, Epstein, Hajer, and Schimmelfennig all have at the core of their studies how actors seek to pursue policies and limit alternatives through shaping policy discourse using strategic narrative.[44]

In international relations, narratives are a dynamic and ever-negotiated social product based on states' interactions both with their societies and with external significant others.[45] Leaders cannot create a narrative out of nothing, off the cuff. The parameters of a state's strategic narratives are bounded by prevailing domestic and international understandings and expectations of that state, readings of its history, and evaluations of its reputation.[46] So part of the task of strategic narrative is to give narrativity to events as they unfold within these constraints. It is a relentless task, but one that promises the potential to influence others in a strategic way. To what issues associated with strategic narratives does the communication process—formation, projection, and reception—point us?

FORMATION OF STRATEGIC NARRATIVES

Explaining the formation of strategic narratives involves understanding actors' strategic goals and types of communication.[47] Agenda setting, legitimation, diverting attention, securing acquiescence, enhancing popularity, and mobilization are examples of communicative goals. Strategic narratives may be designed with short-term and/or long-term goals in mind. Beyond goals, political actors can use different types of communication in the construction of strategic narratives, including persuasion, argument, and representational force.

Understanding an actor's strategic aims is a central issue in the study of strategic narratives, and politics more broadly. At the domestic level, in each phase of the policy-making process—agenda setting, decision making, and implementation—political actors seek to set the terms of debate, affect the process of thinking about and deciding on a policy, and guide how policies play out. Recognizing the importance of the domestic context and policy legitimacy, Alexander George's conception of policy legitimacy suggests that actors must convince others that a policy is achievable and normatively desirable.[48] Policy legitimacy "is tied to the role of political elites and public opinion because these forces play a powerful role in decision-making and may act as a counterweight to leaders and their agendas."[49] If, then, policies can be described as fitting squarely within an accepted narrative describing problems that should and can be addressed, and actions that should be taken and can be achieved, policy legitimacy can be enhanced. If an actor can focus attention on what is perceived to be hypocrisy—or a mismatch with an accepted narrative—a target may be discouraged from taking particular decisions. This is related to role theory's understanding of altercasting—a method of socialization—"in which the relevant others cast a social actor into a role and provide cues to elicit the corresponding appropriate behavior."[50] Domestic political contestation over strategic narratives is central to political outcomes. In addition, policy legitimacy can be pursued at the international level when conducting foreign policy. Putnam and others note the importance of the two-level game that takes place in this context.

p. 206

Beyond strategic aims focused on agenda setting and policy legitimacy within a policy context, political actors may have broader long-term goals associated with cultivating a positive perception of themselves over time in the international realm. This is related to the concept of soft power that highlights the importance of getting others to "want what you want."[51] As Hayden notes, "How soft power resources are vested with rhetorical capacity. . . . are not elaborated in most depictions of soft power."[52] We address this by arguing that it is a political actor's ability to construct narratives that enhances an appeal for foreign audiences. This echoes Hayden's description of "'policies'. . . as strategic arguments in support of soft power actions and . . . packed with assumptions about the nature of agency [actors], proper vehicles of influence [roles and plot], and achievable outcomes [future goals]."[53] Depending on the type of influence actors want—long- or short-term—actors use media differently and have different expectations. Long-term goals often include the use of strategic narratives to enhance positive opinions about the actor itself. Public diplomacy falls into this category.[54]

Before we discuss the projection of strategic narratives in a new media ecology, it is important to discuss types of communication used by political actors. Communication can have a number of forms, but perhaps the most often cited in the international relations literature are persuasion or argumentation and representational force or coercion. Persuasion is related to argumentation, which is most often associated with reaching a consensus through communicative action over time.[55] Risse, for example, suggests that "[a]rguing and truth-seeking behavior presupposes that actors no longer hold fixed interests during their communicative interaction but are open to persuasion, challenges, and counterchallenges geared toward reaching a reasoned consensus."[56] However, Krebs and Jackson suggest that "persuasion undoubtedly does occur in the political arena, [but] it is also rare."[57]

There are a growing number of scholars whose work focuses on the rhetorical as force. Krebs and Jackson propose such a model of rhetorical coercion: "Rhetorical coercion occurs when this strategy proves successful: when the claimant's opponents have been talked into a corner, compelled to endorse a stance they would otherwise reject. . . . Rhetorical coercion is a political strategy that seeks to twist arms by twisting tongues."[58] Bially-Mattern's work on representational force also focuses on power, arguing that states have conceptions of self "above and beyond a being's particular identities or roles (self-other)" and that "[a] being's subjectivity is subject to (contingent upon) the persistence of the particular configuration of sociolinguistic identity constructs upon which it is based and from whence it is constituted."[59] She suggests that during times of disruption or crisis, representational force consists of the ability to challenge the subjectivity (self) of an actor, thus forcing the target to conform to narratives previously established. This is linked in some ways to metapower, or "how global interactions reconfigure, constitute, or reconstitute identities, interests, and institutions."[60] This use of representational force or metapower is most often associated with times of crisis or disruption while other types of communication are not. Schimmelfennig's notion of rhetorical entrapment, as shown in the case of the European Union and NATO, is not centered on crisis.[61] Neither is Steele's look at reflexive discourse and flattery as counter-power. He argues that a less powerful speaker can stimulate a powerful actor by asking "a targeted audience to justify the disconnect between its narrative understanding of self-identity and the seemingly contradictory actions or inactions."[62] Our conception of strategic narrative is more closely related to this type of communication, as outlined in this chapter. Hence, different types of communication will underpin the formation and motives behind a strategic narrative.

PROJECTION

It is one thing to outline or conceptualize the goals of strategic actors and the types of communication that actors may use, but without attention to the media ecology in which this communication takes place we are missing a crucial component of the process itself. We argue that projection of strategic narratives in a new media ecology presents significant opportunities and challenges for actors. There is no doubt that the mass media environment has become increasingly complex as the twentieth and twenty-first centuries have moved, albeit unevenly, to the era of communication power described by Castells. The literature in communication and political communication acknowledges that the type of media can affect how messages are constructed.[63] From works on the differences in newspaper and television coverage to the new role of the Internet, the characteristics of the medium itself are important to consider. This is directly relevant to the construction of strategic narratives in a number of ways, including increased reach of communication technologies, increased transparency, increased interactivity, and accelerated and distorted time horizons.[64] In addition, a focus on actors requires us to acknowledge that some actors will be more adept at communicating in different media than others.

The development of communication technologies has increased the number of people who can communicate in public. Robin Brown argues that "the diffusion of communications technologies, ranging from the telephone to the Internet, is producing a more open, more public, political environment and that this environment modifies the type of political strategies that work."[65] Actors must take into account an environment in which they may be challenged and their messages contested (see Chapter 4). Steele claims that "forms of technology (such as the Internet) accelerate the dissemination of information so that such information remains slightly 'ahead' of a power attempting to classify and regiment it."[66] The increased reach and availability of communication technologies allows nongovernmental groups to organize and communicate their positions on issues related to foreign (as well as domestic) policies. In this sense, technology has empowered additional actors. Hanson suggests that the development of the Internet has increased transparency of governmental actions and events around the world.[67] In particular, new technologies allow nongovernmental actors to communicate more easily and allow international events to be more broadly transmitted.[68] Livingston categorizes transparency into (1) domestic transparency that focuses on the state's disclosure of information, (2) imposed transparency that attempts to gain access to information from others, and (3) systemic transparency that refers to the proliferation of communication technology.[69] New social media allow greater interactivity and have changed the timing of information. No longer is communication necessarily one-way from communicator to audience. Today audience members can become actors themselves, commenting, liking, and remixing images, information, and narratives. The likelihood of this immediately affecting policy is slim, but there are cumulative effects as well as moments in event and policy cycles when audience members can make a difference.[70] Images and information can (re)appear at unexpected or unplanned (from some actors' perspective) times.[71] This brings us back to states—with which we began this chapter. If new actors have more opportunities to communicate their own narratives or challenge others, what does this mean for states? Price argues that the new media environment has affected sovereignty as "[n]ew media giants, new regional alliances, new geopolitics, all conspire in the remapping of the information space."[72] Rhetorical entrapment may be possible in the short term through use of images or dominating an issue narrative—but in the longer term it is more difficult to actually persuade others and get them to see the world differently, as we explore in more detail below.

RECEPTION WITHIN THE NEW MEDIA ECOLOGY

The concept of media ecology denotes that the term *media* includes environments, actors, and technologies together. Media are understood as akin to organic life forms existing in a complex set of interrelationships within a system that is often balanced but evolving.[73] Technological developments and the emergence of new powerful actors have a ripple effect on these interrelationships, altering and even—in the case of the Gutenberg printing press and perhaps the Internet—transforming the existing balance.[74] Today's new media ecology[75] is marked by a rapid proliferation of digital technologies that are producing a qualitative sense of change *and* observable changes in practices in all spheres of life. The result is that more of physical life matter, social relations, and international relations are recorded, disseminated, and debated, potentially on near-instantaneous and deterritorialized scales. Actors are forced to adapt. We are witnessing the development of participatory, multimodal, and multilingual media ecologies made up of overlapping local, national, and transnational circulations of competing narratives, varying visibilities, and evolving repertories of behavior. These developments are driving the reassessment of classic questions in social and political theory, and institutional concerns in science, government, and academia about how we conduct empirical research. International relations must account for new ways in which media facilitate connectivity between individual and community and the new forms of virtual and actual publics and communities this connectivity enables. Do these connections enable publics to talk to each other and bypass states? How should political leaders best communicate to and through these connected publics and communities? How are processes of legitimation, authorization, and accountability affected? Ultimately, media ecologies condition how communication in international relations functions and are integral to explaining how international interactions proceed and become meaningful to their participants.

Identifying the effect or impact of a narrative on audiences, whether they are elites or publics, requires—at a minimum—analysis of their attitudes, opinions, and behavior before that narrative reached them as well as afterward. To explain any effect requires a richer knowledge of how those audiences consume news and political information, how they compare sources and attribute credibility, and whether they discuss narratives with friends, family, or colleagues in nonpolitical spaces. To explain how audiences receive and interpret narratives requires a thorough understanding of the media ecology those audiences inhabit, the cultural context that causes audiences to be pulled toward certain narratives, and the political context in which leaders are pushing various narratives toward those audiences. Once we take these processes into account, we find that far from being passive recipients of narratives from above, most audiences hold nuanced understandings of the strategic narratives circulating in their media ecology. Not only that, but they are aware of, and take into account, the way those narratives are formed, projected, and mediated. Consequently, audiences are not a blank slate for narratives to be projected onto, and skillful practitioners of strategic narratives must take into account the political and media literacies of their target audiences if they are to create a credible and convincing narrative.

WHEN IS A NARRATIVE STRATEGIC?
THE SPECTRUM OF PERSUASION

Analysis of the role of narratives in international relations requires attention to how actors select from the raw materials of international affairs to lend narrativity to the experience of international affairs so as to try to create the intended meaning to the political past, present, and future. Ryan makes the important distinction between "being a narrative" and "possessing narrativity."[76] International affairs can possess narrativity but no single author because for events to become understood through a narrative depends on audience interpretation. Those events were not narratives in themselves but became recognized as possessing narrativity. There was no author of the end of the Cold War, but events could be interpreted using narrative's semantic features: the *action* of political leaders and activists, a *temporality* defined by the transition out of a historical period into an indefinite new beginning, and numerous attributions of *causality*. Indeed, the economic, domestic, geopolitical, military, and cultural causes are still subject to much debate.[77]

The aim is not simply to analyze the narratives actors use in international relations. Analysis of narratives might be very interesting for their own sake. However, to make claims about the role of strategic narratives in international relations we must ask what actors are trying to do with narratives. Most conceptions of strategy rest on the mobilization of available means to achieve stated aims.[78] In more direct terms, Rumelt suggests that strategy is the "application of strength against weakness."[79] Much of politics involves actors with strategies, facing particular contexts and particular problems, using language to persuade and convince others.[80] Decisions have to be made; actors will use language to try to get each other to take the position they prefer. If actors know there has got to be a decision taken on an issue, those actors will try to influence how each other will vote. Once we analyze communication dynamics in international relations we see actors interacting strategically to maneuver each other toward long-term goals. While use of some aspects of narratives may become habitual, some are consciously reflected upon. Political leaders use narratives, discourse, and frames strategically, thinking through the likely effects or responses at home and abroad.[81] If some actors rely on habit and frame or narrativize a situation in a less than convincing way, their failure demonstrates a lack of skill, not that intentionality and strategy do not exist.

Nevertheless, actors do not have a free hand to craft narratives afresh for each new context and situation. It could be objected that narratives are simply in the ether of international relations, that narratives are free-floating above the control of any actors, or so culturally embedded in political communities that they infuse actors' thoughts subconsciously. We may find that a state's narrative may escape its own projection, for instance Ikenberry's argument that the US post-1945 narrative about the world moving toward an ever more liberal system has been taken up and institutionalized in East Asia independently of any narrative work by the US. East Asian countries have set up regional economic and security systems that are consistent with US values and the liberal order US leaders have promoted.[82] This case, if Ikenberry is correct, leads to important questions about agency and intentionality.

To be precise, narratives can either be understood as structuring the range of thoughts and actions of actors, or as tools that actors use to persuade each other. Given that narratives are central to how actors understand international relations—the units of analysis, the historical trajectories, the character or identities of specific actors—then in some sense actors are born into these structures of meaning, shaping their perspective and behavior.

However, since these understandings of international relations are constantly being challenged and (re)established, we must study how states and other powerful actors project and contest strategic narratives about states and their characters, about the trajectory of history, and about the international system. Narrative structures are not given. If we assumed that the naturalization of the state and the system just happened, with no actors pushing for their meanings to be naturalized in one way or another, then we would ignore a crucial part of international relations. Statecraft is not only about international relations but about constituting the overall meaning of international relations.[83]

We argue that this interplay between narratives as structuring and narratives as tools of agency can best be understood through what we call a spectrum of persuasion, from thin analyses that study the interaction of actors in a given system, to thick analyses that ask how that system and its features are the way they are. The thin approaches are more parsimonious, take certain logics of behavior as given, analyze interactions in a given period and may, based on findings, produce predictions about how actors would likely behave in future situations. For studies of negotiations within a specific time frame, perhaps in the run-up to a major collective decision, such approaches have great utility. They might ask whose strategic narrative carries the day in the new treaty, or whose strategic narrative most effectively wins the support of public opinion. The thick approaches are necessarily richer in terms of historical detail since they seek to account for both how actors and their preferences, and structures and their effects, came into being in the first place, as well as how they shape interactions in a given period. For example, a thin analysis of strategic narrative might take for granted that a set of states possess coherent strategic narratives and analyze how they take each other's narratives into account as they seek to reach agreement on an international issue or crisis. A thicker analysis might ask how the formation of those narratives bears upon how they fare in the interaction phase. Perhaps when constructing their national narrative, a state's elites glossed over certain problematic historical events, events that other states then put onto the table of debate in order to undermine that state's negotiating position. Or, the researcher producing thicker analysis might ask whether a hegemonic or imperial state constructed the narrative of the entire international system that others take for granted and work within, since that process might strongly condition how any interactions play out. They might be concerned that the powerful state has won before the game begins.

These are all analytical choices that depend on what strategic narrative processes the researcher wishes to explain. Below, and drawing on Brent Steele's survey of IR theory and communication,[84] we set out four positions on the spectrum of persuasion.

- *VERY THIN:* Rationalist. Theories that analyze interactions between actors with given preferences within a given structure of anarchy. Persuasion is usually secondary to material inducement (coercion, bargaining) and communication is understood as signaling intentions, or cheap talk used to manipulate impressions. However, persuasion is possible by trapping others into committing to action through rhetorical skill or by producing a road map or blueprint to which others agree to commit. Rhetorical maneuvering can thus stop short of inculcating a shared a point of view to achieved its desired effect.[85] The media ecology is understood simply as an arena within which actors transmit information. Some actors hold more power in media systems and can exert more control of who knows what and when.

- **THIN:** Communicative action. Studies that begin with rational actors seeking to persuade one another by making convincing claims. Attention is paid to the nature of the media ecology, conceptualized as a public sphere, because the distribution of access and voice and the norms of civility, style, and genre all shape how debates unfold. Media are not a neutral space. The process of debate weeds out weak and unconvincing claims, socializes participants into the art of rational debate, and allows actors with the most compelling arguments to persuade others to follow their proposals. The process of debate has the main effect, however, of refining actors' identities into the norms and standards of the community of interlocutors. These shifts might be modest but are real.[86] This remains thin analysis because at the start of analysis all players are still taken to be coherent, rational actors with relatively stable preferences and identities.

- **THICK:** Reflexive. The communication and action by some triggers responses in others; mutual monitoring as actors learn to mutually respond to one another in advantageous ways—power begets counter-power, a web of anxiety.[87] Deft and decisive action by one actor to undermine the identity and status of another can lead that other to alter behavior and revise self-understanding.[88] These communication processes involve more than the exchange of rational claims. Actors exploit the media ecology to use gestures and symbolic acts to contest each other's status, reputation, identity, and image. The media ecology is far more than an arena within which actors exchange information or claims. It is an unpredictable, textured, and recursive set of overlapping ecologies in which visuality, symbolism, emotion, and affect are central to persuasion.

- **VERY THICK:** Poststructural. The strategic actor (to the extent this is possible) projects a discourse that features subject positions that others fill, giving them a clear identity from which they then speak and act. These discourses can be presented in various forms, whether material or representational, including narratives.[89] Discourses form structural conditions that change only very slowly and function through generative power (producing and constituting identities and meanings of systems) rather than strictly behavioral power of one actor over another. Media ecologies are one more system of discourse, with enduring rules and roles that result in stable forms of news and political information through which the meanings of international relations are reproduced.

Our argument is that once you get to the thick end, rational action kicks back in. Actors' identities may have been generated through structures that only change very slowly, but those structural conditions can themselves be the subject of narrative contestation and struggles over the discourses that under-pin those narratives. David Campbell[90] described the move from a rationalist to a poststructural discourse analysis approach to studying foreign policy as "*from* a concern of relations *between* states which takes place across ahistori-cal, frozen and pre-given boundaries, *to* a concern *with the establishment of boundaries* that constitute, at one and the same time, the 'state' and the 'inter-national system.'"[91] But given that actors in international relations are at least partially reflexive about how their understandings of the system are formed, there comes a point at which actors in powerful states may feel they are able to start wielding their power to do something about what Campbell calls the boundaries that constitute the state and the international system.[92] If they are unhappy about the prevailing way in which borders, human rights, collective action, the basis of rule, or any other foundation of political order is done, then these can be contested. And this involves forming an alternative narrative about international relations that puts these core aspects in a new light.

The upshot for researchers is this. Since these boundaries are constantly being challenged and (re)established, then we need to study how states and other powerful actors project and contest strategic narratives *about* the state and *about* the international system. If we believed that the naturalization of the state and the system just happened, with no actors pushing for their meanings to be naturalized in one way or another, then we would ignore a crucial part of international relations. Hence, we must study the establish-ment of these boundaries and identities (constitutive power) but also how actors use their agency, within specific situations and historical relation-ships, to entrench the meaning of these boundaries and identities in order to steer other actors toward certain behavior (behavioral power).

This compound, recursive theory of action in international relations is further complicated by our use of poststructuralist studies of discourse in international relations. There are three points to make about how discourse functions in IR and how our understanding of the ontology of discourse enables us to analyze contestation. First, discourses are sustained through repetition; science, law, and nationhood are discourses reproduced through practices in laboratories, courts, and public events. Since these are human practices, there is always scope for error, divergent understandings, creativ-ity, and discovery, as well as the interaction of multiple discourses around one event. Consequently, discourses are never quite fixed. Since a discourse produces relations of power, and some actors benefit more from these rela-tions that others, then there will always be some groups with an incentive to challenge the discourse or terms of debate that an issue is being discussed within. This unfixed-ness creates space for politics and contestation. Second, discourses give meaning to material objects and institutions that then become anchors of those discourses. In modern international relations, Jonathan Bach argues, a certain configuration of "the sovereign state" has become the anchor of how relations between political communities are understood and this depends on material and legal arrangements through phenomena such as citizenship, borders, and war. This state-form becomes naturalized, "as *a priori* and unhistoric," and so much of international affairs follows from that.[93] Bentley's study of how certain weapons become weapons of mass destruction at different historical junctures equally shows the contingent and ultimately political and power-infused manner in which objects gain meaning through discourse.[94] However, there is again no essential correspondence between material object or institution and how it is described in language or experienced. The same object can be interpreted in competing ways, giving rise to argumentation and antagonism. Third, discourses create subject-positions that actors fill: laboratory assistant or journal editor in science, judge or defendant in law, citizen or illegal immigrant in nationhood.[95] Many fill these positions, creating in- and out-groups who assert competing identities and interests.

The unfixidity of discourse and its contingent framing of objects, as well as its production of identity groups, all create politics. In our analysis, political leaders then step in to craft these discourses into narratives. If the raw materials of narrative themselves produce political differences and struggles, then so too will the narratives formed from them. Hence, the very stuff of narratives, their ontological foundations, make political contestation inevitable.[96] (It is for this reason that a degree of ambiguity, a level of abstraction that obscures lower-level discursive differences, may increase the attractiveness of strategic narratives to multiple audiences.) Consequently, "winning" any battle of narratives is not easy. Or as the former diplomat Robert Cooper pithily commented: "Influencing foreigners is difficult."[97]

Our argument here is novel and, we hope, exciting because it means strategic narratives have a twofold power effect. Strategic narratives are an instrument of power in the traditional Weberian or *behavioral* sense of A getting B to do what B otherwise would not; of shaping behavior in an observable way. If your strategic narrative is convincing, allies will commit resources, publics will reelect your party to continue your foreign policy, and enemies will realize their prospects are bleak unless they change course. But strategic narratives are also an instrument of power by *constituting* the experience of international affairs and thus the identity of its actors and the meaning of the system. If states believe that international security is best achieved by coalitions forming to protect or repair the human rights of populations during moments of crisis, then they may identify themselves *as* states-who-protect or at least states-who-support-protection. Their policies will then follow from this identity. Hence, these two processes work hand in hand: if your narrative comes to constitute an important part of the identity of another state, this will shape their behavior. Alternatively, if one convinced another state to commit to specific policies and actions on a consistent basis, then that other state may come to take on the identity of a state that carries out such policies naturally, as an expression of their values. For example, Epstein has explained how environmental NGOs managed to convince states of a shift in their interests and identity: to move from supporting a pro-whaling narrative, industrial whaling practices, and being seen as "whaling states" to expressing an anti-whaling narrative and feeling a need to verbalize and demonstrate their anti-whaling credentials.[98] They unquestionably bought into the new narrative, as was evident from their policy behavior and their communication and representation of themselves and whaling states. Identity and behavior work in tandem and must be explained together.

HOW OUR ARGUMENT PROCEEDS: CHAPTER OUTLINE

In this book our primary aim is to theorize strategic narrative and establish the scope and limits for actors to use narratives to achieve their goals. To do this, we focus on four major concepts in international relations theory through which we can conceptualize what narratives are and how they are used strategically: actors, order, contestation, and infrastructure. We realize infrastructure is not yet taken as a key concept, but once we account for the role of the communications environment in the formation, projection, and reception of strategic narrative, it becomes a concept worth taking very seriously. The scope of these concepts takes our focus beyond subfields such as foreign policy analysis, the study of policy legitimation, or public diplomacy, although it contributes to these fields. In a subsequent volume we present a series of empirical case studies and reflect on the methods needed to explain the impact narratives do or do not have.[99] However, we have included case studies in each of the four chapters of this book to help illustrate our arguments and demonstrate how strategic narrative works.

In Chapter 2 we investigate how political actors are affected by the intersection of power and social interaction in a new media ecology. The chapter addresses great powers, rising powers, weak states, and international organizations—including NGOs and other nonstate actors such as terrorist groups—by exploring how international politics shapes and is shaped by the narrative construction of these actors and these actors' strategic narratives. This chapter ties narratives to issues associated with identity in the international relations literature. This focuses attention on identity in relationship (self-other) and in terms of subjectivity (self), the agency-structure debate, and issues associated with collective and individual identity. In addition, we examine how political actors use narratives that address actors' intersubjectivity and subjectivity (conception of self) *strategically* in pursuing foreign policy goals. The European Union member states, for example, are using strategic narratives to help shape integration processes themselves. We conclude with an overview of the construction of the US great power narrative in the 1940s and show how the continuation of deeply embedded great powers' strategic narratives structure foreign policy behavior in a post–Cold War system. A new communication environment significantly affects these strategic narratives, adding to the challenges associated with political actors' use of narratives.

Chapter 3 examines how narrative is central to conceptions of international order and to the process of how actors challenge or reinforce order.[100] Narratives are used by states to explain unfolding events to shape international responses. This is particularly the case in crises, during which actors fall back on established narratives to explain to their domestic and international audiences how the crisis should be overcome. Strategic narratives within crises present a story about the nature of the crisis, what the resolution of the crisis should involve, and what the postcrisis landscape does and should look like. We illustrate this through an examination of the Libya crisis of 2011. This episode divided international opinion but ultimately involved NATO enforcing a no-fly zone under the mandate of United Nations Security Council Resolution 1973. We demonstrate how the strategic narrative of France and the UK shaped the responses of other states to persuade them to agree to the passing of UN1973. The narrative contestation that defined the debate on Libya serves as a microcosm of narratives of international order. Strategic narratives contribute in three main aspects to our understanding of international order. First, strategic narratives shape how order is conceived. Second, they play a role in the production of order, for example, strategic narratives of hierarchy that claim status is there for a reason, which creates roles, expectations, and relations of authority. Finally, the analyses of narratives help explain how order is maintained.

Having offered our theorization of actors and international order, in Chapter 4 we ask what happens when narratives clash and what counts as victory. Different IR scholars have addressed a variety of forms of contestation, from short-term trapping of one state by another around a particular issue[101] and numerous studies of framing, to long-term discursive shifts through which actors purposefully seek to define the core terms through which international relations can be understood.[102] This chapter presents two dimensions that offer analysts clear research paths to finding out what is being contested and how. The first dimension is the spectrum of persuasion introduced above, from thin to thick analyses. The second is concerned with the numerous aspects of narrative contestation, including the content of the narrative, its relation to actual events, and its process of formation, projection, and reception. There are indeed innumerable points at which a strategic narrative can be contested. These dimensions are illustrated using three examples of narrative contestation in the last half century: the narrative contests that have emerged during Israel's conflicts with its neighbors, the narrative work involved when a bulk of the world's states and citizens shifted from pro-whaling to anti-whaling in the 1960s and 1970s, and contestation of Iran's nuclear program. We use these analyses to highlight how strategic narratives draw upon long-standing discourses and the raw material of news and events, and the role of different types of actors in narrative contests. We aim to identify conditions that facilitate shared narratives, as well as factors that determine which narratives prevail. Understanding how strategic narrative works is valuable for those working in international relations, whether for the state, for an international organization, or for a nongovernmental organization (NGO). But, we conclude by cautioning against the quest for an overly simplified model or template of narrative success.

In Chapter 5 we turn to the role of media and communications in the use of strategic narratives by actors in the contemporary international system. Here, we directly address the terrain of communication power that Castells has laid out through his theorization of network society. Strategic narratives are conceived by policy makers as tools to influence overseas publics, in a new great game in which "the people" are reified as the site of power and hope and whose energies must be harnessed. Our state departments are playing a twin-track strategy. They must exploit the media ecologies of the day, distributing their narrative within national and transnational public spheres. But they must also compete to shape the very infrastructure of these ecologies, since that infrastructure privileges certain voices and certain ways of communicating over others. The United States pursues an agenda of Internet freedom that deploys both tracks: a narrative *in media ecologies* about freedom, and an effort to *shape media ecologies* so more voices can support the freedom narrative. Other countries are engaged in the same game. The UK government openly fears it is losing the battle of the narratives. This chapter will look at some of the difficulties that are emerging as states seek to both exploit and produce this new hierarchy of international political communication. It focuses on Obama's 2009 Cairo Speech and the BBC World Service's use of its Arabic language service. These difficulties include policy makers' conceptions of "the people," their conceptions of influence, and their inability to control media ecologies, which are being transformed more by commerce and technology than by geopolitical sensitivities. There are also tensions between the value of intercultural dialogue for its own sake versus the instrumental, interest-oriented goals of public diplomacy—goals that overseas publics are well aware of. Consequently, we see the spectrum of persuasion being played out in the actual policies of media and foreign policy organizations, who seek both to shape immediate opinion and behavior but also the long-term conditions and structures through which people understand their identity and interests.

We conclude the book in Chapter 6 by summarizing our argument and outline potential future avenues for the application of strategic narrative. We argue that strategic narrative offers a conceptual framework to build on existing literature in the fields of communication and international relations.

We specify the questions and analytical problems strategic narrative can help address. We aim to bring insights from communications and international relations together to better understand the forces pulling and shaping the contemporary world.

OUR CONTRIBUTION

The precise contribution we want to make to the understanding of communication and power in international relations is to explain how narratives are used strategically. We build upon two decades of often excellent work in international relations by those who have mapped the prevailing ideas, norms, discourses, frames, and narratives held by actors and explained their origin, formation, promotion, diffusion, translation, emulation, institutionalization, and contestation. Others have shown how narratives are central to actors' identities,[103] how they represent their allies or enemies,[104] and how actors achieve ontological security.[105] Some have explored how actors articulate policy through narratives.[106] All of these studies have demonstrated how important narrative is to international relations, principally because of the human propensity both to understand the world through narrative and to give narrativity to events. Our focus is on how actors try to use narratives. While actors are born into a world of narratives and understand themselves and their environment through narratives, this does not rule out the possibility that actors seek to use narratives in a strategic way to influence others' attitudes and behavior. Indeed, given how important narratives are to actors' identity and action, it would be foolhardy for political leaders *not* to try to use narratives to influence others.

To explain how actors try to use narratives strategically, it is essential to account for the media ecologies through which narratives are projected, received, and interpreted. Communication in international relations does not take place in a vacuum. Many of the roles media and communications play in international relations have been explored. There are impressive bodies of work about agenda setting and whether political leaders follow journalists or vice versa. The increased transparency of international affairs—symbolized by Wikileaks and the Abu Ghraib scandal—have renewed interest in questions of who has what information and who *should* have what information in the daily business of international affairs. The emergence of the Internet and Web 2.0 have triggered interest in new patterns of connectivity. We appear to inhabit a world characterized by both national media systems and cultures *and* transnational, emergent dynamics that often take political leaders by surprise. The temporality of connectivity has also been destabilized. Digitization radically increases the potential for the reevaluation and reinscription of events and timelines that in previous eras would have been more settled. State narratives about a conflict can be reinforced as digital images are later recovered from participants, but equally those narratives can be disrupted. As Abu Ghraib showed, a narrative of victory can quickly turn to one of shame. Overall, then, processes through which the flow and flux of information about international relations are organized, such as agenda-setting, gatekeeping, and archiving, are all qualitatively transformed by new media ecologies. However, this involves both continuity and change: traditionally powerful actors still exert control but the increase in the number of actors and the contingency of control give the processes through which the meaning of events is created a different quality.

The status of the image would seem to exemplify these trends. Scholars have recently claimed that international relations appear marked by a new visuality.[107] Since satellite television emerged in the 1990s, the likelihood of real-time, immediate news coverage of events has created an imperative for political leaders to control the look or image of any and every event that might affect the legitimacy of their regime and policies.[108] The prevalence and circulation of user-generated images—whether actual or only anticipated—has only intensified this imperative. Since leaders must seek to manage and respond to this visual aspect of international relations, this entails learning how to visualize narrative and fit visuals of ongoing events into long-term strategic narratives—something Al-Qaeda operatives were highly skilled at doing in the mid-2000s, as we discuss in Chapter 2.

All of these media dynamics might even be creating a new ontology of international relations. There is more information, being narrativized by more actors, in new patterns that do not simply map onto hierarchies of material power. For instance, in Chapter 3 we argue that the construction of strategic narratives of order by political actors provides a compelling explanation of how orders emerge and are maintained, as well as their demise. Critically, the construction of order has taken on greater complexity with the emergence of the new media ecology and the greater dispersal of power and authority in the world. If, for instance, we accept a poststructuralist ontological primacy of language, since language makes the stuff of international relations meaningful, and digital communication means there is simply far more language about international affairs produced, recorded, archived, searched, used, and manipulated, then it does become possible to ask whether the basic ontology of international relations is shifting. If the current international order and its hierarchy are sustained through practices of legitimation, and legitimation is produced through communication, and communication is itself transformed, then we must retheorize communication, legitimacy, and hierarchy in a fundamental way. This is an ontological matter, an implication of our argument with which we hope readers will engage.

To reiterate, state leaders and publics experience international affairs through narratives.[109] Humans find sense and thus a degree of control of existence by putting events into order, by organizing temporality and the things that happen in it. This is done through language.[110] Part of the work of being a leader in international affairs is therefore to craft and communicate a strategic narrative through which others will come to experience events.

The task is constructing the reality of events for audiences. If allied states or domestic publics genuinely believe progress is being made in Afghanistan or that the future of international security will be achieved through coalitions carrying out military interventions and development programs, then they will act as if this is common sense. Ultimately, they will consent to policies that promise to realize these narratives. This is why we speak of strategic narratives. They are strategic because they help realize a goal. The goal is that one's audience will behave in ways they otherwise would not have. The narrative becomes the means to an end: the end of other states or publics acting in accordance with the narrator's wishes.

Our understanding of the role of narratives, language, and discourse in international relations has become theoretically strong and realized through a large body of empirical work in the last two decades. In many ways we seek to build upon these traditions and bring these scholars with us. We hope our focus on the *strategic* nature of narratives, the role of narratives in structuring experience of international relations, and how these processes depend on the media ecology through which narratives pass, all add important new dimensions to the work of these scholars.

NOTES

1. Abramo F. K. Organski, *World Politics* (New York: Knopf, 1958).
2. Jeffrey W. Legro, *Rethinking the World: Great Power Strategies and International Order* (Ithaca, NY: Cornell University Press, 2005); John M. Owen IV, *The Clash of Ideas in World Politics: Transnational Networks, States, and Regime Change, 1510–2010* (Princeton, NJ: Princeton University Press, 2010).
3. Manuel Castells, *Communication Power* (Oxford: Oxford University Press, 2009).
4. Manuel Castells, *The Rise of the Network Society: The Information Age: Economy, Society, and Culture*, Vol. 1 (Oxford: Wiley-Blackwell, 2011); Manuel Castells, *The Power of Identity: The Information Age: Economy, Society, and Culture*, Vol. 2 (Oxford: Wiley-Blackwell, 2011); Manuel Castells, *The Internet Galaxy: Reflections on the Internet, Business, and Society* (New York: Oxford University Press, 2003).
5. Manuel Castells, "Communication, Power and Counter-Power in the Network Society," *International Journal of Communication* 1, no. 1 (2007).
6. Manuel Castells, *Networks of Outrage and Hope* (Cambridge: Polity, 2012).
7. Brent J. Steele, *Defacing Power* (Ann Arbor: University of Michigan Press, 2012), 85; Nik Gowing, "Time to Move On: New Media Realities—New Vulnerabilities of Power," *Media, War & Conflict* 4, no. 1 (2011).
8. Manuel Castells, *Communication Power* (Oxford: Oxford University Press, 2009), 155–189.
9. Castells, *Networks of Outrage and Hope*, 105.
10. Lawrence Freedman, "Networks, Culture, and Narratives," *Adelphi Papers Series* 45, no. 379 (2006): 22.
11. Wayne Porter and Mark Mykleby, *A National Strategic Narrative* (Washington, DC: Woodrow Wilson International Center for Scholars, 2011), accessed

May 23, 2013, http://www.wilsoncenter.org/sites/default/files/A%20Na tional%20Strategic%20Narrative.pdf.

12. Anne-Marie Slaughter, introduction to Porter and Mykleby, *A National Strategic Narrative*, 4.

13. Note that some scholars distinguish between narrative and story, describing a story as focusing on an event or situation while narrative has a temporal arch, with specific actors, plot, and setting. See Daniel Leonard Bernardi, Pauline Hope Cheong, Chris Lundry, and Scott W. Ruston, *Narrative Landmines: Rumors, Islamist Extremism, and the Struggle for Strategic Influence* (New Brusnwick, NJ: Rutgers University Press, 2012).

14. Joseph Nye, "Soft Power," *Foreign Policy* 80 (1990): 153–71.

15. Hans J. Morgenthau, *Politics among Nations* (New York: Knopf, 1963); Hans J. Morgenthau, *Truth and Power* (London: Pall Mall Press, 1970).

16. Ian Manners, "Normative Power Europe: A Contradiction in Terms?" *Journal of Common Market Studies* 40, no. 2 (2002): 235–58.

17. Sven Biscop, "The Value of Power, the Power of Values: A Call for an EU Grand Strategy," Egmont Paper No. 33 (2009): 4. http://www.egmontinstitute .be/paperegm/sum/ep33.html. Accessed 15 July 2013.

18. Mary Kaldor et al., "Human Security: A New Strategic Narrative for the EU," *International Affairs* 83, no. 2 (2007): 273–88.

19. Freedman, "Networks, Culture, and Narratives"; Frank Scott Douglas, "Waging the Inchoate War: Defining, Fighting, and Second-Guessing the 'Long War,'" *Journal of Strategic Studies* 30, no. 3 (2007); Brian Fishman, "Using the Mistakes of al Qaeda's Franchises to Undermine its Strategies," *Annals of the American Academy of Political and Social Science* 618, no. 1 (2008); Jens Ringsmose, and Berit Kaja Børgesen, "Shaping Public Attitudes towards the Deployment of Military Power: NATO, Afghanistan and the Use of Strategic Narratives," *European Security* 20, no. 4 (2011): 505–28.

20. Ministry of Defence, "Strategic Communication: The Defence Contribution," Joint Doctrine Note 1/11, 2011, accessed May 22, 2013, http://www.mod .uk/NR/rdonlyres/7DAE5158-63AD-444D-9A3F-83F7D8F44F9A/0/ 20110310JDN111_STRAT_COMM.pdf: 2–10.

21. Andreas Antoniades, Alister Miskimmon, and Ben O'Loughlin, "Great Power Politics and Strategic Narratives." March 2010. Working paper no. 7, Centre for Global Political Economy, University of Sussex. Accessed 15 July 2013. http://pcmlp.socleg.ox.ac.uk/sites/pcmlp.socleg.ox.ac.uk/files/great powerpolitics.pdf.

22. James Pamment, *New Public Diplomacy in the 21st Century: A Comparative Study of Policy and Practice* (London: Routledge, 2012).

23. Kaleavi J. Holsti, "National Role Conceptions in the Study of Foreign Policy," International Studies Quarterly 14, no. 3 (1970): 233–309; Cameron G. Thies, "International Socialization Processes vs. Israeli National Role Conceptions: Can Role Theory Integrate IR Theory and Foreign Policy Analysis?" Foreign Policy Analysis 8, no. 1 (2012): 25–46; Cameron G. Thies, "The Roles of Bipolarity: A Role Theoretic Understanding of the Effects of Ideas and Material Factors on the Cold War," International Studies Perspectives (2012), Article first published online: 21 August, DOI: 10.1111/j.1528-3585.2012.00486.x; Stephen G. Walker, "Role Theory and Foreign Policy Analysis: An Evaluation," in Role Theory and Foreign Policy Analysis, edited by Stephen G. Walker, 241–259 (Durham, NC: Duke University Press, 1987).

24. Seymour Martin Lipset, *American Exceptionalism: A Double-Edged Sword* (New York: Norton, 1997).

25. Daniel Woodley, "Radical Right Discourse Contra State-Based Authoritarian Populism: Neoliberalism, Identity and Exclusion after the Crisis," in *Analysing Fascist Discourse: European Fascism in Talk and Text*, edited by Ruth Wodak and John E. Richardson, 17–41 (New York: Routledge, 2013).

26. Jeffrey T. Checkel, "Social Constructivisms in Global and European Politics: A Review Essay," *Review of International Studies* 30, no. 2 (2004): 234.

27. Marc Lynch, *State Interests and Public Spheres: The International Politics of Jordan's Identity* (New York: Columbia University Press, 1999), 18.

28. Tzvetan Todorov, *The Poetics of Prose* (Paris: Ithaca, 1977), 45.

29. Geoffrey Roberts, "History, Theory and the Narrative Turn in IR," *Review of International Studies* 32, no. 4 (2006): 703–714.

30. Daniel Bernardi et al., *Narrative Landmines*.

31. Morgenthau, *Politics among Nations*, 73; See also Morgenthau, *Truth and Power*.

32. Many, but not all, scholars make a distinction between narrative and story. Halverson, Corman, and Goodall, for example, describe a narrative as a "system of stories." Jeffry R. Halverson, H. Lloyd Goodall, and Steven R. Corman, *Master Narratives of Islamist Extremism* (Basingstoke: Palgrave Macmillan, 2011).

33. Gearóid ÓTuathail, "Theorizing Practical Geopolitical Reasoning: The Case of the United States' Response to the War in Bosnia," *Political Geography* 21, no. 5 (2002): 627.

34. ÓTuathail, "Theorizing Practical Geopolitical Reasoning," 609.

35. Monroe Price, "Al-Obedi's Tripoli Surprise and the Packaging of Libya's Future," *Huffington Post*, April 20, 2011, accessed May 22, 2013, http://www.huffingtonpost.com/monroe-price/strategic-narratives-of-t_b_851701.html.

36. Andrew Hoskins, *Televising War: From Vietnam to Iraq* (London: Continuum, 2004); Andrew Hoskins, "Temporality, Proximity, and Security: Terror in a Media-drenched Age," *International Relations* 20 (2007): 453–66; Hoskins and O'Loughlin, *Television and Terror* (London: Palgrave Macmillan, 2009).

37. Antoniades et al., "Great Power Politics and Strategic Narratives."

38. Michel Foucault, *The Archaeology of Knowledge*, trans. A.M. Sheridan Smith, (London: Tavistock, 1972); Michel Foucault, *Power/Knowledge: Selected Interviews and Other Writings, 1972–1977* (London: Vintage Books, 1980); Michel Foucault, *The History of Sexuality: An Introduction*, trans. Robert Hurley (London: Penguin, 1984).

39. Robert M. Entman, *Projections of Power: Framing News, Public Opinion, and US Foreign Policy* (Chicago: University of Chicago Press, 2009), 5. Emphasis is his.

40. Robert M. Entman, review of *Framing Public Life: Perspectives on Media and Our Understanding of the Social World*, edited by Stephen D. Reese, Oscar H. Gandy, Jr., and August E. Grant (Mahwah, NJ: Lawrence Erlbaum, 2001), in *Political Communication* 23, no. 1 (2006): 121; Hsiang Iris Chyi and Maxwell McCombs, "Media Salience and the Process of Framing: Coverage of the Columbine School Shootings," *Journalism & Mass Communication Quarterly* 81, no. 1 (2004): 22–35.

41. Gadi Wolfsfeld, *Media and the Path to Peace* (Cambridge: Cambridge University Press, 2004); Derek B. Miller, *Media Pressure on Foreign Policy: The Evolving Theoretical Framework* (Basingstoke: Palgrave Macmillan, 2007).

42. Michael Pfau, Michel M. Haigh, Theresa Shannon, Toni Tones, Deborah Mercurio, Raina Williams, Blanca Binstock, "The Influence of Television News Depictions of the Images of War on Viewers," *Journal of Broadcasting &*

Electronic Media 52, no. 2 (2008): 303–322; Thomas E. Nelson, Rosalee A. Clawson, and Zoe M. Oxley, "Media Framing of a Civil Liberties Conflict and Its Effect on Tolerance," *American Political Science Review* 91, no. 3 (1997): 567–583; David Domke, David Perlmutter, and Meg Spratt, "The Primes of Our Times? An Examination of the 'Power'of Visual Images," *Journalism* 3, no. 2 (2002): 131–59; Thomas Petersen, "Testing Visual Signals in Representative Surveys," *International Journal of Public Opinion Research* 17, no. 4 (2005): 456–72.

43. Roberts, "History, Theory and the Narrative Turn in IR," 712.

44. Janice Bially-Mattern, *Ordering International Politics* (New York: Routledge, 2005); Charlotte Epstein, *The Power of Words* (Cambridge: The MIT Press, 2008); Maarten Hajer, *The Politics of Environmental Discourse: Ecological Modernization and the Policy Process* (Oxford: Oxford University Press, 1995); Schimmelfennig, *The EU, NATO and the Integration of Europe: Rules and Rhetoric* (Cambridge: Cambridge University Press, 2003).

45. Alister Miskimmon, Ben O'Loughlin, and Laura Roselle, "Forging the World: Strategic Narratives and International Relations," Royal Holloway/ Elon University Working Paper, accessed May 22, 2013, http://newpolcom. rhul.ac.uk/storage/Forging%20the%20World%20Working%20Paper%20 2012.pdf; Ted Hopf, *Social Construction of International Politics: Identities & Foreign Policies, Moscow, 1955 and 1999* (Ithaca: Cornell University Press, 2002); Maja Zehfuss, *Constructivism in International Relations: the Politics of Reality*, Vol. 83 (Cambridge: Cambridge University Press, 2002).

46. Jack Snyder, *Myths of Empire: Domestic Politics and International Ambition* (Ithaca, NY: Cornell University Press, 1991).

47. We are not arguing that these are distinct processes. In fact, we see these as inextricably linked. We distinguish among them here for conceptual clarity.

48. Alexander George, "Domestic Constraints on Regime Change in US Foreign Policy: The Need for Policy Legitimacy," in *American Foreign Policy: Theoretical Essays*, edited by G. J. Ikenberry, 583–608 (Glenview: Scott, Foresman, 1989).

49. Laura Roselle, *Media and the Politics of Failure: Great Powers, Communication Strategies, and Military Defeats* (Basingstoke: Palgrave Macmillan, 2006), 9.

50. Cameron Thies, "Role Theory and Foreign Policy," Working Paper, 2009, accessed May 22, 2013, http://myweb.uiowa.edu/bhlai/workshop/role.pdf.

51. Joseph S. Nye, *The Power to Lead* (New York: Oxford University Press, 2008), 29.

52. Craig Hayden, *The Rhetoric of Soft Power: Public Diplomacy in Global Contexts* (Lanham, MD: Lexington Books, 2012), 51.

53. Hayden, *The Rhetoric of Soft Power*, 56.

54. Hayden, *The Rhetoric of Soft Power*; Jan Melissen, *The New Public Diplomacy* (Basingstoke: Palgrave Macmillan, 2005); Philip Seib, *Real-Time Diplomacy: Politics and Power in the Social Media Era* (Basingstoke: Palgrave Macmillan, 2012).

55. Thomas Risse, "International Norms and Domestic Change: Arguing and Communicative Behavior in the Human Rights Area," *Politics & Society* 27, no. 4 (1999); Thomas Risse, "'Let's Argue!': Communicative Action in World Politics," *International Organization* 54, no. 1 (2000): 1–39.

56. Risse, "'Let's Argue!'"

57. Ronald R. Krebs and Patrick Thaddeus Jackson, "Twisting Tongues and Twisting Arms: The Power of Political Rhetoric," *European Journal of International Relations* 13, no. 1 (2007): 36.

58. Krebs and Jackson, "Twisting Tongues and Twisting Arms," 36, 42.

59. Janice Bially Mattern, *Ordering International Politics: Identity, Crisis, and Representational Force* (London: Routledge, 2005), 97.
60. J.P. Singh. "The Meta-Power of Interactions: Security and Commerce in Networked Environments," in *The Meta-Power Paradigm: Impacts and Transformation of Agents, Institutions, and Social Systems: Capitalism, State, and Democracy in a Global Context*, edited by Tom R. Burns and Peter M. Hall (New York: Peter Lang, 2012), 472.
61. Frank Schimmelfennig, *The EU, NATO and the integration of Europe: Rules and Rhetoric* (Cambridge: Cambridge University Press, 2003).
62. Steele, *Defacing Power*, 85.
63. Marshall McLuhan, *Understanding Media: The Extension of Man* (Cambridge, MA: MIT Press, 1994).
64. Andrew Hoskins and Ben O'Loughlin, *Television and Terror: Conflicting Times and the Crisis of News Discourse* (Basingstoke: Palgrave Macmillan, 2007).
65. Robin Brown, "Getting to War: Communication and Mobilization in the 2002–03 Iraq Crisis," in *Media and Conflict in the Twenty-First Century*, edited by Philip Seib (New York: Palgrave, 2005).
66. Steele, *Defacing Power*, 52.
67. Elizabeth Hanson, *The Information Revolution and World Politics* (Lanham: Rowman and Littlefield, 2008).
68. Philip Seib, ed. *Towards a New Public Diplomacy* (Basingstoke: Palgrave, 2009).
69. Steven Livingston, "Transparency and the News Media," in *Power and Conflict in the Age of Transparency*, edited by Bernard I. Finel and Kristin, 257–85 (New York: Palgrave, 2003), 257.
70. Andrew Chadwick, *The Hybrid Media System: Politics and Power* (New York: Oxford University Press, 2013).
71. Andrew Hoskins and Ben O'Loughlin, *War and Media: The Emergence of Diffused War* (London: Polity, 2010).
72. Monroe E. Price, *Media and Sovereignty: The Global Information Revolution and Its Challenge to State Power* (Cambridge: MIT Press, 2002), 250.
73. McLuhan, *Understanding Media*; Neil Postman, "The Reformed English Curriculum," in *The Shape of the Future in American Secondary Education*, edited by Alvin C. Eurich (New York: Pitman, 1970); Mina Al-Lami, Andrew Hoskins, and Ben O'Loughlin, "Mobilisation and Violence in the New Media Ecology: The Dua Khalil Aswad and Camilia Shehata Cases," *Critical Studies on Terrorism* 5, no. 2 (2012): 237–256.
74. Ronald J. Deibert, *Parchment, Printing, and Hypermedia: Communication in World Order Transformation* (New York: Columbia University Press, 1997).
75. Hoskins and O'Loughlin, *War and Media*.
76. Marie-Laure Ryan, "On the Theoretical Foundations of Transmedial Narratology," in *Narratology beyond Literary Criticism: Mediality, Disciplinarity*, edited by Jan-Christoph Meister, Tom Kindt, and Wilhelm Schernus (Berlin/New York: De Gruyter, 2005), 6.
77. Timothy Garton-Ash, "1989!" *New York Review of Books* 56, no. 17 (November 5, 2009), accessed May 22, 2013, http://www.nybooks.com/articles/archives/2009/nov/05/1989.
78. Lawrence Freedman, *The Evolution of Nuclear Strategy* (London: MacMillan Press, 1981); Luis Simon, *Geopolitical Change, Grand Strategy and European Security* (Basingstoke: Palgrave Macmillan, 2013).
79. Richard Rumelt, *Good Strategy, Bad Strategy: The Difference and Why It Matters* (London: Profile Books, 2011).

80. Michelle Bentley, "War and/of Words: Constructing WMD in US Foreign Policy," *Security Studies* 22, no. 1 (2013): 68–97; Hajer, *The Politics of Environmental Discourse*; Michael Billig, *Arguing and Thinking: A Rhetorical Approach to Social Psychology*, (Cambridge, MA: Cambridge University Press, 1987); Quentin Skinner, *Liberty Before Liberalism* (Cambridge: Cambridge University Press, 1998); Ludwig Wittgenstein, *Philosophical Investigations* (Oxford: Blackwell, 2001).

81. Morgenthau, *Politics among Nations*; Joseph S. Nye, "Soft Power," *Foreign Policy* 80 (1990): 153–171.

82. G. John Ikenberry, *Liberal Leviathan: The Origins, Crisis, and Transformation of the American World Order* (Princeton: Princeton University Press, 2012).

83. Jonathan P. G. Bach, *Between Sovereignty and Integration: German Foreign Policy and National Identity after 1989*, Vol. 23 (Münster: LIT Verlag, 1999), 60.

84. Steele, *Defacing Power*.

85. Krebs and Jackson, "Twisting Tongues and Twisting Arms," 36.

86. Marc Lynch, "Why Engage? China and the Logic of Communicative Engagement," *European Journal of International Relations* 8, no. 2 (2002): 187–230.

87. Steele, *Defacing Power*.

88. Bially Mattern, *Ordering International Politics*.

89. Hajer, *The Politics of Environmental Discourse*; Epstein, *The Power of Words*.

90. David Campbell, *Writing Security* (Minneapolis: University of Minnesota Press, 1992), 26, italics in original.

91. Campbell, *Writing Security*, 69.

92. Campbell, *Writing Security*.

93. Bach, *Between Sovereignty and Integration*, 61.

94. Bentley, "War and/of Words."

95. Epstein, *The Power of Words*.

96. The logic we use here is that set out in theories of the essential contestability of political concepts. Walter B. Gallie, *Philosophy and the Historical Understanding* (New York: Schocken Books, 1964); Glen Newey, "Philosophy, Politics and Contestability," *Journal of Political Ideologies* 6, no. 3 (2001): 245–61. The point has been made differently by Jacques Derrida, *Of Grammatology* (Baltimore: Johns Hopkins University Press, 1974); Charlotte Epstein, "Constructivism or the Eternal Return of Universals: Why Returning to Language Is Vital for Prolonging the Owl's Flight," *European Journal of International Relations* 19, no.3 (forthcoming); Christopher Norris, *Derrida* (London: Fontana, 1987).

97. Robert Cooper, *The Breaking of Nations: Order and Chaos in the Twenty-First Century* (London: Atlantic Books, 2004), 113.

98. Charlotte Epstein, *The Power of Words in International Relations: Birth of an Anti-Whaling Discourse* (Cambridge, MA: MIT Press, 2008); Charlotte Epstein, "Moby Dick or Moby Doll? Discourse or How to Study 'the Social Construction of' All the Way Down," in *Constructing the International Economy*, edited by Rawi Abdelal, Mark Blyth, and Craig Parsons (Ithaca: Cornell University Press, 2010).

99. Alister Miskimmon, Ben O'Loughlin, and Laura Roselle, eds., *Forging the World: Strategic Narratives and International Relations* (Ann Arbor: Michigan University Press, 2014).

100. Roberts, "History, Theory and the Narrative Turn in IR."

101. Krebs and Jackson, "Twisting Tongues and Twisting Arms."

102. Epstein, *The Power of Words*.

103. Steele, *Defacing Power*; Felix Berenskoetter, "Parameters of a National Biography," *European Journal of International Relations* (2012) first published on October 16, 2012 as doi:10.1177/1354066112445290; Hajer, *The Politics of Environmental Discourse*; Catarina Kinnvall, "Globalization and Religious Nationalism: Self, Identity, and the Search for Ontological Security," *Political Psychology* 25, no. 5 (2004): 741–67; Catarina Kinnvall, "European Trauma Governance and the Psychological Moment," *Alternatives: Global, Local, Political* 37, no. 3 (2012): 266–81; Bach, *Between Sovereignty and Integration*.

104. Campbell, *Writing Security*.

105. Steele, *Defacing Power*; Kinvall, "Globalization and Religious Nationalism"; Ayşe Zarakol, "Ontological (In)Security and State Denial of Historical Crimes: Turkey and Japan," *International Relations* 24, no. 1 (2010): 3–23; Ayse Zarakol, *After Defeat: How the East Learned to Live with the West*, Vol. 118 (Cambridge: Cambridge University Press, 2010); Stuart Croft, *Securitizing Islam: Identity and the Search for Security* (Cambridge: Cambridge University Press, 2012).

106. Epstein, *The Power of Words*; Erik Ringmar, "Inter-Textual Relations: The Quarrel Over the Iraq War as a Conflict between Narrative Types," *Cooperation and Conflict* 41, no. 4 (2006): 403–21.

107. Lene Hansen, "Theorizing the Image for Security Studies: Visual Securitization and the Muhammad Cartoon Crisis," *European Journal of International Relations* 17, no. 1 (2011): 51–74; William J. T. Mitchell, *Cloning Terror: The War of Images, 9/11 to the Present* (Chicago: University of Chicago Press, 2011); William J. T. Mitchell, "There Are No Visual Media," *Journal of Visual Culture* 4, no. 2 (2005): 257–266; Ben O'Loughlin, "Images as Weapons of War: Representation, Mediation and Interpretation," *Review of International Studies* 37, no. 1 (2010): 71–91; Cynthia Weber, "Popular Visual Language as Global Communication: The Remediation of United Airlines Flight 93," *Review of International Studies* 34, no. 1 (2008): 137–53.

108. Eytan Gilboa, "Global Television News and Foreign Policy: Debating the CNN Effect," *International Studies Perspectives* 6, no. 3 (2005): 325–41; Hoskins and O'Loughlin, *War and Media*; James Gow and Milena Michalski, *War, Image and Legitimacy: Viewing Contemporary Conflict* (London: Routledge, 2007); Ben D. Mor, "Using Force to Save Face: The Performative Side of War," *Peace & Change* 37, no. 1 (2012): 95–121; Ben D. Mor, "Public Diplomacy in Grand Strategy," *Foreign Policy Analysis* 2, no. 2 (2006): 157–76; Ben D. Mor, "The Rhetoric of Public Diplomacy and Propaganda Wars: A View from Self-Presentation Theory," *European Journal of Political Research* 46, no. 5 (2007): 661–83; Ben D. Mor, "Accounts and Impression Management in Public Diplomacy: Israeli Justification of Force during the 2006 Lebanon War," *Global Change, Peace & Security* 21, no. 2 (2009): 219–39; Ben D. Mor, "Credibility talk in Public Diplomacy," *Review of International Studies* 38, no. 2 (2012): 393–422; Michael C. Williams, "Words, Images, Enemies: Securitization and International Politics," *International Studies Quarterly* 47, no. 4 (2003): 511–31.

109. Bach, *Between Sovereignty and Integration*; Berenskoetter, "Parameters of a National Biography."

110. Bach, *Between Sovereignty and Integration*.

2   Actors in Strategic Narratives

INTRODUCTION

The role of actors in international relations (IR) theory has been wrought with underlying tensions. One tension is that IR theory has focused most squarely on states as political actors even as political leaders and scholars emphasize the proliferation of nonstate actors in the last half century. Another tension involves a focus on material factors as determinative, suggesting that actors are either defined by those material factors or are without agency at all. States have been most often described with adjectives associated with perceived power status in the international system. One need only think about great powers, rising powers, and weak states to see this. Yet, as we recognize this, we have already entered into the realm of narratives because we are describing actors that fit within a narrative about what actors operate in the international system and how. In fact, as realists describe the primary norm of international sovereignty, they define the actors in the system. Stephen Jay Gould has written: "The most erroneous stories are those we think we know best—and therefore never scrutinize or question."[1] A focus on strategic narratives requires one to identify and scrutinize the actors in international relations today. This speaks to Sikkink's call "to articulate more clearly a theory of agentic constructivism."[2]

We argue here that actors are given meaning to themselves and others by narrative. This chapter first ties meaning through narratives to issues associated with identity in the international relations literature. This focuses attention on identity in relationship (self-other) and in terms of subjectivity (self), the agency structure debate, and issues associated with collective and individual identity. Overall, this section sets out our conception of how actors are shaped by narratives within the broader IR literature. Second, the chapter gives an overview of the actors within narratives about IR, and their attributes, actions, and motivations. We address the increase in the number and types of actors and their place in narratives about the international system. The new media environment has changed how narratives can be contested and how different groups, and even individuals, can claim to be purposeful actors on the world stage today. Third, we examine how political actors use narratives that address actors' intersubjectivity and subjectivity (conception of self) strategically in pursuing foreign policy goals. The European Union member states, for example, are using strategic narratives to help shape integration processes themselves. Developing countries are seeking new ways to use strategic narratives, as can be exemplified by climate change negotiations. And nonstate actors seek to use strategic narratives to shape the international policy agenda and mobilize support within individual countries and in transnational communities. New information tools are important in this process as well. Fourth, we briefly look at the strategic narratives of the United States. An overview of the construction of the US great power narrative in the 1940s highlights processes associated with the construction of a Cold War narrative. We argue that the continuation of deeply embedded great powers' strategic narratives structure foreign policy behavior in a post–Cold War system by analyzing US national security strategies and the remarks of Presidents Bush and Obama at the United Nations General Assembly.

ACTORS IN NARRATIVES AND INTERNATIONAL RELATIONS THEORY

The Tie to Identity

Understanding actors in a narrative context focuses our attention most closely on the idea of identity—a central concept in the study of international relations, and especially constructivism. In international relations theory, early constructivist literature on the role of state identity argued that state identity affects foreign policy and international relations.[3] The constructivist literature developed in large part due to the inability of realist and idealist works to explain the end of the Cold War, the growing integration in Europe, the rise of nonstate actors, and changes in norms and practices related especially to human rights.[4] Why did the Soviet Union cease to exist on December 25, 1991? Why was the transition relatively peaceful? Would a European Union grow and flourish? Would the dignity of human beings be valued in the international system?

Attempts to answer these questions have led many to focus on identity. The claim is that realist and idealist lenses do not provide adequate purchase on the questions because the changes in the international system on which these questions focus require attention to ideas and identity. Constructivists focus their attention on how identity affects interest construction, for example, which may then affect behavior. Thus Rousseau and Garcia-Retamero suggest that "power influences people's threat perceptions only after identity between the self and the other has been established."[5] Others go further, arguing that power is not separate from questions of identity, as representational force is power itself: representational force traps others "with the credible threat emanating from potential violence to their" sense of self.[6]

Much of the work on identity focuses on state identity. Identity, wrote Lynch, indicates "how each state understands the meaning and purpose of regional and international organizations, the role the state should play in the world, and the kinds of interests worth pursuing."[7] And assumptions about preferences of states in the international system are based on beliefs, place, reputation, prestige, credibility—all of these are related to state identity. Identities *identify* important characteristics of an actor. This research sees identity as a "claim to . . . attention"[8] or labeling.[9] The specific processes involved in the (re)construction of state identity are less clear and are directly related to communication. Constructivism suggests that identities are complex and multifaceted, and must be (re)constructed over time;[10] we argue this is directly related to communication of narratives, which inevitably include actors. Our attention to actors responds, in part, to the focus on structure in the constructivist literature. As Sikkink has noted, the constructivist literature came to focus on how identity structures actors' behavior in the world rather than on if, when, and how actors play a role in this construction.[11] This is similar to Barnett's critique of constructivism: that it has focused too much attention on ideas or culture and too little attention on the agency of actors within an institutional or strategic context.[12]

As Bially-Mattern says, "Identities are not natural facts, but social constructions that are always in process."[13] A number of scholars have touched on, at least in a general sense, the importance of communication to the process of identity construction. Wendt, for example, argued that "rhetorical practice," through "consciousness-raising, dialogue, discussion and persuasion, education, ideological labor, symbolic action, and so on" could affect identities and interests.[14] Risse's notion of arguing also seeks to explain how identities change.[15] Keck and Sikkink claim that "networks are communicative structures" that help explain changes in norms over time.[16] Yet none of these authors delve into how this communication works. While March and Olsen focus on a "logic of appropriateness" that "sees human action as driven by rules of appropriate or exemplary behavior, organized into institutions,"[17] we suggest that strategic narratives are more helpful in understanding the construction of identity and behavior in international relations due to the narrative structure that includes actors and the agency that narratives afford actors. Narratives set out who the actors are, what characterizes them, what attributes they possess, what actions they take, and what motivates them. Actors are set within an environment or context that affects them even as they often affect the environment. We also claim that political actors can use narratives strategically to shape the behavior of others.

If focused on the state as actor, we argue that there are multiple narratives with which the state engages. These correspond to narrative identities about how the state sees itself as acting in the international system—as great power, rising power, ally, enemy, internationalist, and so forth. Legro, for example, studies "national attitudes toward international society" by looking at three positions—integrationism, separatism, and revisionism—but without an explicit focus on narratives.[18] There are also narratives about the people of the state or the nation itself—freedom-loving, tolerant, efficient, and so forth. Bially-Mattern notes this when she discusses states as having different narratives that may overlap in terms of characteristics that are emphasized. Although we separate these narratives conceptually by focus (as does Bially-Mattern) either relationally (self-other) or subjectively (self), expectations about actors may overlap in these narratives. For example, the narrative of American exceptionalism that is characterized by liberty, egalitarianism, individualism, populism, and laissez-faire also sets out a call to share this with the world.[19] (This idea of American exceptionalism stands in contrast to actors depicted as normal or normalizing, such as in the cases of Russia and Germany discussed below.)

National identity has been addressed in the literature as "a constructed *and* public national self-image based on membership in a political community as well as history, myths, symbols, language, and cultural norms commonly held by members of a nation."[20] In his work on coalition building, Snyder notes that because these "myths are necessary to justify the power and policies of the ruling coalition, the leaders must maintain the myths or else jeopardize their rule."[21] These myths are not simply used strategically by groups as political instruments, although that certainly is true: "Often the proponents of these strategic rationalizations, as well as the wider population," notes Snyder, "came to believe them."[22] These beliefs then affect future policy decisions.[23]

There are a growing number of scholars who have looked at the nation-state as situated within and shaped by narrative(s). These include Berenskoetter, who identifies a biographical narrative of the state that designates "an experienced space (giving meaning to the past) intertwined with an envisioned space (giving meaning to the future) and delineated through horizons of experience and of possibility, respectively."[24] Bially-Mattern argues that "narrative is prior to and necessary for all other forms of communicative exchange."[25] For most of these scholars the use of narrative as a conceptual underpinning for understanding identity lies in the structure of narratives that set out an actor within a context, and includes a temporal and spacial dimension.

Agency/Structure

Narratives structure behavior even as actors are afforded agency and thus our conception of strategic narratives bridges the divide between those who focus on agency and those who focus on structure. Bially-Mattern notes that this divide exists in both international relations theories and narrative theories.[26] In regard to structural IR theorists, many note that Waltz and other structuralists "smuggle" or "sneak in" agency (via nationalism, for example).[27] On the other end of the spectrum, there are international relations scholars who focus attention on agency at the expense of structure, context, and information requirements. Game theorists, for example, take as given many especially interesting concepts related to international behavior, including interests, variability in information, and social dynamics. We agree with Bially-Mattern and Sikkink in rejecting both extremes: "the two [agency and structure] are mutually constitutive";[28] "structures and agency are mutually determined."[29] An example of this is found in Cruz's analysis of postcolonial Costa Rica and Nicaragua.[30] Costa Rican political elites used a narrative that stressed the peaceful and diligent nature of the people, "creating in the process sufficient space for intraelite consensus building and, ultimately, the political stability necessary to craft and execute developmental policies."[31] A structure was thus created that encouraged certain ways of working together and facilitated certain policies. In Nicaragua a very different narrative was strategically employed, which "created incentives among political rivals for preemptive, particularist bids, thus closing off space for effective developmental leadership."[32]

Collective/Individual Actors

Another conceptual matter important in international relations is how to understand and distinguish between and among collective and individual identities. Individuals have identities that psychologists have studied extensively. These can be different from collective identities, but can be related as well. This is associated with the distinction between collective and individual memory.[33] Collective identity "is a set of ideas that are generally accepted by any group of actors as defining what their collectivity is and the general rules under which it operates."[34] Leavy, in highlighting the role of media in the construction of collective identity, argues that "[n]arrative is the technique whereby collective memory is created, shaped, and reinforced, how meaning is imparted."[35] Eder goes farther, suggesting that "collective identities are narrative constructions which permit the control of the boundaries of a network of actors."[36] We argue here that a collective narrative can be identified, even if it is created through a process involving individuals in the midst of domestic contestation. As Steele argues: "The narrative itself is an outcome of intrasocietal debates, but because it emanates from the agents of states, it nevertheless most closely approximates the identity commitments a state will pursue in international relations."[37] Thus, state narratives are articulated by state leaders. Likewise, collective narratives of other political actors can be identified by analyzing collectives.

ACTORS IN STRATEGIC NARRATIVES OF
INTERNATIONAL RELATIONS

We turn now to an overview of the prominent actors within the narrative of the international system most commonly associated with the post–World War II world. These actors are found in the narratives that political leaders (and scholars) set forth. With each of these actors come characteristics or attributes and expected behavior that we argue is related to identity and structure action. Included here are great powers, normal powers, rising powers, weak powers, and rogue powers that seem to be based on underlying hard power capabilities. It is important to note that we do not argue that hard power capabilities have no place in the construction of actors. We do argue that these types of narrative actors may seek to behave in ways that are consistent with actors' attributes and expectations even if hard power capabilities change. Thus, we give examples of works in international relations that suggest that actors behave in particular ways, not entirely due to power capabilities, but to identities that we suggest are related to actor characteristics within narratives. In this section we also address the rise of nonstate actors and the characteristics and expectations associated with these particular kinds of these actors. Work on narratives suggests that how actors are defined and characterized will influence individuals and groups of people that exist within the foreign policy process, including political leaders, interest groups, bureaucratic actors, diplomats, journalists, and the public.

Unipole/Hegemon

We begin with the unipole or global hegemon because theoretically it is this actor that should be least constrained in an international system—if at all constrained. Finnemore is a singular voice in Ikenberry, Mastanduno, and Wohlforth's edited volume[38] who argues that in spite of the fact that the US is the "closest thing to a unipole we have seen in centuries, [it] has been frustrated in many of its policies since it achieved that status at the end of the Cold War."[39] She explains this by the need, even for a unipole, to seek legitimacy and exist in the social world of institutions. This is difficult and socially constructed and can lead to hypocrisy: "They proclaim adherence to rules or values while violating them in pursuit of other goals."[40] We argue that the concept of strategic narratives helps us understand this more fully. A focus on narratives allows us to understand when, why, and how legitimation is important. Hypocrisy, in other words, is a disturbance to a narrative or narratives that set out what is expected of an actor. Even unipoles have narratives.

Great Powers

There are some that do not accept or agree that unipolarity characterizes the international system today, but will accept that there are great powers that structure the system. In other words, a central actor within the overarching post–World War II international system narrative is the great power. Characteristics associated with a great power within this narrative include an emphasis on sovereignty (independence of action), leadership (structuring the system), and responsibility (to others). As David Lake notes: "Status shapes the behavior of states, with great powers expected to act differently from other states and, especially, to be involved in more alliances, more conflicts, and more conflicts further from their home territories."[41] We argue that narrative helps us understand how status is defined and determined, and is central to setting out expectations about the behavior of states, including great powers. So acceptance of a great power narrative should lead to similar behaviors across political systems at least to a degree. There is evidence to suggest that this is indeed what happens; Oates, for example, shows that US and Russian responses to terrorism (by leaders, media, and audience) are more similar to each other than to British responses.[42] Roselle also argues that the US and Russia behaved similarly during withdrawals from failed wars, despite different political and media systems.[43] The explanation for similarities in US and Russian behavior can be attributed to each state's understanding of what is expected of states in the international system.

The notion that great powers are expected to act in a particular way highlights the importance of narratives. If indeed power granted a state the ability to pursue any course of action it chose, then why would there be particular expectations about the behavior of great powers? Why wouldn't powerful states that had not achieved military objectives simply admit this and move on? Some scholars suggest that credibility lies at the heart of this dilemma because past actions can influence if and how others trust you in the future.[44] Press disputes this, arguing instead that a "country's credibility, at least during crises, is driven not by its past behavior but rather by [hard] power and interests."[45] However, Press acknowledges that his research "presents a new puzzle"—"the very same leaders who are so concerned about their own country's credibility that they are loath to back down reflexively ignore the enemy's history for keeping or breaking commitments."[46] We argue that a focus on strategic narratives resolves this puzzle. Narratives about what powerful states can and should do constrain behavior beyond a focus on hard power.

The cases of the US failure in Vietnam and USSR failure in Afghanistan serve as one example of how identifying as a great power affects political behavior.[47] In these cases, the same story was told to domestic audiences: great powers did not lose, did not turn their backs on their allies, and acted with honor. Leaders designed and supported Vietnamization and Afghan national reconciliation as policies to strengthen allies so that they could defend themselves. In both cases, leaders knew their allies remained weak, yet withdrawal continued apace. In each case the story of withdrawal fit with what was perceived to be the proper and the rightful role of a great power in the international system—a great power narrative. In neither case did leaders say that the state had failed to achieve its goals. In both cases, honor was the most important phrase, connected to fulfilling a duty to defend others, a task central to the identity of a great power. The powers did not subsequently acknowledge their respective roles in South Vietnam's fall and Afghanistan's descent into chaos. In fact, in the US, the public expected and predicted a South Vietnamese defeat by the North. In the Soviet Union the military expected Afghanistan to deteriorate into chaos. Still, both superpowers insisted that withdrawal was accomplished with honor, and they constructed the same kinds of stories to explain and justify it. In fact, Dwight Chapin, deputy assistant to President Nixon, in a memo to White House Chief of State H. R. Haldeman, said of the media strategy associated with the signing of the Paris Peace Accords in 1973: "What we should have for the people is a story of the war that they can understand and live with."[48]

Normal Powers

Another actor prominent in international narratives is that of a *normal power*. This is perhaps seen most often in regard to Russia during and after the dissolution of the Soviet Union,[49] but has also been used in the context of Germany and China.

One can see the power of actors in the narrative in an analysis of the transition of the Soviet narrative about the international system from one that emphasizes dueling economic systems as actors to one in which the Soviet Union becomes a normal great power in the international system. As Legro notes, the dominant Soviet "belief" or *narrative* was about "the inevitable competition between the capitalist and socialist blocs, that the correlation of forces would favor socialism, leading to its eventual victory and the formation of a new international system."[50] Included in the narrative that Gorbachev and his supporters championed was the state as the primary actor. Perhaps most important to the changing narrative was a change from the communist identity of the Soviet Union. Instead of economic systems or classes as actors, with the Soviet state as the exemplar of a great socialist system, the new narrative set out states as the primary actors in the international system and proclaimed that the Soviet Union would be a normal great power within that state-centric system. This notion of normal—*normalno*—was resonant in the USSR.

It is important to recognize that in both narratives (Communist and State) the USSR was depicted as a great power—with the concordant attributes and expected behaviors—as discussed above. Changes included a different understanding of behavior within the international system. Normal great powers are involved in international negotiations and seek recognition on the world stage. A Communist narrative emphasizes the inevitable conflict between economic classes and systems. A narrative focusing on state actors—rather than economic actors—fit within a broader international—and dominant narrative—about how the international system worked. As Legro notes, "The United States and Western European governments and nongovernmental organizations threw their status-granting support and resources behind new thinking and Gorbachev."[51] This is because the Soviet Union was changing its narrative to one more in line with Western narratives about the international system. With this came rewards.

Interestingly, Germany is also wrestling with a narrative that includes notions related to normalization. Instead of looking to be a normal state in Europe, however, Germans use the term *normalizing* as a process. Germany's post–WWII development has been understood as rejecting many of the expectations of rationalist IR. Germany has been reluctant to use aggressive military force to the point that Maull describes Germany as a "civilian power."[52] Germany has also embedded itself deeply within multilateral institutions, which has limited its unilateral room for maneuver.[53] (West) Germany lived Thomas Mann's dictum of a "European Germany, not a German Europe." However, since the late 1990s the sense that Germany is going through a process of normalization has taken hold, understood as the emergence of a more identifiably national-interest-driven policy style.[54] Bulmer and Paterson, for example, argue that,

> Normalization, by contrast, is reflected in a greater willingness to undertake unilateral demarches, the adoption of a discourse of the national interest in policy statements, and the use of power to keep certain items off the agenda. In terms of power resources, political and economic weight are associated with more fixed, structural properties and are less susceptible to change; however, greater resort to advancing compelling demands would be associated with normalization.[55]

So normalization entails more focus on German interests in the context of a European integration. A narrative of a normal state, then, is one that suggests that states should act in a more self-interested way. The concept of self-interest demands that states determine what that means—and this, we know from constructivists, clearly relates to more than an undefined sense of security.

Finally, some have depicted China as becoming a normal state in the international system. Once again, the shift from states as actors—rather than economic systems—signifies a significant shift in the narrative. This comes before—and perhaps is more important than—whether rising powers are then set out as peaceful or aggressive, because the narrative of a state-centric international realm suggests that actions can affect the conditions under which states are peaceful or aggressive. As Legro notes: "At least since the time of Deng Xiaoping's leadership, the prevailing trend in China's orientation [narrative] toward the existing rules, institutions, and norms of the international system has been toward integration."[56] China sees itself as a normal great power.[57]

Rising Powers

In addition to a normal state, however, China is often described or narrated as a rising state.[58] In addition to China, there are a number of states that identify as rising powers. For example, the BRICS—Brazil, Russia, India, China, and South Africa—are grouped together in a narrative about rising economic power in a post–Cold War world. Two of these (Brazil and India) have called for a place on the United Nations Security Council—suggesting that this is a proper role for them because of their rising status. The very fact that some Chinese political leaders identify China as a rising power in the international system suggests that an underlying narrative about the international system has been accepted by the Chinese themselves. But what does a rising power do in the international system? As Legro notes, there are concerns about rising powers: what will they do with their *power* and *independence*.[59] Some are concerned that rising powers will attempt to change the system.[60] Thus, rising powers are seen as dangerous, which leads to specific assumptions about threat that then affect decision making and foreign policy behavior. A narrative of China as a normal power may suggest a very different future.

A number of scholars note that simply understanding changes in material factors within a country does not tell policy makers enough about a state's behavior to form clear and compelling policies. In fact, assumptions about how rising powers will behave may lead to outcomes that are suboptimal in that they become self-fulfilling prophecies. Legro argues that China's

> influence depends on a third meshing gear—national ideas about how to achieve foreign policy goals. Such ideas perform three critical functions: they empower certain domestic interests groups over others, they generate expectations against which performance is assessed, and they either facilitate or impede the possibility for a new strategy to emerge.[61]

The national ideas Legro discusses are, to our minds, narratives. They are about the past, present, and future of China in the world.

It is these narratives that Callahan examines when he argues that "[t]he heart of Chinese foreign policy . . . is not a security dilemma, but an 'identity dilemma.'"[62] Callahan recognizes and emphasizes the narrative of Chinese exceptionalism, pitting Chinese civilization against outside barbarians, but he also recognizes that there are other narratives—such as the "harmony of civilizations" narrative—that may compete with the exceptionalism narrative. So, again, we see the need to understand *narratives* about the rising state to understand international relations. For in addition to understanding narratives that constrain and influence Chinese foreign policy, as Leonard points out, Chinese narratives may come to influence narratives about the international system itself.[63]

Weak States/Rogue States

A final group of states that are grouped as actors in many of the international narratives of today are weak states[64] and rogue states.

Rotberg describes weak states as including

> a broad continuum of states that are: inherently weak because of geographical, physical, or fundamental economic constraints; basically

strong, but temporarily or situationally weak because of internal antagonisms, management flaws, greed, despotism, or external attacks; and a mixture of the two. Weak states typically harbor ethnic, religious, linguistic, or other intercommunal tensions that have not yet, or not yet thoroughly, become overtly violent.[65]

This definition implies that different understandings—or narratives—are important to understanding weak states. Strongly contested narratives or groups associated with different narratives contribute significantly to the weakness of the state beyond measures of hard power.

Perhaps one can see the implications of narratives about state actors most vividly when analyzing what policy makers, especially in the United States, have called rogue states. In terms of narrativity, the very concept of a weak/rogue state suggests we're at Time A when it's rogue and we need to get to Time B when it's not rogue, and there'll be some causal transformation in the plot that will get everyone to the desired ending. Narratives about rogue states set out expectations about threat emanating from states that do not follow the rules of the international system, often by pursuing nuclear weapons, for example.[66] Litwak suggests that this narrative can be a problem:

[T]he rogue state designation—that is, demonizing a disparate group of states—significantly distorts policymaking. It perpetuates the false dichotomy that sets up containment and engagement as mutually exclusive strategies.[67]

Alexander George,[68] as Litwak notes, suggests that what is important to understand is the "socialization" of states into the system, or we would say, to an acceptance of the broader narrative about goals and behavior. For example, in Chapter 4, "Contestation," we see how the EU and US try to socialize Iran into a multilateral system of nuclear energy control, but fail for a number of reasons. In addition, contemporary struggles in weak or rogue states like Syria, Iran, and Burma get given meaning to international society through the great powers' preferred system narratives.[69] O'Loughlin suggests, for example, that "for China, Russia and other states promoting an international order based upon the primacy of sovereignty, independent states, Syria, Iran and Burma become instances pivotal to the realization of that order."[70] Likewise the United States and European Union placed events in Tunisia, Egypt, and Libya as pivotal to their own narratives that emphasize the promotion of democracy and the protection of human rights.

NEW ACTORS IN THE INTERNATIONAL NARRATIVE

One of the challenges for the construction of new narratives is when new actors are included in these narratives. The literature in international relations has brought in a number of new actors for examination,[71] but it is rare that scholars have paid explicit attention to how these nonstate actors' roles are constructed. Nonstate actors challenge traditional conceptions of international relations that are focused on the state, and highlight the importance of understanding narratives and narrative power. Transnational advocacy networks, multinational corporations, and terrorist organizations are probably most often cited as important new actors in the world. Included here are also other types of actors, such as diaspora groups, individuals, and virtual groups, including those comprised entirely online and underground groups such as Anonymous. We argue that these too are contained within narratives about how the world does, could, or should work. This leads too to insights on how the new media ecology is changing the context for narrative construction in the world. A challenge for the construction of new narratives and/or for the maintenance of an old narrative about the international system is the proliferation of actors within the context of a technology-connected world. Although Chapters 4 and 5 will focus more explicitly on this new technological ecology, it is important to note that the increasingly interconnected world has affected the ability of groups and individuals to claim actorhood and attempt to set out narratives that may challenge or support dominant (and traditional) elite narratives.

Nonstate actors are increasingly cited as important to international relations. Keck and Sikkink's seminal work on *transnational advocacy networks*, for example, argued that nonstate actors can effect change in the international system by using "the power of their information, ideas, and strategies to alter the information and value contexts within which states make policies."[72] Keck and Sikkink do not, however, specifically explain what makes information or ideas powerful or resonant. They do argue that transnational advocacy networks and other nonstate actors that are concerned about issues within a state may influence political actors outside of a state to take action to effect change. This boomerang model, in essence, argues that advocacy groups can tap into narratives outside of the state, for example, related to human rights, and then states as actors can influence others through both hard power and use of strategic narratives related to order in the international system. Central to this ability is, of course, the ability to communicate across international borders. Groups can find, engage with, and solicit support from supporters online. What is not addressed thoroughly in the literature is whether or not there are specific expectations about transnational advocacy groups as such. Is there an expectation, for example, that these groups will be focused on certain issues (human rights, for example), or that they can communicate only in specific ways?

Terrorists provide another example of an actor that has become more prominent in narratives related to the international system, but expectations about their goals are assumed as malevolent. In response to the emergence of transnational terrorism, innovative recent studies have addressed the diffusion and contestation of communications by or about terrorist groups across national borders and how media and how citizens in different countries transfer and translate stories across different channels and platforms.[73] In the 2000s, the threat posed by Al-Qaeda related radicalization was taken as serious by national security agencies not only because of the potential physical harm terrorism can bring. Rather, Al-Qaeda's very networked structure enabled it to perpetuate a narrative that for some years security agencies did not know how to contest. How Al-Qaeda worked was unknown, creating anxiety for policy makers. A cumulative narrative process was achieved by Al-Qaeda members who, as individuals or as parts of cells, formed "global microstructures" through which the narrative of resistance to the West could be sustained independently of Al-Qaeda leadership.[74] This was enabled by the information infrastructure, through which emergent events were rapidly assimilated into already established narratives in a diffused way through the digital tools (blogs, social networking sites, videos) employed by amateurs as well as by official Al-Qaeda media productions.[75]

Al-Qaeda's narrative sought to convince Muslim audiences to understand ongoing conflicts as part of a wider historical global attack on Islam by a belligerent Zionist-Crusader alliance. Al-Qaeda's Jihadists claimed to serve as the sole and crucial vanguard against this attack. This narrative remained coherent and consistent over time. As Awan and colleagues note,[76] Osama bin Laden's earliest message to the world in his 1996 *Declaration of War against the Americans Occupying the Land of the Two Holy Places*[77] argued:

> The people of Islam had suffered from aggression, iniquity and injustice imposed on them by the Zionist-Crusaders alliance and their collaborators; to the extent that the Muslim's blood became the cheapest and their wealth as loot in the hands of the enemies. Their blood was spilled in Palestine and Iraq. The horrifying pictures of the massacre of Qana, in Lebanon are still fresh in our memory. Massacres in Tajikistan, Burma, Kashmir, Assam, Philippine, Fatani, Ogadin, Somalia, Eritrea, Chechnya and in Bosnia-Herzegovina took place, massacres that send shivers in the body and shake the conscience.[78]

This narrative offered great certainty for those confused or disappointed by world events. It was not difficult to characterize the US and its allies as nefarious when war in Iraq based on forged dossiers and fabricated evidence was leading to civilian deaths, when George W. Bush used the term "crusade"[79] and the spectacles of Guantanamo and Abu Ghraib "demonstrated" the West's motives. For instance, in the lead-up to the invasion of Iraq in 2003, bin Laden argued that "the Bush-Blair axis claims that it wants to annihilate terrorism, but it is no longer a secret—even to the masses—that it really wants to annihilate Islam."[80] Al-Qaeda recognized that the binary narrative projected by the US ("with us or against us") mirrored and reinforced their own narrative. Hence, they welcomed President Bush's election to a second term and endorsed his fellow Republican Senator John McCain in the 2008 US presidential election.[81]

At the same time as Al-Qaeda was narrating world affairs, Western news media regularly constructed narratives about the radicalization of its members, usually featuring a "turn to religion" and change in outward appearances such as the growing of a beard as signifying radicalization. News reports about members who were convicted and spent time in jail often added a "recovery" or "repentance" phase to the narrative.[82] These former Al-Qaeda members were on occasion recruited by states to become counter-narrative agents, using the same digital media spaces as Al-Qaeda members to argue with their interpretation of scripture and their narration of ongoing international politics. In this way, the battle of the narratives involved a complex mix of state and nonstate, political and religious actors, conducted through the Internet as well as in offline relationships, and simultaneously on local and global scales. Chapter 4 will expand on the dynamics of strategic narrative contestation.

US GREAT POWER NARRATIVES

The strategic narrative construction of the US great power narrative provides an illustrative example of how strategic narratives function in international relations. The example is not meant to serve as an exhaustive history, but gives an idea of how we apply a focus on strategic narratives to the reading of history. It is contrasted with the difficulty in constructing a narrative in a post–Cold War environment, which follows from our discussion about the changing information environment and the proliferation of strategic narrative actors. In the immediate post–World War II period, the media environment was dominated by newspapers and radio. Still, political actors had to take into account the projection of strategic narratives for domestic and international audiences. Media considerations, and the importance of public opinion and Congressional support, required the projection of strong narratives with broad strokes. As George notes, "As one moves from the highest level of policy making to the mass public, one expects to find a considerable simplification of the set of assertions and beliefs that lend support to the legitimacy of foreign policy."[83] But the new media ecology complicates this simplification of narratives by adding actors, increasing interactivity, complicating audiences, and warping time and space.

Establishing the United States as a Great Power

In looking at the development of a US great power narrative in the post–World War II context, two separate episodes will serve here to give an overview of the processes of US strategic narrative construction: the Greek and Turkish crisis of 1947 (leading to the Truman Doctrine) and the drafting of

NSC 68 in 1950. Through these cases we see how domestic considerations, public opinion, and media influenced, changed, shaped, and constrained narratives. We also show how political actors used narratives for strategic purposes. Thus, the creation of the US as a great power actor set within a Cold War narrative provides an example of the mutually constituted nature of narratives and shows how strategic intentions play into the construction. We do not claim that two moments in time will create a narrative, but that a narrative about US great power status in a Cold War system was (re)constructed over the 1940s and 1950s.

By 1947, George Kennan had already written his Long Telegram and was pushing the doctrine of what would be called containment that said that the United States should challenge communist actions with a specific focus on Europe. The US administration under President Harry Truman had become tougher on the USSR before 1947, but as Gaddis notes,

> the significance of the Greek-Turkish crisis was rather that this was the first situation in which special appropriations were necessary to carry out the Administration's program. It was this need for congressional sanction of a policy already in effect which caused the Administration to state its intentions—or overstate them—in universal terms.[84]

The British decision not to continue its financial support for Greece and Turkey, announced in February 1947, spurred some in the American political elite to act to clearly articulate a narrative that would set out US commitments as a great power. However, Americans were not in favor of rescuing Greece and Turkey, the US armed forces had been significantly demobilized by 1947, and the Republicans were more focused on reducing taxes than providing aid abroad.[85] In fact, according to Isaacson and Thomas, the Republicans had gained control of Congress in November 1946 by promising a return to normalcy, not an assumption of international commitments associated with great power.

In spite of this, we see a strategic construction of a narrative about the role of the United States as a great power within a dangerous international system characterized by a bipolar confrontation. Bostdorff lays this out quite nicely in her work on the Truman Doctrine.[86] This construction came about through the statements and speeches made by the political leaders. It is clear that domestic politics affected the construction of the narrative, as supporters of aid to Greece and Turkey had to overcome Congressional opposition to secure the votes for the funding. For example, Republican Senator Vandenberg of the Senate Foreign Relations Committee told President Truman that he had to convince Congress and the American people, who were weary after the sacrifices of World War II: "Mr. President, the only way you were ever going to get this is to make a speech and scare the hell out of the country."[87] When Truman's speech was drafted, General George Marshall was one of quite a few that asked that the text be toned down.

The reply from Truman was that without the rhetoric, Congress would not approve the money.[88] Isaacson and Thomas put it this way, explaining Clark Clifford's editing of the speech: "He understood that to grip the American people, the issue had to be framed as a contest between the forces of darkness and light."[89] A narrative of good and evil was taking shape.

Dean Atchison, who was undersecretary and then secretary of state (in 1949), did not take the Truman doctrine literally.[90] Gaddis notes this as well. Isaacson and Thomas claim that "overstatement was to Acheson merely a tool for manipulating balky, unsophisticated congressmen into paying for legitimate policies."[91] The words of the speech, however, set out a compelling narrative about the state of the world and the role of the United States in it:

> The seeds of totalitarian regimes are nurtured by misery and want. They spread and grow in the evil soil of poverty and strife. They reach their full growth when the hope of a people for a better life has died. We must keep that hope alive.
>
> The free peoples of the world look to us for support in maintaining their freedoms. If we falter in our leadership, we may endanger the peace of the world and we shall surely endanger the welfare of our own nation.
>
> Great responsibilities have been placed upon us by the swift movement of events.[92]

The problem with having to shape the narrative within a context that took into account this domestic political situation, was that this stark narrative—without nuance—contributed to the shape of future policies and narratives. The narrative was reinforced in 1950 in the secret security paper NSC-68 also showing the importance of strategic narratives. NSC-68 emphasized the danger of the Soviet Union, delineated the responsibility of the US as a great power in confronting the USSR, and called for a massive increase in military spending:

> In a shrinking world, which now faces the threat of atomic warfare, it is not an adequate objective merely to seek to check the Kremlin design, for the absence of order among nations is becoming less and less tolerable. This fact imposes on us, in our own interests, the responsibility of world leadership. It demands that we make the attempt, and accept the risks inherent in it, to bring about order and justice by means consistent with the principles of freedom and democracy.[93]

The report was secret (until 1975)—but scholars report that "initially, (Nitze and) the Policy Planning Staff had intended to make large portions of the document public. Indeed, that was why the language was so loud and simplistic."[94] In fact, Atcheson said that it was necessary to make the narrative "clearer than the truth."

It is important to recognize that NSC 68 alone did not lead to a sustained or developed strategic narrative, but Korea in June 1950 pushed it along.

John Lewis Gaddis claims that the real commitment came with Korea, but the narrative was in place to support that intervention.[95] He argues that the overblown rhetoric did not match a more measured policy (pre-Korea), but "having pictured the Soviet Union as seeking world domination, and having described Communist parties throughout the world as puppets of the Kremlin, Administration officials found it difficult to explain why the United States should not resist communism wherever it appeared."[96] In other words, political leaders were caught in their own narratives.

Thus strategic narratives were developed after World War II that stressed a confrontation of great powers. The US was depicted as the hero in a struggle of good and evil. Domestic politics, in particular, contributed to the simplification of that narrative—as did the relatively constrained media system. What does this tell us about the construction of narratives? First, strategic considerations were important to the process. There were internal debates about the role of the United States, the characterization of the Soviet threat, and the contours of the international system, and political actors structured language in particular ways to increase the likelihood that their narrative would be accepted and form the underpinning for US foreign policy. This points to the importance of understanding domestic politics, audiences, and information environments. Second, political leaders can be caught in their own narratives, which may constrain or shape future options. Narratives can be created and be binding.

A Post–Cold War Context

So what has happened to the American great power Cold War narrative after the dissolution of the Soviet Union? For much of the twentieth century, the United States and the Soviet Union were locked in a competition marked by ideological, political, and economic differences. Building competing alliance structures, claiming superiority, and encouraging their citizens to see their own state as superior to the other, the US and the Soviet Union claimed great power status in a bipolar world. If narratives are important in shaping the contours of both international relations and foreign policy, then we should expect the Cold War narrative to continue to influence post–Cold War diplomacy at least in some ways, even as new space may open for contestation over new narratives. And in fact we do see that both continuity and change mark the enacting of great power identity in a post–Cold War system. In addition, the changing media ecology has significantly complicated the projection of strategic narratives.

An analysis of US national security strategies shows a continuing reliance on elements associated with great power narratives. Examining leadership speeches gives one a first cut at strategic narrative because of the authoritative voice of leaders and the attention paid to their communication.[97] Specifically, actors and plot (actions and goals) are broad categories that comprise the story told about the international system today. As in the case of the immediate postwar period, it is important to analyze strategic narratives in context, identifying the actors, their goals and roles, and their place in the world described.

The 2002 and 2006 national security strategies of the United States under President George W. Bush set out a strategic narrative about the international system.[98] In 2002 President Bush had already sent troops to Afghanistan and his administration was preparing to launch military operations against Iraq. By 2006 opposition to the war in Iraq had grown in the United States and around the world. President Bush's 2002 strategic narrative emphasized the threat of nonstate actors such as terrorists and rogue states in the international system and what the United States—as world leader—and other states should do to combat this threat. The narrative shifted, however, from 2002 to 2006 with a greater emphasis on the promotion of democracy as part of the US role in the system. US television continued to "reproduce the framing and assumptions of political discourses advanced by elected officials,"[99] but the broader media environment in which Bush projected his strategic narrative became increasingly complicated from 2002 to 2006 as alternative actors could contest his narrative. Al Jazeera, for example, provided a different narrative of the wars in Iraq and Afghanistan,[100] the Internet disseminated other viewpoints and images, and a broader range of actors could weigh in on the credibility of the US strategic narrative, as the case of Al-Qaeda, discussed above, attests. This highlights a changing environment for the conduct of hypocrisy in international relations.[101]

A comparison of President Bush's address to the United Nations in 2008 and President Barack Obama's address to the United Nations in 2009 shows continuity even across presidents. In this case there is change in presidents and parties in government. Much has been written on the changes that President Obama promised and has brought in philosophy and message. Obama's strategic narrative emphasizes a more respectful US state seeking to work with others in the international system. However, the continuing narrative tells the story of the United States as the leader of the free world, in an increasingly complex world. Obama's narrative centers on shared interests and challenges—going well beyond the threat of terrorists. Still, in narratives across the Bush and Obama presidencies, US leadership in the international system is emphasized, and a new media ecology challenges the ability of the US to project its strategic narrative.

President George W. Bush—Strategic Narratives of the National Security Strategies of 2002 and 2006

The executive branch in the United States periodically issues a document detailing US national security strategy. This was mandated by Section 603 of the Goldwater-Nichols Defense Department Reorganization Act of 1986, and requires:

> A comprehensive description and discussion of the foreign policy worldwide commitments and national defense capabilities of the United States; the proposed short-term and long-term uses of the elements of national

power required to protect and promote the interests and achieve the stated goals and objectives; and to provide an assessment of the capabilities of the United States to implement its national security strategy.[102]

Under President George W. Bush, two such documents were released—one in 2002 in the aftermath of 9/11 and one in 2006 after intervention in Iraq and Afghanistan had carried on for years. As Peter Feaver has said:

> Precisely because it is a public document, it [the National Security Strategy] must authentically reflect the administration's world-view; it is not a fortune cookie prediction of what the administration will do in any particular setting, but it is an authoritative statement of the principles that guide the president.[103]

The US president pays particular attention to the national security strategy, as do the rest of the government and the military. It sets out the strategic narrative of the United States from the executive's perspective, and carries significant weight even if others in society may challenge its narrative. An analysis of the 2002 and 2006 documents shows a coherent and consistent strategic narrative in some areas and some differences as well.

States, countries, or nations are clearly depicted as the primary actors in the international system. For example, the 2002 *National Security Strategy of the United States of America (NSS 2002)* says: "In the twenty-first century, only nations that share a commitment to protecting basic human rights and guaranteeing political and economic freedom will be able to unleash the potential of their people and assure their future prosperity." On the one hand these states are tied together in the international system against a common enemy:

> Today, the international community has the best chance since the rise of the nation-state in the seventeenth century to build a world where great powers compete in peace instead of continually prepare for war. Today, the world's great powers find ourselves on the same side—united by common dangers of terrorist violence and chaos.[104]

On the other hand, the focus is clearly on the United States as "the United States enjoys a position of unparalleled military strength and great economic and political influence."[105] In *National Security Strategy of the United States of America (NSS 2006)* a shift occurs as democracies are cited much more often as actors central to the strategic narrative. This ties in to more emphasis in the narrative on democratic states as champions or heroes.

The adversaries in the strategic narrative set out in the national security strategies are consistent over the 2002 and 2006 documents. Terrorists, extremists, and to a degree rogue states, are actors within the system that challenge not only states, and especially democracies, but the very system itself.

As President Bush says in the introduction to the 2002 document, "shadowy networks of individuals can bring great chaos and suffering to our shores for less than it costs to purchase a single tank."[106] These enemies, however, are enemies shared by great powers, according to the national security strategies, and this opens up opportunities for collaboration and cooperation. As will be discussed below, the strategic narrative suggests that the rise of these enemies challenges fundamental concepts associated with the international system, including deterrence.

There are more references to alliances, coalitions, and friends in the 2002 document than in the 2006 document. This may reflect the concern for building coalitions in 2002 and the reality of international critiques of US behavior in Iraq in 2006. In terms of individual countries important to the international system, there are shifts, some subtle and some major, in the Bush narratives. In 2002, different areas of the world and specific countries are depicted as important in the system. Africa, Europe (and NATO), China, Russia, and India are the most often cited in the document. Russia, China, and India are depicted as rising powers in the international system in the midst of internal transitions of their own:

> We are attentive to the possible renewal of old patterns of great power competition. Several potential great powers are now in the midst of internal transition—most importantly Russia, India, and China. In all three cases, recent developments have encouraged our hope that a truly global consensus about basic principles is slowly taking shape.[107]

Europe is depicted as a partner in opening trade and in security issues through the international organization of NATO. Fragile states in Africa must be supported, according to the narrative in 2002. This highlights the importance of states as central to the appropriate functioning of the international system.

By 2006, the focus of the narratives shifts significantly. Afghanistan, Iraq, and Iran take center stage. By this time, of course, the United States has been engaged militarily in Afghanistan and Iraq for years. The narrative outlines the successes since 2002 in these states even as military conflict continues: "The peoples of Afghanistan and Iraq have replaced tyrannies with democracies."[108] By this time as well, there have been significant challenges to the US strategic narrative from news organizations abroad (e.g., Al Jazeera), online sources that depicted US behavior in Iraq as directly contradicting the US narrative emphasizing freedom and human rights, and sources challenging the effectiveness of US policy. One important example was the distribution of the photographs of torture and prisoner abuse at Abu Ghraib. These images, taken by US soldiers themselves, directly undermined any US claim to a higher moral purpose in Iraq—or anywhere. As Hoskins and O'Loughlin note: "[M]ilitary headquarters and major media organizations cannot guarantee the success of their framing or narrative because of [this] key phenomena, 'emergence': namely the massively increased potential for media data literally to 'emerge.'"[109]

In terms of a description of the broader international system, the US strategic narrative continues to note the importance of China and Asia more generally:

> As China becomes a global player, it must act as a responsible stake-holder that fulfills its obligations and works with the United States and others to advance the international system that has enabled its success: enforcing the international rules that have helped China lift itself out of a century of economic deprivation, embracing the economic and political standards that go along with that system of rules, and contributing to international stability and security by working with the United States and other major powers.[110]

The narrative suggests that China should work within the international system and through international organizations in part because the system has allowed it to flourish. Finally, while still discussed in the narrative, there is less emphasis on India and Europe.

Overall, the narrative describes the international system as one of states as primary actors with the US as a leader. The antagonists are nonstate actors—terrorists and rogue states—that threaten not only the United States and others in the system, but the very system itself. This sets the stage for the narrative to suggest that the United States will be ready to act unilaterally to pursue its own self-defined interests. This US strategic narrative is under considerable challenge by the end of Bush's second term, in part due to changes in the media ecology that allow different narratives to contest US assertions about the actors, roles, and goals in the world and because it was through media that US actions contrary to its own narrative could be seen and witnessed by publics in the US and globally.

Presidents George W. Bush and Barack Obama—Strategic Narratives at the United Nations

Each fall the United Nations plays host to political leaders from around the world. This section analyzes the differences and similarities of presidential narratives about the international system by President Bush in 2008 and President Obama in 2009. Barack Obama ran on a platform that stressed change in both domestic and foreign policy realms. He asserted that his administration would be different from that of President Bush in that the United States would no longer assert what others should do, but would listen to others in the international system. An analysis of these two UN speeches shows that President Obama's narrative about the international system was different from that of President Bush in the challenges faced by states as primary actors within the international system. The responsibility of all states for the maintenance of the system is emphasized in Obama's narrative. Still, President Obama faced challenges associated with the new media ecology that challenged the effectiveness of a refined strategic narrative.

Similar to that of the 2006 national security strategy, President Bush's narrative in the 2008 United Nations speech focuses on terrorists or extremists as threatening the international order itself, saying that "[b]y deliberately murdering the innocent to advance their aims, these extremists defy the fundamental principles of international order."[111] In fact, Bush states that "the ideals of the [UN] Charter are now facing a challenge as serious as any since the U.N.'s founding—a global movement of violent extremists" (2008). Bush's narrative then focuses on how multilateral organizations within the international system *should* respond, saying: "The objectives I've laid out for multilateral institutions—confronting terror, opposing tyranny, and promoting effective development—are difficult, but they are necessary tasks."[112]

Obama's narrative in 2009, while still emphasizing security for states in the system, does not center on terrorism, but gives a much broader description of the international system and the challenges it confronts. Recognizing the implicit rules of the international system of sovereign states, Obama says that "my responsibility is to act in the interest of my nation and my people, and I will never apologize for defending those interests."[113] Yet, the focus of the narrative is on the responsibilities of the states that are members of the United Nations to work together to confront a whole host of challenges that exist in the world. These challenges include conflicts (including the conflict between Israel and Palestine), climate change, economic crisis, the spread of nuclear weapons, and extremist violence.

Obama's narrative is explicit in its recognition of criticisms of past United States behavior and suggests that US behavior will change. This behavior will change, according to the narrative, because the view of the international system is presented as more complex. Many challenges to states in the system are shared and go well beyond the threat of terrorists.

> Some of our actions have yielded progress. Some have laid the groundwork for progress in the future. But make no mistake: this cannot be solely America's endeavor. Those who used to chastise America for acting alone in the world cannot now stand by and wait for America to solve the world's problems alone. We have sought—in word and deed— a new era of engagement with the world. Now is the time for all of us to take our share of responsibility for a global response to global challenges.[114]

Obama also uses a quote by Franklin Roosevelt to make this point as well.

> This body was founded on the belief that the nations of the world could solve their problems together. Franklin Roosevelt, who died before he

could see his vision for this institution become a reality, put it this way—
and I quote: "The structure of world peace cannot be the work of one
man, or one party, or one Nation. . . . It cannot be a peace of large
nations—or of small nations. It must be a peace which rests on the cooperative effort of the whole world.[115]

Finally, in the narrative of the international system in the twenty-first century, Obama clearly addresses common assumptions about the international
system that he describes as having changed profoundly.

Responsibility and leadership in the 21st century demand more. In an
era when our destiny is shared, power is no longer a zero sum game.
No one nation can or should try to dominate another nation. No world
order that elevates one nation or group of people over another will succeed. No balance of power among nations will hold. The traditional
division between nations of the south and north makes no sense in an
interconnected world. Nor do alignments of nations rooted in the cleav-
ages of a long gone Cold War. The time has come to realize that the
old habits and arguments are irrelevant to the challenges faced by our
people. They lead nations to act in opposition to the very goals that they
claim to pursue, and to vote—often in this body—against the interests
of their own people.[116]

Therefore, the actions needed are cooperative and the aim is to enhance that
cooperation.

Interestingly, however, some analyses of more recent Obama speeches
show a shift in the narrative, especially when the audience is domestically
based. For example, in his first State of the Union address to the nation on
January 27, 2010, Obama stressed the following:

Meanwhile, China's not waiting to revamp its economy. Germany's not
waiting. India's not waiting. These nations aren't standing still. These
nations aren't playing for second place. They're putting more emphasis
on math and science. They're rebuilding their infrastructure. They are
making serious investments in clean energy because they want those
jobs.
Well, I do not accept second-place for the United States of America.[117]

In the United Nations speeches in 2008 and 2009, security as a goal or
value is central to the narratives of both presidents. In terms of other values
or goals, there is a significant difference in the narratives of the two. President Bush emphasizes democracy, freedom, liberty, markets, and obligations
as important values of the United States in the international system. President Obama, while mentioning many of these, focuses more attention on
peace, responsibility, and change.

Both narratives also frequently spoke about the people of the world and the responsibilities of states for giving opportunities to the people. This is where the commonalities end, however, as Bush more frequently included extremists, terrorists, and democracies in the narrative than did Obama. Bush's narrative covers what he considers to be the most important actors in the international system: states and multilateral organizations, including the UN, in a struggle against extremists. Obama, for his part, was significantly more likely to speak of "America" than did Bush and to use the personal pronoun "I." However, Obama's narrative focuses on an interdependent international system where states share interests and responsibility so all states are seen as important to the addressing the problems of the planet. In terms of the countries found in the narrative, there were also differences. Bush focused on Afghanistan and Iraq, while Obama focused on Israel and Palestine.

Under President Obama, the media environment continued to challenge the ability of the US president to project a strategic narrative. One telling example—the Cairo Speech and attempts to change the narrative within the Middle East—is covered in Chapter 4. The administration has sought to address the new media ecology, for example, through new initiatives to incorporate public diplomacy, including a twenty-first-century statecraft initiative that asserts that the US is responding to "a decentralization of power away from government and large institutions and toward networks of people."[118]

> The reaction of the U.S. and many other governments is to align policies and actions with greater openness. In some ways, this is merely accepting the inevitable. These changes are upon us. They cannot be contained. The disruptions we have witnessed bring both new opportunities and new threats. They come wrapped together and we can neither stop nor control them. We can either choose to embrace them and try both to amplify the positive and to mitigate the negative—or we can be buffeted back and forth by changes for which we are not prepared.[119]

Yet this acknowledgement of a change in the media ecology does not guarantee that strategic narrative reception will be effective—as will be discussed in more length in Chapter 4 on contestation.

CONCLUSION

These US narratives set out how the executive branch constructs the structure of the international system if these words become materialized in the policies through which the US shapes international order. Narratives set the stage for understanding specific US foreign policies and actions because the narrative may structure the range of the possible. It is important, then, to understand the conditions under which the narrative about the international system suggests possible and acceptable behavior and/or policies and the conditions under which narratives make unacceptable others. This is not to say that narratives cannot change according to decisions to conduct particular policies, that is, to legitimize policies, but the use of a broader narrative about the international system makes this more difficult. This is similar to Snyder's suggestion that even if the elite does not believe its own myths (or narratives), "it may nonetheless become politically entrapped in its own rhetoric."[120]

This chapter addresses how political actors are narrated, narrate, and are affected by the intersection of power and social interaction in a new media environment. Narratives about actors highlight the expectations and behavior of those actors, for example, great powers, rising powers, weak states, international organizations (including nongovernmental organizations), and other nonstate actors (including terrorist groups). A new communication environment significantly affects these strategic narratives, adding to the challenges associated with the use of narratives. Contestation is covered as a separate chapter in this work, but it is important to recognize that there is agency in this contestation. Actors contest for various reasons and with various outcomes, and it is to this we turn next.

NOTES

1. Stephen Jay Gould, *Full House: The Spread of Excellence from Plato to Darwin* (Harvard University Press, 2011), 57.
2. Kathryn Sikkink, "Beyond the Justice Cascade: How Agentic Constructivism Could Help Explain Change in International Politics" (revised paper from a keynote address, Millennium Annual Conference, October 22, 2011, "Out of the Ivory Tower: Weaving the Theories and Practice of International Relations," London School of Economics, presented at the Princeton University IR Colloquium, November 21, 2011), 35.
3. Peter J. Katzenstein, ed., *The Culture of National Security: Norms and Identity in World Politics* (New York: Columbia University Press, 1996); Yosef Lapid and Friedrich V. Kratochwil, eds., *The Return of Culture and Identity in IR Theory* (Boulder, CO: Lynne Rienner, 1996); Alexander Wendt, *Social Theory of International Politics* (Cambridge: Cambridge University Press, 1999); Vendulka Kubálková, *Foreign Policy in a Constructed World*, Vol. 4 (Armonk, NY: M.E. Sharpe, 2001); Ted Hopf, *Social Construction of International Politics: Identities & Foreign Policies, Moscow, 1955 and 1999* (Ithaca, NY: Cornell University Press, 2002); Jeffrey T. Checkel, *Ideas and International Political Change: Soviet/Russian Behavior and the End of the Cold War* (New Haven: Yale University Press, 1997); Jeffrey T. Checkel, "Social Constructivisms in Global and European Politics: A Review Essay," *Review of International Studies* 30, no. 2 (2004): 229–44.
4. Margaret E. Keck and Kathryn Sikkink, *Activists beyond Borders: Advocacy Networks in International Politics* (Ithaca, NY: Cornell University Press, 1998).
5. David L. Rousseau and Rocio Garcia-Retamero, "Identity, Power, and Threat Perception: A Cross-National Experimental Study," *Journal of Conflict Resolution* 51, no. 5 (2007): 749.

6. Janice Bially Mattern, *Ordering International Politics: Identity, Crisis, and Representational Force* (New York: Routledge, 2005), 96.
7. Marc Lynch, *State Interests and Public Spheres: The International Politics of Jordan's Identity* (New York: Columbia University Press, 1999), 22.
8. Amartya Sen, *Identity and Violence: The Illusion of Destiny* (London: Penguin Books, 2007).
9. Mary Kaldor, *New & Old Wars: Organized Violence in A Global Era* (Stanford, CA: Stanford University Press, 2007), 80.
10. Checkel, "Social Constructivisms."
11. Sikkink, "Beyond the Justice Cascade."
12. Michael Barnett, "Culture, Strategy and Foreign Policy Change: Israel's Road to Oslo," *European Journal of International Relations* 5, no. 1 (1999): 5–36.
13. Bially Mattern, *Ordering International Politics*, 9.
14. Alexander Wendt, "Identity and Structural Change in International Politics," in *The Return of Culture and Identity in IR Theory*, edited by Yosef Lapid and Friedrich V. Kratochwil (Boulder, CO: Lynne Rienner, 1996), 57.
15. Thomas Risse, "'Let's Argue!': Communicative Action in World Politics," *International Organization* 54, no. 1 (2000): 1–39.
16. Keck and Sikkink, *Activists beyond Borders*, 3.
17. James G. March and Johan P. Olsen, *The Logic of Appropriateness* (ARENA Working Papers 04/09, Centre for European Studies, University of Oslo, 2004), 2, http://www.sv.uio.no/arena/english/research/publications/arena-publications/workingpapers/working-papers2004/wp04_9.pdf.
18. Jeffrey W. Legro, *Rethinking the World: Great Power Strategies and International Order* (Ithaca, NY: Cornell University Press, 2005).
19. Seymour Martin Lipset, *American Exceptionalism: A Double-Edged Sword* (New York: Norton, 1997).
20. John Hutcheson, David Domke, Andre Billeaudeaux, and Philip Garland, "US National Identity, Political Elites, and a Patriotic Press Following September 11," *Political Communication* 21, no. 1 (2004): 28.
21. Jack L. Snyder, *Myths of Empire: Domestic Politics and International Ambition* (Ithaca: Cornell University Press, 1991), 17.
22. Snyder, *Myths*, 2.
23. We do not claim that all (re)construction of national identity is strategic—a point to which we will return elsewhere. Michael Billig's *Banal Nationalism* points to the ways that everyday and lived experience can contribute to national identity.
24. Felix Berenskoetter, "Parameters of a National Biography," *European Journal of International Relations*, Online First Version, October 16, 2012, 3.
25. Bially Mattern, *Ordering International Politics*, 107.
26. Bially Mattern, *Ordering International Politics*, 119.
27. Bially Mattern, *Ordering International Politics*; Berenskoetter, "Parameters of a National Biography"; Sikkink, *Beyond the Justice Cascade*.
28. Bially Mattern, *Ordering International Politics*, 119.
29. Sikkink, *Beyond the Justice Cascade*, 3.
30. Conseulo Cruz, "Identity and Persuasion: How Nations Remember Their Past and Make Their Futures," *World Politics* 52, no. 3 (2000): 275–312.
31. Cruz, "Identity and Persuasion," 278.
32. Cruz, "Identity and Persuasion," 279.
33. Patricia Leavy, *Iconic Events: Media, Politics, and Power in Retelling History* (Lanham, MD: Lexington Books, 2007); Michael Schudson, *Watergate in American Memory: How We Remember, Forget, and Reconstruct the*

Past (New York: Basic Books, 1992); Iwona Irwin-Zarecka, *Frames of Remembrance: The Dynamics of Collective Memory* (Somerset, NJ: Transaction, 1994).

34. Anne L. Clunan, *The Social Construction of Russia's Resurgence* (Baltimore: Johns Hopkins University Press, 2009), 28.

35. Leavy, *Iconic Events,* 12.

36. Klaus Eder, "A Theory of Collective Identity Making Sense of the Debate on a 'European Identity,'" *European Journal of Social Theory* 12, no. 4 (November 2009): 427.

37. Brent J. Steele, *Defacing Power: The Aesthetics of Insecurity in Global Politics* (Ann Arbor: University of Michigan Press, 2012), 77.

38. We are not necessarily accepting the Ikenberry, Mastanduno, and Wohlforth narrative about the unipolarity of the international system here. We are analyzing it in terms of actors within a narrative.

39. Martha Finnemore, "Legitimacy, Hypocrisy, and the Social Structure of Unipolarity: Why Being a Unipole Isn't All It's Cracked Up to Be," in *International Relations Theory and the Consequences of Unipolarity,* ed. G. John Ikenberry et al. (Cambridge: Cambridge University Press, 2011), 67–98.

40. Finnemore, "Legitimacy, Hypocrisy," 84.

41. David A. Lake, *Hierarchy in International Relations* (Ithaca, NY: Cornell University Press, 2009). See also Jack Levy, *War in the Modern Great Power System* (Lexington: University Press of Kentucky, 1983).

42. Sarah Oates, "Through A Lens Darkly?: Russian Television and Terrorism Coverage in Comparative Perspective," paper prepared for "The Mass Media in Post-Soviet Russia" International Conference, University of Surrey, April 2006.

43. Laura Roselle, *Media and the Politics of Failure: Great Powers, Communication Strategies, and Military Defeats,* 2nd ed. (New York: Palgrave Macmillan, 2011).

44. Paul Huth and Bruce Russett, "What Makes Deterrence Work: Cases from 1900 to 1980," *World Politics* 36 (1984): 496–526; James D. Fearon, "Signaling Versus the Balance of Power and Interests," *Journal of Conflict Resolution* 38 (1994): 68–90.

45. Daryl G. Press, *Calculating Credibility: How Leaders Assess Military Threats* (Ithaca, NY: Cornell University Press, 2005), 1.

46. Press, *Calculating Credibility,* 60.

47. Roselle, *Media and the Politics of Failure,* 2011.

48. Roselle, *Media and the Politics of Failure,* 59.

49. Robert G. Herman, "Identity, Norms, and National Security: The Soviet Foreign Policy Revolution and the End of the Cold War," in *The Culture of National Security: Norms and Identity in World Politics,* edited by Peter Katzenstein (New York: Columbia University Press, 1996), 272–316; Roselle, *Media and the Politics of Failure.*

50. Legro, *Rethinking the World,* 143.

51. Legro, *Rethinking the World,* 154.

52. Hanns W. Maull, "Germany and Japan: The New Civilian Powers," *Foreign Affairs* 69, no. 5 (Winter 1990): 91–106.

53. Peter Katzenstein, ed., *Tamed Power: Germany in Europe* (Ithaca, NY: Cornell University Press, 1997); Ulrich Krotz and Joachim Schild, *Shaping Europe: France, Germany, and Embedded Bilateralism from the Elysee Treaty to Twenty-First Century Politics* (Oxford: Oxford University Press, 2012).

54. Adrian Hyde-Price and Charlie Jeffery, "Germany in the European Union: Constructing Normality," *Journal of Common Market Studies* 39, no. 4 (November 2001): 689–717.

55. Simon Bulmer and William E. Paterson, "Germany and the European Union: From 'Tamed Power' to Normalized Power?" *International Affairs* 86, no. 5 (2010): 1059.
56. Legro, *Rethinking the World*, 173.
57. Legro, *Rethinking the World*, 173.
58. Jeffrey W. Legro, "What China Will Want: The Future Intentions of a Rising Power," *Perspectives on Politics* 5, no. 3 (September 2007): 515–34; William Callahan, *China: The Pessoptimist Nation* (Oxford: Oxford University Press, 2010); William Callahan, "Forum: The Rise of China: How to Understand China: The Dangers and Opportunities of Being a Rising Power," *Review of International Studies* 31 (2005): 701–14; David C. Kang, *China Rising: Peace, Power, and Order in East Asia* (New York: Columbia University Press, 2007).
59. Legro, "What China Will Want."
60. Robert Gilpin, *War and Change in World Politics* (Princeton: Princeton University Press, 1981); John J. Mearsheimer, *The Tragedy of Great Power Politics* (New York: Norton, 2001).
61. Legro, "What China Will Want," 516.
62. Callahan, *China*, 13.
63. Mark Leonard, *What Does China Think?* (New York: Public Affairs, 2008).
64. Michael Handel, *Weak States in the International System* (London: Frank Cass, 1990); Robert I. Rotberg, "Failed States, Collapsed States, Weak States: Causes and Indicators," in *State Failure and State Weakness in a Time of Terror*, edited by Robert I. Rotberg (Washington, DC: World Peace Foundation, 2003), 1–25.
65. Rotberg, "Failed States," 4.
66. Robert Litwak, *Rogue States and U.S. Foreign Policy: Containment after the Cold War* (Baltimore: Johns Hopkins University Press, 2000).
67. Litwak, *Rogue States*, xiv.
68. Alexander George, *Bridging the Gap: Theory and Practice in Foreign Policy* (Washington, DC: United States Institute of Peace Press, 1993).
69. Ben O'Loughlin, "Small Pivots: Should Local Struggles Take On Global Significance?" *Global Policy*, April 29, 2013, http://www.globalpolicyjournal.com/blog/29/04/2013/small-pivots-should-local-struggles-take-global-significance.
70. O'Loughlin, "Small Pivots."
71. John Agnew, *Globalization and Sovereignty* (Lanham, MD: Rowman and Littlefield, 2009).
72. Keck and Sikkink, *Activists beyond Borders*, 16.
73. Cristina Archetti, *Understanding Terrorism in the Age of Global Media: A Communication Approach* (Basingstoke: Palgrave Macmillan, 2013); Steven R. Corman, Angela Trethewey, and H.L. Goodall, Jr., *Weapons of Mass Persuasion: Strategic Communication to Combat Violent Extremism*, Vol. 15 (New York: Peter Lang, 2008); Andrew Hoskins, and Ben O'Loughlin, *Television and Terror: Conflicting Times and the Crisis of News Discourse* (London: Palgrave/Macmillan, 2009); Akil Awan, Andrew Hoskins, and Ben O'Loughlin, *Radicalisation and Media: Connectivity and Terrorism in the New Media Ecology* (London: Routledge, 2011).
74. Karin Knorr-Cetina, "Complex Global Microstructures: The New Terrorist Societies," *Theory, Culture & Society* 22, no. 5 (2005): 222.
75. Awan et al., *Radicalisation and Media*.
76. Awan et al., *Radicalisation and Media*.
77. Whilst Osama bin Laden had released other statements prior to the 1996 *fatwa*, these earlier messages are considered to have been addressed to more

local Saudi audiences such as the *Ulama* (scholars) or wider appeals to Arab or Muslim constituencies.

78. Osama bin Laden, *Declaration of War against the Americans Occupying the Land of the Two Holy Places*, 1996, available at http://www.mideastweb .org/osamabinladen1.htm.
79. In a speech given on September 16, 2001, President George W. Bush stated, "This is a new kind of—a new kind of evil. And we understand. And the American people are beginning to understand. This crusade, this war on terrorism is going to take a while." Available at http://georgewbush-white house.archives.gov/news/releases/2001/09/20010916–2.html.
80. From the sermon "Among a Band of Knights," February 14, 2003, cited in Bruce Lawrence (ed.), *Messages to the World: The Statements of Osama bin Laden* (London: Verso, 2005).
81. See Tim Reid, "Al-Qaeda Supporters Back John McCain for President," *The Times*, October 23, 2008.
82. Hoskins and O'Loughlin, *Television and Terror*.
83. Alexander George, "Domestic Constraints on Regime Change in US Foreign Policy: The Need for Policy Legitimacy," in *American Foreign Policy: Theoretical Essays*, edited by G. J. Ikenberry (Glenview: Scott, Foresman, 1989), 585.
84. John Lewis Gaddis, "Was the Truman Doctrine a Real Turning Point?" *Foreign Affairs* 52, no. 2 (January 1974): 389.
85. Walter Isaacson and Evan Thomas, *The Wise Men: Six Friends and the World They Made* (New York: Simon & Schuster, 1986).
86. Denise Bostdorff, "Harry S. Truman, 'Special Message to the Congress on Greece and Turkey: The Truman Doctrine' (12 March 1947)," *Voices of Democracy* 4 (2009): 1–22.
87. Isaacson and Thomas, *The Wise Men*; Bostdorff, "Harry S. Truman," 11, suggests that the sourcing of this quote is unclear, but does agree that "Truman's address was frightening."
88. Isaacson and Thomas, *The Wise Men*, 397.
89. Isaacson and Thomas, *The Wise Men*, 397.
90. Isaacson and Thomas, *The Wise Men*, 390.
91. Isaacson and Thomas, *The Wise Men*.
92. Truman Doctrine, http://www.ourdocuments.gov/doc_large_image.php?doc =81.
93. NSC-68, 14 April 1950. https://www.fas.org/irp/offdocs/nsc-hst/nsc-68.htm.
94. Isaacson and Thomas, *The Wise Men*, 499.
95. Gaddis, "Was the Truman Doctrine," 386.
96. Gaddis, "Was the Truman Doctrine," 394.
97. See Vladimir Shlapentokh, "Perceptions of Foreign Threat to the Regime: From Lenin to Putin," *Communist and Post-Communist Studies* 42, no. 3 (2009): 305–24; Legro, *Rethinking the World*, for further justification for the use of speeches.
98. George W. Bush, *The National Security Strategy of the United States of America (NSS 2002)* (Washington, DC: Executive Office of the President, 2002), http://georgewbush-whitehouse.archives.gov/nsc/nss/2002/; George W. Bush, *The National Security Strategy of the United States of America (NSS 2006)* (Washington, DC: Executive Office of the President, 2006), http://georgewbush-whitehouse.archives.gov/nsc/nss/2006/index.html.
99. Hoskins and O'Loughlin, *Television and Terror*, 98.
100. Philip Seib, *The Al Jazeera Effect: How the New Global Media are Reshaping World Politics* (Washington, DC: Potomac Books, 2008).
101. Finnemore, "Legitimacy, Hypocrisy."

102. Quoted in "Chapter 1: History of the National Strategy in US National Security Strategy 2010," *The National Strategy Forum Review* 19, no. 1 (2009): 1.
103. Peter Feaver, "Holding Out for the National Security Strategy," *Foreign Policy*, January 20, 2010, http://shadow.foreignpolicy.com/posts/2010/01/20/holding_out_for_the_national_security_strategy.
104. Bush, *NSS 2002*.
105. Bush, *NSS 2002*.
106. Bush, *NSS 2002*.
107. Bush, *NSS 2002*.
108. Bush, *NSS 2006*.
109. Andrew Hoskins and Ben O'Loughlin, *War and Media* (Cambridge: Polity, 2010), 9.
110. Bush, *NSS 2006*.
111. George Bush, "President Bush Addresses United Nations General Assembly," 2008, http://georgewbush-whitehouse.archives.gov/news/releases/2008/09/20080923–5.html.
112. Bush, UN 2008.
113. Barack Obama, "President Obama's Address to the UN General Assembly," September 23, 2009, http://www.america.gov/st/texttrans-english/2009/September/20090923110705eaifas0.3711664.html.
114. Obama, UN 2009.
115. Obama, UN 2009.
116. Obama, UN 2009.
117. Barack Obama, "Remarks by the President in the State of the Union Address," January 27, 2010, http://www.whitehouse.gov/the-press-office/remarks-president-state-union-address.
118. "Twentieth Century Statecraft," n.d. http://www.state.gov/statecraft/overview/index.htm.
119. "Twentieth Century Statecraft," n.d. http://www.state.gov/statecraft/overview/index.htm.
120. Snyder, *Myths*, 42.

3   Strategic Narratives of International Order

INTRODUCTION

In the preceding chapter we focused on how actors are given meaning through strategic narrative. We demonstrated that narratives about great powers shape expectations of those states domestically and internationally. We argue that understanding these narratives is essential in explaining US policy since the 1940s and are key to understanding the period of transition in the international system that is currently under way. Other designations of states such as normal, rising powers, BRICS or superpower carry with them expectations that constrain and empower. In this chapter we demonstrate how order is constructed and maintained through the contestation of strategic narrative in international affairs. Order's central place in the study of international relations ensures that a multitude of actors contribute to the shaping of our conception of order, its purpose and utility. The construction of narratives of order by political actors provides a compelling explanation of how orders emerge and are maintained, as well as their demise. The construction of order has taken on greater complexity with the emergence of the new media ecology and the greater dispersal of power and authority in the world. Eric Voegelin contends:

> Conceptions of order . . . are always accompanied by the self interpretation of that order as meaningful . . . that is about the particular meaning that order has. In this sense, self interpretation is always part . . . of the reality of order, of political order, or, as we might say, of history.[1]

This chapter highlights the narrative work undertaken by powerful states to shape international order. Often this narrative work is presented in binaries—good and evil; democratic and authoritarian. These often-simplistic narratives shape our expectations of the emerging order that have decisive influence of government policies. The analysis of power transition and hegemony has been dominated by studies focusing on material conditions.[2] We aim to show that orders are defined by strategic narrative competition. Buzan argues that we are entering a period without superpowers, rather the greater prevalence of great powers in the system.[3] He argues that "decentered" globalism will make it more difficult for superpowers to rise to global hegemony. In fact, this period of uncertainty will entail greater challenges for great powers to project strategic narrative in an international system in which power is diffused more widely. But this by no means implies the foreshadowing of great powers; we argue that their endurance and future role depends on their adaptation to a changing media ecology and their ability to convince others of their narratives of the international system.

This chapter illustrates how actors seek to define international order through their use of strategic narratives. We argue that order is given meaning by narrative. Strategic narrative can help explain the process of defining international order, which is particularly vital in contemporary international affairs. Strategic narrative offers explanation for three aspects of international order. First, strategic narratives contribute to how order is conceived. We outline that the use of strategic narrative is a central component of the development of conceptions of order. Narratives compete to define what order is and terms on which we understand order. Second, strategic narratives play an important role in the production of order. The communication of narratives shapes deliberations on policy choices faced by political actors. Finally, strategic narratives are central to the maintenance of order. They define the nature of existing order(s) in the international system. Strategic narratives are attempts to structure engagement on how we understand order within states, among states and with transnational actors. Strategic narratives can both empower and constrain how actors engage in forming and projecting policy preferences in a highly competitive and diffuse international system. This chapter assesses how strategic narrative analysis can add to our understanding of international relations (IR) by first highlighting how narrative suffuses the paradigmatic theories of the discipline. Subsequently we will examine how strategic narrative plays an explanatory role in how states responded to the Libya crisis of 2011.

STRATEGIC NARRATIVES OF ORDER

Political actors use strategic narrative in an attempt to marshal the center ground of national and international political communication to play an influential role in the constitution of the emerging world order, at a time when other voices are gaining weight. Narratives are negotiated both domestically and internationally. Strategic narratives cannot outstrip the domestic will in engaging with third parties, which is further complicated by their diffusion in the media. In this way Robert Putnam's two-level game analogy suggests that political actors' concentration on the domestic and international win set is crucial in the pursuit of international agreements.[4] Such a segregation of domestic and international is, however, difficult to maintain. Gourevitch[5] suggests that domestic polities are permeable and therefore the link between the domestic and international is more fluid than domestic interest analyses might suggest.[6] We contend that actors have agency—albeit constrained—to seek to shape the international order according to their preferences.

One impact of the new media ecology on foreign policy is to radically change who is able to project narratives of international order and to allow more open challenge to narratives of great powers in the system.[7] However, whilst some have predicted the "twilight of sovereignty," the state remains a dominant and viable actor in international affairs.[8] The resources available to great powers are such that they have significant potential to narrate the emerging order. Jamieson argues that a successful narrative works by "offering a plausible, internally coherent story that resonates with the audience while accounting for otherwise discordant or fragmentary information."[9] Despite this, the ability to project a narrative that explains the emerging international order has been elusive for powerful states, leading to the conclusion that no unifying narrative of international order may emerge in the coming years. What Freedman refers to as the yearning for a new order to replace the relative stability of the Cold War is not witnessed in any clearly defined new order.[10] To confront the uncertain present and future, narrative is used as an attempt to express continuity during periods of profound change, often stressing past glories, and formative peaceful periods of development.[11]

Despite the diffusion of institutional cooperation between states, the post–Cold War era has not witnessed a shared narrative on the emerging international order. Robert Kagan's provocative statement, "It's time to stop pretending that Europeans and Americans share a common view of the world, or even that they occupy the same world,"[12] suggests that even among close allies, different views of how to organize international affairs can prevail. Binary narratives of capitalism versus communism, East versus West, and good versus evil, no longer generate the cohesive centripetal forces to bind states together as they once did. Narrating the present has always presented actors with challenges, beyond the political slogans of electoral cycles or short-term maneuvering of diplomatic pronouncements. Hans Morgenthau, regarded as one of the developers of the modern study of international relations after World War II, understood the limitations of material power and the complexity of communication. In "The Principles of Propaganda," Morgenthau argued,

> All foreign policy is an attempt to influence the will of other governments on behalf of interests believed to be of paramount importance. To that end, foreign policy makes use of different media. It may use the media of diplomatic suasion. It may use the medium of military pressure. It may use the medium of the benefits of aid and trade. Or it may use the medium of propaganda in order to impress not only the governments but also and primarily the man in the street of other nations with the sum total of the qualities of the nation and of its policies.[13]

In a precursor to Nye's "soft power," Morgenthau pleaded that the United States

> must finally recognize that whatever improvements we might make within our information policy will be of little avail as long as the substance of our foreign policy and our national life as a whole are lacking in the qualities for which American throughout its history has been admired and emulated by other nations. America must rediscover itself and its mission in the world.[14]

Likewise, a widely read Wilson Centre paper from 2011 entitled *A National Strategic Narrative* suggested a new basis for emulation of the United States.[15] This plea for US domestic and foreign policy to be founded on attraction to persuade others is a powerful theme in strategic narrative projection of order. Normative power Europe,[16] China's "peaceful rise," the projection of the BRICS group, and the US claim for global leadership all have at their heart a wish for others to emulate political and economic models that define order in the international system. This process, we argue, is not passive. Political agents seek to encourage emulation through the creation of shared meanings by projecting narratives to policy elites and through the new media ecology.

UNDERSTANDING ORDER IN INTERNATIONAL RELATIONS

Order is a central concept in the academic literature in a number of interrelated disciplines that have influenced the study of international relations. The application of narrative approaches to the study of order can be seen in history,[17] legal studies,[18] political science,[19] public policy,[20] and sociology.[21] Narratives have real impact on international affairs by guiding states toward certain goals and strategies. This can have positive or negative outcomes. Layne suggests that,

> for most of the last century, Washington has consistently followed an expansionist and interventionist grand strategy. But why? The answer is that liberal ideology—Wilsonianism in its foreign policy guise—is the U.S. "myth of empire." Wilsonianism defines security in ideological terms, positing that the United States can be secure only in a world composed of democracies, and thus inevitably injects a crusader mentality into U.S. foreign policy.[22]

Narrative conceptions of order manifest themselves in the foreign policy choices governments make. Order is often conceived through the metaphor of balance. Balance is achieved when the structure of international relations is characterized by the balance of power among the powerful units in the system.[23] Balance of power is central to many approaches to international order—achieving balance is seen as a necessary goal of international affairs. The post–Cold War world has not witnessed a balance of power even for those who see an era of US primacy, a narrative that reinforces a unipolar conception of order and sidelines alternative narratives of institutional co-operation or nonstate actors.[24] For example, despite perceived US primacy, Waltz argues, "[W]e must prepare to bid bipolarity adieu and begin to live without its stark simplicities and comforting symmetry."[25] Whilst debates rage over the scale and longevity of US unipolar hegemony and whether it remedies the absence of symmetry, the lack of balance has taken on a normative quality in the literature concerning whether unipolarity and US hegemony might ultimately be benign and valuable for maintaining order in the absence of counter-balancing states.[26] Conversely, US global dominance has brought with it concerns that the US is exploiting that dominance to the detriment of its future standing, according to scholars such as Bacevich,[27] Layne,[28] and Nye.[29] The US, it is argued, is afflicted with the condition of great power hubris, which has the potential to damage its transition to greater balance of power in the system.[30] With this in mind a literature emerged attempting to understand why states have not sought to balance American power.[31] Balance of power is viewed by much of the literature to be the goal of international affairs. Indeed, Waltz argues, "As nature abhors a vacuum, so international politics abhors unbalanced power."[32] Being off-balance is viewed as a negative. In the post–Cold War era:

> The world is off balance. . . . Not since Rome has one nation loomed so large above the others. Indeed the word "empire" has come out of the closet. Respected analysts on both the left and the right are beginning to refer to "American empire" approvingly as the dominant narrative of the 21st century. And the military victory in Iraq seems only to have confirmed this new world order.[33]

Conversely, Brooks and Wohlforth see US unipolarity as a unique opportunity to shape the world in America's image before the rise of challengers.[34] Realist conceptions of order, then, focus on power and the extent to which hegemonic actors can use military force to secure the existing hierarchy and deter challengers.[35] Lake argues that social power is insufficient to establish and maintain order. Rather, it is the ability to offer material incentives that reinforces hierarchy and authority in the system.[36] However, the US declinism literature paints a picture of American hubris and relative power loss in light of the rise of (re)emerging powers.[37]

Liberal theories of order focus on how the state is caught up with economically driven transnational forces, which represent the interests of dominant actors. The most prominent scholar working from a liberal perspective on world order is G. John Ikenberry. Ikenberry has argued that the liberal order established by the US in the aftermath of World War II has been a success precisely due to the lack of coercion involved in enforcing this liberal order.[38] It is the co-opting of other states within the US liberal order that accounts for its success and will result in its longevity, even in the era of relative decline and emerging challengers. Ikenberry's argument sets himself against realism and its focus on balance and rivalry among great powers. In Ikenberry's *Liberal Leviathan* he sets out to tell the tale of "the unfolding drama of the liberal international project."[39] Indeed, "One of the great dramas of world politics over the last two hundred years has been the rise of liberal democratic states to global dominance."[40] The heroes of Ikenberry's story are the United Kingdom and the United States, each of whom led for a time in implementing "the liberal vision" in the international system.[41] The villains were "rival autocratic, fascist, and totalitarian great powers."[42] However, this is really a drama of great powers that followed "a common logic"[43] of playing out the role of great powers. He argues that, "By the 1990s, the American-led order was at its zenith. [. . .] Today, the American-led liberal hegemonic order is troubled."[44] But Ikenberry has a surprise—a happy ending: the order will continue even as US unipolarity recedes, which goes against the established wisdom of realist scholarship. This, for Ikenberry and the US, is "the desired global order":[45]

> If America is smart and plays its foreign policy "cards" right, twenty years from now, it can still be at the center of a one-world system defined in terms of open markets, democratic community, cooperative security, and rule-based order. This future can be contrasted with less-desirable alternatives familiar from history: great-power balancing orders, regional blocs, or bipolar rivalries.[46]

Ultimately, Ikenberry wants to show what is required for the liberal system to endure. To achieve this, he argues, "we need a new bargain, not a new system."[47] Global public goods such as security and markets must be provided, but we currently do not have the authority system to organize this.[48] Hierarchy is in transition; it is therefore not clear how intervention can be legitimated, and it is also not clear how and when international authority should override democratic domestic authority.

This is a crisis of authority *within* the liberal international system, not a crisis *of* that system, which echoes Gilpin's concept of systemic change, not systems change.[49] To explain why entails identifying the drivers of international political change, and showing how they indicate that the renewal of liberal order is the most likely outcome. Ikenberry suggests that the US-led liberal international order is unstable because its basis—the Westphalian system—is eroding.[50] Global interdependence created processes with which the international system cannot cope.[51] According to Ikenberry we need a new governance architecture: the US must remake the global milieu.[52] Drawing on Wolfers, Ikenberry distinguishes between "milieu-oriented grand strategy" and "positional grand strategy."[53] *Milieu-oriented* means remaking the environment itself: "building the infrastructure of international cooperation."[54] *Positional* means countering or containing other great powers who can challenge hegemonic actors. This is important as the US builds the institutional *and* communication infrastructures today, via Google and other organizations (explored in Chapter 5). The objective was a "world environment in which the American system can flourish."[55] Therefore, not America, but its system based on whoever operates in an American way, is essential for the future and maintenance of the liberal order.

Ikenberry builds explicitly on Gilpin's *War and Change* and Organski's *World Politics* through a cyclical theory of power transition in which hegemonic war leads to the establishment of a new order. Power shifts germinate below the surface, to the point where it makes sense for emerging powers to challenge the existing hierarchy and order. While great powers use prestige and ideology to perpetuate hegemony or to legitimize a new order they create upon winning a hegemonic war, ultimately they are undone by hard power.[56] Conflict is central to changing orders. It is in postwar contexts that the rules and institutions of a new order are settled.[57] A constitution of sorts is created.[58] States' behavior is then patterned and stable according to the logic of that order type. "International order breaks down or enters into crisis when the settled rules and arrangements are thrown into dispute or when the forces that perpetuate order no longer operate."[59]

The role of communication is unexplored in *Liberal Leviathan*. Ikenberry argues that given the crisis of authority in the international system, an "opening exists for America's postwar vision of internationalism to be updated and rearticulated today."[60] But Ikenberry does not ask how this would work or how it would be persuasive. His book also underplays how competing visions might challenge America's vision. Ikenberry's argument could feasibly be understood as narrative analysis—he both describes and prescribes: it is a justification of liberalism as well as a description of how liberal orders function.[61] The logics of anarchy and hierarchy, of consent/control/command, are each "a grand narrative of the rise and transformation of the international system."[62] So Ikenberry is using IR theories to construct his own overarching grand narrative.

Ikenberry follows Jervis[63] in arguing that a unipolar state seeks to "remake the world in its own image, or rather in its desired self-image."[64] Hence, it matters who leads that unipolar state and "the ideas that these leaders have."[65] Roosevelt and Truman drew on ideas that resonated with US political culture.[66] Those ideas also resonated with European liberal democracies. And it had a clear Other in the USSR to help define this, hence a binary narrative opposite.[67] This identity enabled the construction of the West in a way that made sense to those in that community.[68] Further questions emerge from Ikenberry's analysis. He follows Slaughter[69] in arguing that the US is well placed to organize hegemony because of its "capacity for connectivity."[70] It is open to nongovernmental organizations (NGOs), entrepreneurs, business groups, and activists, so it is a state through which others can get things done. Slaughter outlines a number of ways in which this liberal order is institutionalized that define the evolving order:

> The state is not the only actor in the international system, but it is still the most important actor. The state is not disappearing, but it is disaggregating into its component institutions, which are increasingly interacting principally with their foreign counterparts across borders. These institutions still represent distinct national or state interests, even as they also recognize common professional identities and substantive experience as judges, regulators, ministers, and legislators. Different states have evolved and will continue to evolve mechanisms for re-aggregating the interests of their distinct institutions when necessary. In many circumstances, therefore, states will still interact with one another as unitary actors in more traditional ways. Government networks exist alongside and sometimes within more traditional international organizations.[71]

Both Ikenberry and Slaughter agree the US and the institutions it leads are a hub through which others can help themselves and others. But he does not ask how this enables a shared narrative to emerge. If the US is integrative, it needs to weave in others' narratives. This is the ideational dimension to such integration. How does this work and through what platforms? Ikenberry is insistent that the US did not intend to lead the post-1945 order, it just happened: "The order was not conceived in a singular vision and imposed on the world. It was cobbled together in a rolling political process"[72] At the same time, he details how the Roosevelt and Truman administrations knew their order would be "expansive" since it was progressive and potentially universal.[73] Rather than an ad hoc response to changing international conditions, Hogan[74] argues that Truman constructed a successful narrative that forged acceptance of the US international commitments after World War II. Without this, Truman would not have been able to mobilize domestic political opinion. Containing Soviet Union ambitions became the central narrative of US foreign policy after World War II.

HOW STRATEGIC NARRATIVES AID OUR UNDERSTANDING OF ORDER

Strategic narratives play a central role in how actors view international order. Strategic narratives can construct, affect, and shape expectations of the nature and workings of the international system. This can indicate a number of interrelated aspects of international order such as actors' understandings of polarity and the identification of great powers; it highlights expectations about the behavior of kinds of states, for example great powers and rogue states; it outlines the desirability and possibility of collaboration, cooperation, and integration in the order; it makes predictions about rising and falling powers, threats, enemies, and allies; it assesses identification of interests; and finally strategic narratives can outline the scope for the socialization of political actors.

Owen[75] argues that changes from one order to another have been defined by the ideas and narratives that they represented as well as the changing allocation of material power in the system. Owen suggests that regime transition needed a justifying narrative to outline the new ground rules of the polity,[76] which were often reinforced by narrative binaries to reinforce the distinction between old and new regimes—such as Roman Catholics and Lutherans—to shore up support.[77] Narratives are then also a means to bridge uncertainty and require actors and networks to spread.[78] Legal scholars explain the reinforcement of order due to the embedding of narratives. Karin Fierke[79] cites legal scholar Robert Cover's contention that, "No set of legal institutions or prescriptions exists apart from the narratives that locate it and give it meaning . . . Once understood in the context of narratives that give it meaning, law becomes not merely a system of rules to be observed, but a world in which we live."

During the French Revolution the cry of *liberté, égalité et fraternité* conveyed a narrative to define change from the old monarchical order.[80] George H. W. Bush's declaration of a "New World Order" in 1991 was a strategic narrative of positive change after the fall of the Berlin Wall on the eve of the Gulf War. Likewise Fukuyama's "end of history" narrative sought to indicate the success of liberalism as the cause of the end of the Cold War and to reinforce its dominance as the organizing principle of the post–Cold War order. As McEvoy-Levy suggests, Fukuyama's narrative was one of orderly transition.[81] However, Fukuyama's Hegel-inspired contention that the argument whether liberal order was the dominant had been won with the fall of the Berlin Wall in 1989 was immediately contested. Rather than providing a hegemonic narrative of transition, the 1990s witnessed contestation over the legacy of the Cold War and lacked a blueprint for transition. Uncertainty has continued to define our understanding of world order both in academia and policy circles. It is within this context of uncertainty that China, the EU, the US, and other leading actors have sought to project their narratives. Rather than witness the diffusion of the US narrative, the end of bipolarity and its apparent binary choices has been replaced with multiple complexities and uncertainty. Our focus is on the agency of major powers in narrating the emerging order amidst uncertainty to the satisfaction of domestic and international audiences. As Beck argues,

> We find ourselves at a difficult historical juncture, one in which we should remind ourselves once again of Gramsci's definition of a crisis. Crisis, Gramsci says, "consists precisely in the fact that the old order is dying and the new cannot be born." But this transitional phase is fraught with confusion. That is our situation today: it is a caesura, an interregnum, a simultaneous collapse and a new beginning—and an uncertain end.[82]

Schweller and Pu argue that prestige and the demand for influence of emerging states drives efforts to discredit—or in their terms delegitimize—the hegemon's global authority and order.[83] Drawing on the work of Modelski, they argue, "delegitimation occurs after the hegemon (or unipole) has begun its relative decline. In Modelski's scheme, delegitimation is followed by a 'deconcentration/coalition building' phase, in which power becomes even more diffuse and balance of power alliances start to form. This is essentially what we argue, but there are some differences regarding timing and the fact that the current system is the first truly unipolar, not just hegemonic, structure."[84] Schweller and Pu's emphasis on proposing an alternative to the existing hegemonic order fits with our conception of strategic narrative. They argue that relative material decline of an existing hegemon is not in itself a decisive condition for power transition, but that ideational change must take place, which is where we view the importance of strategic narrative. Schweller and Pu suggest that,

> While the consensus opinion is that U.S. power is eroding, the legitimacy of the United States' international order and authority to rule have not, to this point, been seriously undermined. Any challenger that seeks to restore global balance-of-power dynamics, therefore, must put forward an alternative idea of order that appeals to other powerful states. Delegitimizing U.S. unipolarity and proposing a viable new order are prerequisite exercises for traditional balancing behavior to commence.[85]

A hegemon's ability to define the basis of an order will be repeatedly challenged by the less powerful or potential rivals.[86]

Making sense of complexity is an increasingly difficult thing for policy makers to do, which is why strategic narrative is an attractive policy concept and explanatory tool. The formation and projection of multiple views of order are enabled by the new media ecology. This challenges states to be proactive in their engagement with defining the terms of international order. In 1919 world leaders could negotiate the new world order out of the immediate gaze of the world's media.[87] Today the "global battle of ideas"[88] creates both the perception and actuality of a more competitive and contested marketplace for governments who must learn how to compete with or harness a plethora of voices. States no longer have the option to conduct relations with the world in grand diplomatic set pieces, controlling who is in and who is not in the room. Monroe Price[89] argues that although leaders can choose not to engage in shaping hearts and minds of citizens, the incentives to do so and the contestation of ideas that shape the world require activism on the part of states. As Richard Holbrooke once commented to Michael Ignatieff in an interview, "Diplomacy is not like chess. . . . It's more like jazz—a constant improvisation on a theme."[90] The ability to devise and implement a coherent strategic narrative rests on the vagaries of events and the views of others.

Bially-Mattern's major contribution to theorizing the power of communication within international relations rests on the concept of *representational force*. She contends that:

> representational force leaves its victims no choice but to *live the experience* of the re-produced identity. Therefore, representational force not only re-produces the epistemological order, but also the expectations and behaviors, and so the international order, that derive from them. Identity, as such, can impose order upon disorder; it can be a source of order. But at least during crises, it does so through force. *It forces order.*[91]

Orders can be inclusive or exclusive. The North Atlantic security community that emerged after World War II forged a shared identity in the face of a perceived threat from the Soviet Union and its allies.[92] From an inclusive perspective the English School of International Relations has at its core the goal of the emergence of an international society of sovereign states, mediating the negative consequences of anarchy.[93] The difficulty in contemporary international affairs is that the we-ness is more complex to maintain. Instead of the Cold War binary, there is a more diverse system emerging with new more diverse voices. However, it could be argued that the world is more united by shared media practice.[94] Ikenberry's argument that we are entering a period defined by what he calls Liberalism 3.0 might come to pass, but the diversity of opinions and views—and the very fact of their circulation and political leaders' vulnerability to them—might have a more profound influence than currently imagined.[95] We-ness might not be the result of interconnection among great powers—nor might we expect a Huntington style clash of civilizations.[96] Barry Buzan's compelling argument that we are not likely to see the emergence of new superpowers as a result of systemic change is an important contribution to debates on power transition. Buzan asserts that the conditions for the emergence of new superpowers do not exist and that the result of this will be that power will be concentrated regionally among a spread of new and existing great powers. Buzan focuses on the US as an existing superpower and the European Union and China as potential superpowers in the making. Buzan argues that:

> loss of material capability is probably not going to be the main factor moving the US away from sole superpower status. The key factors in this move will be social, and they are working both within the US, where the will to support a superpower role may well be waning and outside it, where the US is likely to find ever fewer followers, whether it wants to lead or not. . . . Changes in social support on either the domestic or international level could thus quite quickly shift the US from superpower to great power status.[97]

Buzan argues that the fates of China and the US will be intertwined and define policy choices. Buzan states:

> To the extent that realist thinking dominates in Washington, and the US retains its commitment to not tolerating any peer competitors, then a rising China, whether peaceful or not, *must* appear threatening to the US. The nature of the China that rises, however, will be crucial to whether others share US perceptions of China as a threat. In the absence of any common cause, it is far from clear that other powers will feel threatened by China's challenge to US hegemony.[98]

Buzan goes further to argue that,

> If they can carry off their design for a "peaceful rise" then it becomes possible that US perceptions of China as threatening will not be shared widely, if at all. . . . If China's rise is benign but the US securitizes it anyway, Japan will face very difficult choices. . . . If China plays its hand cleverly, it could put the US more on its own in relation to great power politics than it has been since before the First World War.[99]

Robert Cooper's analysis divides the world into modern and postmodern orders, requiring different styles of engagement to combat challenges in each.[100] Goldman's logic of internationalism suggests that, "Communication across borders is apt to make interests less incompatible in two ways, according to the theory of internationalism as interpreted here. One is to diminish misperception; the other is to increase empathy."[101] Following on from there, Lynch argues, "Communicative approaches to deliberation go beyond this conception of the public as an exogenous constraint. Public dialogue within overlapping national and international public spheres does more than simply provide information about preferences; it allows interested actors and expert observers to contest truth claims and interest claims."[102] Communication, we argue, does not always increase empathy. Narratives that are framed as inclusive may not be interpreted as such by others. Lynch quotes a speech by Bill Clinton that is telling: Clinton argued that "we cannot allow a healthy argument to lead us toward a campaign-driven Cold War with China; for that would have tragic consequences . . . the debate we're having today about China is mirrored by a debate going on in China about the United States . . . and we must be sensitive to how we handle this."[103]

With the advent of the new media ecology, governments are able to communicate directly with citizens in other states on a near-instantaneous and continual basis. There has been a decisive move from a two-step model of communication—involving political actors projecting narratives and frames to news media, which then filter that content by interaction with niche groups—to a one-step model where communication technologies allow for direct targeting by political actors.[104] It is within the capabilities of major powers to engage directly with citizens of other states. Indeed the salience of strategic narratives rest on their credibility, which needs to be established by political actors. As Ramo argues, "If China wants to achieve Peaceful Rise, it is crucially important that it gets other nations to buy into the world view it proposes."[105] Felix Ciută argues that narrative is a vehicle for change as well as the vessel that carries the changing categories of meaning, shaping security practice.[106] Likewise, whilst we would not contend that material power is insignificant, examining relative shifts in material power does not tell the whole story when it comes to the establishment of order.[107]

MILITARY INTERVENTION: STRATEGIC NARRATIVES OF ORDER IN ACTION

Strategic narratives of order can be traced in how great powers narrate their positions in times of crisis management. Even for the United States, forging a coherent narrative in the post–Cold War era has been difficult.[108] The apparent certainties of the Cold War era and President H. W. Bush's short-lived New World Order have been replaced by great complexity and a lack of clarity concerning what the US position in the world is.[109] There is, however, no obvious alternative to the US liberal narrative of international order. The unity of the post-9/11 response quickly dissipated with the controversy of the 2003 Iraq War and disagreements over Afghanistan. Despite developments in government communication, the US has found it as challenging as any other major state to influence others and communicate its conception of order.[110] We can chart the use of strategic narrative through the narratives that states draw on in arguing for the use of military force in international crises. Divergent views on military intervention have pitted great powers against one another since the end of the Cold War. The debate over United Nations Security Council Resolution 1973 in March 2011 divided the international community and highlighted different national views on military intervention and international order. This section will focus on how the British and French constructed a strategic narrative of intervention that ultimately persuaded the US to agree to enforce the no-fly zone.

The agency of France and the UK will be highlighted as a means to illustrate the formation, projection, and reception of strategic narratives. Orford's work charts how narratives of intervention can create compelling arguments for greater Western use of military force and precedents in international law for such actions.[111] We illustrate how France and the UK were able to mobilize a strategic narrative for intervention that ultimately resulted in agreement or abstention on the UN Security Council Permanent 5 (P5) member states. The debate on UN 1973 highlights the different conceptions of maintaining order of UN P5. France and the UK's strategic narrative of responsibility to protect (R2P) ultimately won out and forced US consent and the acquiescence of Russia and China, with most hardened criticism from Germany.[112] How Libya was communicated among elites and publics in the UN Security Council and publics beyond it also demonstrates different reception dynamics.[113] Strategic narrative analysis suggests that a focus on R2P narratives backed with a coordinated British-French position was able to mobilize sufficient support within the Security Council to agree to UN1973.

The debate within the EU concerning the decision to enforce a no-fly zone in Libya in 2011 represents an interesting test case for demonstrating the complexity major powers face to project a strategic narrative. The diplomatic response to the events that emerged in Libya in February 2011, culminating in the very public vote on UNSCR 1973 in the UN Security Council, was characterized by political debate concerning ideas underpinning what the appropriate response should be.[114] Rather than presenting a unified EU position, Germany diverged from France, the US, and the UK on whether a no-fly zone should be enforced militarily under the remit of UNSCR1973 and its precursor UNSCR1970. A strategic narrative analysis of the Libya no-fly zone decision demonstrates that whilst France and the UK were ultimately able to project an effective narrative able to influence the US position, it came at some detriment to EU cohesion. The Libya case also highlights the divergence of opinion among the UN Security Council permanent member states regarding interventionist military force. The following section will outline in brief the central pillars of the British, French, and German narratives on the Libya crisis to highlight how these shaped national and international responses to the diplomacy surrounding the proposed no-fly zone.[115] Regarding the spectrum of persuasion as outlined in our introduction, the Libya case demonstrates that only thin persuasion took place, with fundamental differences concerning principles of military intervention underlying the divergent positions of the key actors.

France

France's role as a cosponsor of the resolution put it center stage in international diplomacy.[116] This was further enhanced through its presidency of the G8, which France attempted to mobilize to generate support within the UN. Despite this structural influence, France was unable to mobilize substantial support within the G8 due to German and US reluctance to consider a no-fly zone. At the G8 meeting in Paris on March 13–14, 2011,[117] the summit statement did not include a statement of support for a no-fly zone and indeed German foreign minister Westerwelle made statements reinforcing Germany's opposition to a military option.[118] France's diplomacy therefore rested on gaining acceptance of its narrative. This was initially seen in the efforts of Sarkozy and French philosopher Bernhard-Henry Lévy in calling for action as Gadhafi's forces threatened to attack Benghazi.[119]

Alain Juppé's explanation of France's position on UNSCR1973 stressed timing as being a major motivating factor for support of the no-fly zone:

We no longer have much time. It's a matter of days; it may be a matter of hours. With every day, every hour that goes by, the forces of repression are closing the net around a civilian population who long for freedom, particularly the population of Benghazi. Every day, every hour that goes by increases the weight of responsibility on our shoulders. Let's be sure not to arrive too late![120]

Sarkozy pressed the French narrative as the bombardments began in the days after the passing of UNCR1973. On March19, 2011, Sarkozy asserted the self-determination of Arab peoples and the determination of France to end the violence to allow their freedom as being the main motivations of his government:

I say this solemnly. Everyone must now shoulder their responsibilities. It is a grave decision that we have had to take. Alongside her Arab, European and North American partners, France is determined to assume her role in history.[121]

Steven Erlanger of the *New York Times* quotes Sarkozy in the days immediately after the vote on UNSCR1973:

France had "decided to assume its role, its role before history" in stopping Colonel Qaddafi's "murderous madness," Mr. Sarkozy said solemnly on Saturday, standing alone before the television cameras and pleasing those here who still have a strong sense of French exceptionalism and moral leadership.[122]

The French narrative of responsibility for leadership, Gadhafi's unsuitability for power, and his illegitimate suppression of opposition along with the situating of the Libya crisis within wider developments in the Middle East indicates great similarity with the UK's narrative, as discussed below. These exchanges demonstrate that the R2P discourse created subject positions—states who take responsibility—that Sarkozy adopted and spoke from. He narrativized events by framing a problem, characterizing himself and France (we take responsibility), and projecting an imagined terrible ending ("Let's be sure not to arrive too late!"). Thus Sarkozy was the vehicle for, face of, and narrator of, France's strategic narrative.

France's narrative defines a perception of order that approximates liberal interventionism. Sarkozy drew on France's long history of military intervention in Africa and its role as a shaper of the EU's emerging crisis management capabilities in making the case that calls for intervention in Libya did not contradict existing foreign policy narratives. France's determination to enforce order within Libya came from a sense of French responsibility to Libyan citizens and of France's role as a European power to react to instability in the region. France's strategic narrative assumes responsibility for leadership and bringing security to the people of Libya. France's strategic narrative placed her in the center of a diverse coalition of states to prevent the repeat of what it viewed as historical failures to react to attacks on civilians in Africa.

Germany

Germany's decision to abstain on UNSCR1973 resulted in stinging criticism of the German government from within Germany and internationally. Germany's foreign policy narrative was deemed to have been contradicted by Germany's decision not to aid Libyans who were suffering at the hands of Colonel Gadhafi. Germany's decision to take part in Operation Allied Force in Kosovo was deemed to be a signal of greater German responsibility for international crisis management to protect human rights. Germany's abstention over Libya was criticized for not continuing this narrative.

In the statements before the vote on UNSCR1973 Peter Wittig, Germany's Permanent Representative to the UN stated the following to explain Germany's reason for abstaining:

> Decisions on the use of military force are always extremely difficult to take. We have carefully considered the options of using military force, its implications as well as its limitations. We see great risks. The likelihood of large-scale loss of life should not be underestimated. If the steps proposed turn out to be ineffective, we see the danger of being drawn into a protracted military conflict that would affect the wider region. We should not enter a military confrontation on the optimistic assumption that quick results with few casualties will be achieved. Germany, therefore, has decided not to support a military option as foreseen particularly in OP 4 and OP 8 of the resolution. Furthermore, Germany will not contribute to such a military effort with its own forces.[123]

Like Sarkozy, Wittig offers a projection of the future, but his terrible ending is a different one—a "protracted military conflict that would affect the wider region." Foreign Minister Gudio Westerwelle's (FDP) rationale for abstaining can be seen in a number of interviews he gave, which stressed his concern of unforeseen risk inherent in the decision to intervene militarily. Westerwelle argued the following. First, the risk was too great that the enforcing of the no-fly zone would result in military escalation.

> We calculated the risk. If we see that three days after this intervention began, the Arab League already criticises (it), I think we had good reasons. . . . This does not mean that we are neutral, it does not mean that we have any sympathy with Colonel Gaddafi, but it means that we see the risks.[124]

He went on to argue that,

> It is not because we have some sort of lingering soft spot for Gaddafi's system that we decided not to send German troops to Libya, but because we also have to see the risks of a lengthy mission.[125]

Second, Westerwelle asserted that he did not consider military intervention to be correct strategy for dealing with Libya and that a military response could have the potential to create growing expectations for a greater crisis management role for Europeans in the future. He was offering a further projected negative or unwanted ending to the narrative. To this Westerwelle urged the following:

> I warn against having a discussion in Europe about a military intervention every time there is injustice in north Africa or in Arabia. . . . I am convinced that there can only be a political solution in Libya. . . . At the end of the day it is important that we clearly stand by the democrats. . . . But it is also clear that we cannot threaten military action against every country in north Africa where there is injustice.[126]

Defense Minister Thomas De Maiziere (CDU) was even more forthright in his opposition to UNSCR1973. In an attempt to rebuff the criticism of Germany, De Maiziere argued that Germany's decision had been well thought out and rational. He said,

> Our decision not to participate in the military part of the Libya mission was based on carefully considered reasons. It remains correct.[127]

More fundamentally, however, de Maiziere outlined very explicitly his skepticism toward the principal of responsibility to protect (R2P), which had gained traction in the late 1990s with the decision to intervene in the Kosovo crisis of 1998–99. De Maiziere stated:

> The responsibility to protect a country's civilian population if its government violates human rights is firmly anchored in international law. But does that mean we are allowed to intervene? Or does that mean we're actually required to? I believe that each military operation must be analysed to determine whether its goals can be achieved with appropriate means and within an appropriate time frame as well as how one gets out at the end. Every one.[128]

Westerwelle and De Maiziere's statements were a direct challenge to the British and French diplomacy pushing for military intervention, as we outline below. The German response suggested a rejection of the principals promoted by British-French diplomacy and indicated a future-oriented reticence to see Libya as a model for future crisis management operations. They were in essence laying out what is possible and what is not for German foreign policy, based on their reading of events and informed and shaped by German foreign policy experience. This is a pillar of Germany's national identity narrative, which has been highly resistant to change, despite cautious involvement in military crisis management operations as part of the EU and NATO.[129]

Germany's narrative stressed the importance of diplomacy and sanctions. German elites underplayed a narrative of crisis as a means to limit the military response of the international community. Using insights from Buzan and Waever's securitization concept,[130] Germany's narrative was desecuritizing the crisis, making the problem and solution the stuff of domestic politics rather than international crisis management. This desecuritizing narrative met with stiff resistance from the UK and France's narrative insistence that a military response was necessary. In a poll by Emnid for *Bild am Sonntag* on March 20, 2011, 62 percent of respondents were for a military mission in Libya with 31 percent against. But, when asked whether the German armed forces should participate, 65 percent of respondents answered no with 29 percent responding yes.[131] The German narrative of selective intervention complicated the effectiveness of Germany's narrative within Germany, among its partners in France, the UK and the US, and within Libya itself.

Germany has long had a conception of order based on legally grounded multilateral institutional cooperation among states. Building long-term regional and global institutional infrastructure, as witnessed in the European Union, has been the top priority of German governments since 1949. Due to tragic historical experience, using military force to advance German interests has been rejected by post–World War II German governments. The deeply embedded set of preferences and skepticism of the utility of military force to achieve policy goals comes under significant pressure when faced with international crises. With the exception of NATO's Operation Allied Force against Serbia in 1999,[132] Germany has often resisted calls from its allies to play a larger role in the aggressive use of military force. These differences were laid bare in Germany's strategic narrative concerning its abstention on UN1973.

The United Kingdom

The United Kingdom's narrative on the Libya crisis was perhaps a midway point between German reticence and French enthusiasm for a military response to the crisis in Libya. The UK's diplomacy was much more defined by a problem-solving tone than the more emotional appeals of Juppé and Sarkozy. The UK's intervention policy in recent years was defined by Tony Blair's Chicago speech of 1998. Public skepticism toward military intervention in the wake of Iraq and Afghanistan and Conservative Party criticism of Blair's interventionist policies ensured that Prime Minister David Cameron and Foreign Minister William Hague's narrative needed to balance a desire for leadership alongside France with an understanding of the UK public concern not to become embroiled in another protracted military campaign. Another factor that is important to bear in mind is the singularity of Libya-UK relations. Gadhafi's support of the Irish Republican Army and his involvement in the Lockerbie bombing had ensured that for many years Gaddafi had been an opponent of the UK government. Blair's decision to bring Gadhafi in from the cold coupled with the release on contested medical grounds of Abdelbaset al-Megrahi—who was implicated in the Lockerbie bombing of 1988—saw UK-Libya relations reestablished and indeed promoted.

When Gadhafi responded to the uprising in Libya by seeking to quash it, the UK government was able to criticize the former Labour government's policy to reintegrate Gadhafi into the international community and signal a UK leadership role with France, a country with which the UK had committed to working closely in security and defense policy since the British-French agreement of November 2010. The UK's Permanent Representative to the UN, Mark Lyall Grant, outlined the UK's rationale for supporting UNSCR1973. In marked difference to Peter Wittig's comments focusing on risk, Grant focused on outlining Gadhafi's crimes and the implications of letting these continue unchecked; he outlined the UK's efforts to achieve regional support for the no-fly zone initiative; he finished on the need to support the Libyan people to deflect counter-narratives of UK national interests being advanced; his statement also outlined the scope and limitations of the military operation and discounted foreign occupation.[133]

William Hague's statement in response to the UN's decision to pass UNSCR 1973 outlined the UK's negative assessment of Gadhafi's actions and the criteria set out by the UK, which they considered needed to be fulfilled—a clear demonstrable need for action, a clear legal basis for involvement, and finally, broad support from within the region from the Arab league.[134] This narrative was reinforced in the House of Commons by Hague on March 24, 2011, when he argued that the UK's policy was for the benefit of not only Libyans, but the wider Middle East:

> [T]he United Kingdom believes that the people of all these countries must be able to determine their own futures. That is why in all of them we argue for reform not repression, and why in Libya, supported by the full authority of the United Nations, we have acted to save many lives threatened by one of the most repressive regimes of them all. This will continue to be our approach as change continues to gather pace in the Middle East.[135]

The UK was careful not to be openly critical of Germany's abstention on UNSCR1973. In response to question from Gisela Stuart (Labour) about Germany following a statement on Libya, Hague replied:

> It is a crucial partner of this country in the European Union and in NATO. The different countries in NATO have of course taken varying

decisions about their level of participation, and indeed on whether to participate, but Germany has not been unhelpful or obstructive and has not attempted to block the work we need to do in NATO. It set out its position at the UN Security Council and did not vote for the resolution, which we must respect, but it has not been unhelpful in so many other ways. I hope that it will attend the conference in London.[136]

The UK's role as a cosponsor of UNSCR1973 put it at the center of efforts to find a majority within the UN for a no-fly zone. UK officials were very keen to stress the broad acceptance of their narrative and avoid focusing on UK interests. In his evidence to the House of Commons Select Committee on Defense, Mark Lyall Grant was keen to stress that it was not only the UK's efforts that secured a majority, but also the "narrative work" of other actors. Lyall Grant focused particularly on the defection of Libya's UN ambassador and the statements he made within the UN on Gadhafi. Lyall Grant stated,

> The Libyan ambassador to the UN defected in a very public way. In the Security Council, a very public forum, he started comparing Gaddafi to Pol Pot and Hitler, and that obviously had quite a dramatic impact on Security Council members.[137]

This narrative connection with Pol Pot and Hitler drew historical analogies— or as D'Andrade and Strauss argue, cognitive schemas—from two reviled figures and provided a powerful context for generating support for military action against Gadhafi's forces.[138] It gave texture to the narrative by using these historical frames or templates to characterize the enemy actor in a way that warranted action to stop him.

The United States: Obama's Reticence

The Libya crisis presented the Obama administration with a number of challenges. As a break from Bush, Obama's foreign policy narrative was founded on drawing down US military commitments overseas and seeking partnerships with other nations to maintain international order. During Obama's inauguration speech in 2009, he asserted his commitment to withdrawal from Afghanistan and Iraq. Obama's inauguration speech demonstrated a foreign policy position caught between a narrative of American military withdrawal and a narrative of American leadership and responsibility that reflected US great power identity, as explained in Chapter 2.[139] Pressure to withdraw from Iraq and Afghanistan clashed with the potential implications of involvement in Libya, with no clear sense of the scope of the military operation. The scaling back of US military operations coupled with the desire to have other states share in maintaining international order soon became the key pillars of Obama's foreign policy doctrine.[140] Cited in the *Financial Times,* Anne-Marie Slaughter stated,

This is a president who could still run in 2012 on the grounds that he got us out of two wars. . . . He's not going to do things that distract us from Afghanistan. And that's totally consistent with what I call the Obama doctrine—that other countries are going to have to do more in a more diverse international order.[141]

For Obama, the advocacy of France and the UK in making the case for UN1973 was helpful for Obama's narrative of cautious engagement in crisis management. Even though, as events demonstrated, the US still needed to undertake the majority of the heavy lifting for the military operations in Libya, the involvement of France and the UK, along with the Arab League and eventually NATO, allowed Obama to present a strategic narrative of multilateral engagement and shared responsibility. Obama's decision to support UN1973 was criticized on procedural grounds, however, for not including Congress in discussions leading up to the vote. Thus, the process of forming the US strategic narrative was contested. Obama was also criticized for apparent indecision in responding to events in Libya, at a time when France and the UK became more assertive in their narrative of the crisis.[142]

Obama's reticence on involvement in Libya persisted right up until the vote in the UN.[143] No substantive discussions took place on Libya in the US Senate, leading one scholar to estimate that although Libya was raised for debate, this could not have last more than approximately thirty-five seconds.[144] Despite this, the Senate recommended the imposition of a UN-sponsored no-fly zone on March 1, 2011 to protect Libyan civilians,[145] although no explicit statement of US involvement was made. Even on March 9, Obama and his national security team were reported to still consider involvement in Libya as being filled with too many uncertainties.[146] US Secretary of State Hillary Clinton stressed the need for a multilateral effort led by NATO or the EU, not by the US.[147] At the G-8 Ministerial summit in London on March 15, 2011, no common position on Libya could be agreed.[148]

The final US position on UN1973 outlined in the remarks of Ambassador Susan Rice stressed,

> Colonel Qadhafi and those who still stand by him continue to grossly and systematically abuse the most fundamental human rights of Libya's people. On March 12, the League of Arab States called on the Security Council to establish a no-fly zone and take other measures to protect civilians. Today's resolution is a powerful response to that call—and to the urgent needs on the ground. . . . The United States stands with the Libyan people in support of their universal rights.[149]

The powerful narrative of the international communities' responsibility to protect, the role of the Arab League, and the centrality of universal human rights as motivations for action all mirrored the Franco-British narrative.

A good indication of why Obama ultimately decided to become involved in the Libya no-fly-zone operation can be seen in his speech of March 28, 2011, at the National Defense University in Washington, DC.[150] In his speech Obama sought to justify his decision to become involved a number of ways. The speech focused on outlining the need for US involvement and how the US led the response to the crises in a timely manner—Obama argued that it took only 31 days to put together a response, in contrast to the year it took the international community to respond to the Bosnia crisis in the 1990s. He also highlighted the breadth of the international response and the role of NATO. Viewed as a strategic narrative, Obama sought to counter criticisms of an uncertain response to the crisis and a lack of US leadership. Obama argued that,

> Confronted by this brutal repression and a looming humanitarian crisis, I ordered warships into the Mediterranean.[151] European allies declared their willingness to commit resources to stop the killing. The Libyan opposition and the Arab League appealed to the world to save lives in Libya. And so at my direction, America led an effort with our allies at the United Nations Security Council to pass a historic resolution that authorized a no-fly zone to stop the regime's attacks from the air, and further authorized all necessary measures to protect the Libyan people.[152]

It was this commitment to all necessary measures that alienated the German position, which was keen to contain the scope of any military involvement.[153] Obama continued to stress that it was Gadhafi's actions that made US involvement unavoidable. He asserted, "It was not in our national interest to let that happen. I refused to let that happen."[154] The international nature of the forces reinforced Obama's legitimacy and responsibility to act:

> In this effort, the United States has not acted alone. Instead, we have been joined by a strong and growing coalition. This includes our closest allies—nations like the United Kingdom, France, Canada, Denmark, Norway, Italy, Spain, Greece, and Turkey—all of whom have fought by our sides for decades. And it includes Arab partners like Qatar and the United Arab Emirates, who have chosen to meet their responsibilities to defend the Libyan people.[155]

Obama's robust defense of UN1973 and US involvement in the enforcement of the no-fly zone was necessary for his foreign policy narrative of withdrawal whilst signaling his international leadership profile. Obama's narrative stresses US leadership in enforcing order at the head of a large coalition of like-minded states. The US responsibility to maintain international order was central to Obama's strategic narrative, both to claim international leadership and to convince the US public of his rationale for involvement in the no-fly zone.

China and Russia's Abstentions

China and Russia's abstentions on UN1973 came as no surprise and were in many ways consistent with their responses to Western-led military operations over recent years. China and Russia have been skeptical of military intervention to uphold international order. The post-Kosovo increases in liberal interventionist operations, whether by the EU or NATO, have been resisted by China and Russia. China and Russia's narrative on military intervention have stressed the importance of international law and national sovereignty. China's foreign policy narrative of peaceful rise has ensured that the Chinese government has been reluctant to involve China in military crisis management operations. China's UN ambassador outlined a position that was supportive of UN Security Council action and cooperation with the Arab League, but retained reservations over the contents of the resolution:

> China is seriously concerned over the worsening situation in Libya. We support the Security Council in taking appropriate and necessary action to stabilize the situation in Libya and put an end to the acts of violence against civilians at an early date.[156]

China also stressed a regional solution to the crisis:

> China attaches great importance to the decision made by the 22-member Arab League on the establishment of a no-fly zone over Libya. We also attach great importance to the positions of African countries and the African Union.[157]

China's explanation for the abstention accepted much of the Franco-British narrative of the crisis. However, Russia's ambassador stuck a more critical note in his comments to the Security Council. The Russian ambassador did not accept the British, French, and US narrative of responsibility to protect Libyans in Benghazi, turning this narrative on its head by arguing,

> Our position as to the clear unacceptability of the use of force against civil population in Libya remains unchanged. Any attacks against civilians and other violations of international humanitarian law and human rights must be immediately and unconditionally stopped.[158]

Churkin went on to state,

> The work on this document was not in keeping with the Security Council standing practice. A whole range of essentially specific and absolutely relevant questions raised by the Russian Federation and other Security Council members remained unanswered, such as how the no-fly zone would be enforced, what the rules of engagement and limits of the use of force would be.[159]

Most interesting about Russia's decision to abstain was perhaps the reported disagreement between President Medvedev and Prime Minister Putin.[160] Medvedev's decision to abstain contrasted with Putin's more strident criticisms of the UN resolution, leading to a very public disagreement with one another. Medvedev's cautious acceptance of UN1973 in the days after the UN vote suggest that Churkin's comments in the Security Council were a means to present a narrative of Russian abstention that included the views of both the Russian president and prime minister. Rachman contrasts the missionary zeal of the Western powers' decision on UN1973 with the egocentrism of China and Russia, still cautious of Western intervention since the experiences with Tiananmen and Chechnya.[161] China and Russia's narratives were more about fundamentals of their foreign policy narratives than the individual case before them. A disconnect between national narratives of international order and the West's interventionist narrative ensured that whilst there are clear efforts to express concern for the situation, they could not openly support the resolution.

DISCUSSION

An analysis of strategic narratives of the P5 and Germany uncovers quite substantial differences of how to respond to the crisis as well as underlying differences on the utility of military force in crisis management. A skeptical view of British-French intentions would suggest that their response to Libya was driven by attempts at sidelining of Germany from international leadership as a response to a perceived increase in Germany's power in Europe since the onset of the Eurozone crisis.[162] From this reading of motives, France and the UK were driven to assert influence over the international community's response to the Arab Spring and to profile their international position as leading players in the region. Our focus here is to understand how France, Germany, and the UK tried to shape international understanding of the crisis through their strategic narratives. Ultimately, although Germany and the US shared similar views of the crisis until the eve of the vote on UN1973, Germany was left isolated when Obama decided to support the resolution.

We argue that a strategic narrative involves three interconnected and complementary dynamics, understood as the processes of narrative formation, narrative projection, and narrative reception. France and the UK were successful in their efforts to have UNSCR1973 accepted, despite the abstention of a number of important Security Council members. Their narrative was successful in influencing the US to support their proposals despite publicly stated reservations of President Obama and Secretary of State Clinton. France and the UK were also able to carry domestic opinion, albeit by a slim majority that waxed and waned throughout the operations. Their narrative, although unsuccessful in influencing Germany's vote within the UN Security

Council, did resonate within political elites and German public opinion, despite overall public support for Westerwelle's abstention.

Taking each stage in the process of strategic narrative development, we can pinpoint differences and similarities in national positions and, most importantly, chart the reception or rejection of these competing visions of the crisis. In terms of formation, domestic political culture and national strategic cultures defined the formation of national narratives of the crisis.

Each country's government sought to project its narrative in different ways. France and the UK coordinated early on in the crisis and thus the timing and content of the narratives were broadly similar. Germany's focus for its diplomacy was in the G-8, UN, and the EU once it felt excluded from UK-French bilaterals. At each step France and the UK sought to multilateralize diplomacy, and focused on the importance of having a wide range of support within the Security Council and lessening the exclusivity of their bilateral discussions. Through this process each government sought to structure diplomacy in a manner to benefit their objectives in the Security Council. Cameron and Sarkozy used media reports to strengthen their hand and sought legitimacy for their involvement in the region through the Arab League.

Reception in this context is largely understood in the degree of support for each of the positions outlined by France, Germany, and the UK. The UK and France were able to generate a large coalition in favor of the no-fly zone, particularly once the US had come on board. In France, public opinion was very much skeptical until the decision on UNSCR1973 in the UN. After that public support rose and remained generally supportive throughout the campaign.[163] From looking at the speeches and debates within France and the UK it appears that Germany's narrative had little impact in those countries. Germany's focus on a political solution to the crisis was not out of step with France and the UK. Rather, different threat perceptions and fundamentally different responses to R2P ensured normative dissonance between the EU big three.

Here the role of the US is of great interest. Interviews by one of the authors in the Auswaertiges Amt, Bundesministerium der Verteidigung, and the Kanzleramt in Berlin in the summer of 2011 uncovered a sense of surprise within policy circles when President Obama decided to support the draft resolution. This last-minute decision exposed German diplomacy and heaped more pressure on Berlin to explain its decision. For Germany to take a different position to France, the UK, and the US, its closest allies, marked a significant moment in recent German foreign policy. After March 17, 2011, Westerwelle had to explain why Germany's position was out of step with Germany's main allies, which led to Westerwelle's assertion that his policy, of politics first, was the correct one and that military engagement under the banner of R2P operations was not sustainable.

China has been consistently against intervention, but cautious about how this is presented. China's strategic narrative of peaceful rise is an important brake on a more expansive foreign policy to include multilateral

Table 3.1 Strategic Narrative Formation

Strategic Narrative Formation	France	Germany	United Kingdom	USA
Policy goals	No-fly zone; removal of Gadhafi	Diplomacy and sanctions; removal of Gadhafi	No-fly zone; removal of Gadhafi	Diplomacy and sanctions; removal of Gadhafi; eventually support of NFZ
Role of domestic politics	Largely the most supportive according to opinion poll data	Supportive of NFZ but not of German role in it; domestic politics criticism was led by the Greens	Marginally supportive and shifting	Little discussion of Libya; only non-binding resolution in Senate on 1/3/2011; Obama central to final decision
Constraints on historical narrative	Supportive narrative of French intervention across the world; France as a leading player in world affairs	Coming to terms with military intervention but with lingering reticence	Narrative of UK forces involved in crisis management across the world; UK responsibility; the UK's global reach	Pressures of living up to great power narrative and leadership; Obama's concern to distinguish his foreign policy from G. W. Bush
Events	Fukushima; Sarkozy's precarious political domestic support.	Fukushima; Eurozone crisis; domestic electoral cycle pressuring governing coalition; resignation of Defense Minister zu Guttenberg due to allegations of plagiarism of his PhD thesis	Fukushima; acceptance rather than overwhelming support of government position; relations between UK and Libya very delicate after Lockerbie; Gadhafi's supply of arms to IRA	Concern to respond to Arab Spring and set agenda in the region whilst encouraging partners in maintenance of order
Conception of order	Order can be maintained through the use of military force akin to Liberal Interventionism outlined in Tony Blair's Chicago speech of 1998.	True international order rests on legally binding multilateral institutional arrangements among states. The use of military force to reestablish order in times of crisis has the potential to exacerbate the crisis and postpone the renewal of order in the system.	Order can be maintained through the use of military force akin to Liberal Interventionism outlined in Tony Blair's Chicago speech of 1998.	Order can be maintained through the use of military force akin to Liberal Interventionism outlined in Tony Blair's Chicago speech of 1998. The United States bears responsibility to maintain the post–World War II order.

Table 3.2 Strategic Narrative Projection

Strategic Narrative Projection	France	Germany	United Kingdom	USA
New media technologies	Sarkozy only beginning to make use of new media with the appointment of Nicolas Princen. Does not appear to have been a major focus.	Media blitz by Westerwelle to explain abstention after March 17, 2011 vote.	Perception in UK government that they were lagging behind US in use of social media.[1]	Extensive use of public diplomacy to attempt nonmilitary solution (Stratton, 2011).
Timing of communication	Central role for summitry in G8 and UN to focus attention on France's role in diplomatic efforts; preemptory recognition of Libyan rebels in run-up to UN vote before EU agreement	Timing revolved around domestic elections in Germany. An abstention was considered important for Westerwelle's party in regional elections in which the FDP were under pressure.	UK placed great importance in UN diplomacy; this was followed up by the London conference in late March 2011 and then ultimately in NATO. UK supported France's efforts within the G8 and in run-up to vote in UN. Both Cameron and Hague phoned their opposition numbers in Berlin in last-minute attempts to persuade a yes-vote in UN.	Obama's decision to support UN1973 only in the final hours; supportive of Franco-UK lead and of Arab League
Dissemination networks	Staging of UN Security Council and media coverage of Juppé's passionate speech; establishment of Libya Contact Group	Germany pursued its policy of diplomacy within the UN and the EU. Provided low-key support within NATO.	Staging of UN Security Council and media coverage of meeting; establishment of Libya contact group; EU summitry, although once Germany had abstained and Baroness Ashton had appeared to contradict Sarkozy and Cameron, the EU became less of a forum and NATO took over as the central organ for diplomacy	UNSC, NATO, and the London conference March 29, 2011 as well as Obama's speech outlining his reasons for supporting UN1973 on March 28, 2011

[1] Allegra Stratton, "Inside Politics: How US Diplomats Are Tweets ahead of British," *The Guardian*, March 17, 2011, 19.

Table 3.3 Strategic Narrative Reception

Strategic Narrative Reception	France	Germany	United Kingdom	USA
Credibility of messages for audiences	Largely the most supportive according to opinion poll data	Skepticism in German elite and public discourse over Westerwelle's role in diplomacy	Mixed message according to opinion poll data as to how credible the domestic narrative was	Position as most powerful nation; claim to leadership
Effects of competing narratives	Supportive domestic opinion and Sarkozy's leadership ensured that he did not have to deal with a significant counter-narrative. Opinion polls suggest support for government policy.	Pressure on government to explain abstention; skepticism of Westerwelle's claim that Germany's policy had contributed to the overthrow of Gadhafi. Information that emerged suggesting Germany was involved in helping targeting within NATO, which contradicted the German government's position.[1]	Opinion polls suggest there was concern and potential mistrust of government narrative over the scope of the mission.	Obama had significant room to maneuver as Commander in Chief, allowing him to hold back on final agreement.
Types of reception: support, acquiescence, protest, appropriation	Largely supportive of, Sarkozy and Juppé despite electoral pressures on government.	Support for not being involved, despite events surrounding the abstention. Elite debates in Bundestag suggested quite diverse opinions on Westerwelle's decision.	Acquiescence in the main; public opinion split but not significantly against mission.	Largely supportive domestic audience.
Contingent factors affecting reception	Mission was considered to be very successful[2]	Germany's opposition to military involvement balanced with perceived contribution to diplomatic and political effort viewed to be positive	Mission was considered to be very successful[3]	Mission was considered to be very successful[4]

[1] Matthias Gebauer, "Are German Soldiers Secretly Helping Fight Gadhafi?" *Spiegel Online*, August 19, 2011, accessed September 1, 2011, at http://www.spiegel.de/international/world/0,1518,781197,00.html.

[2] This was echoed in the NATO and the USA's assessment of the outcome. Ivo H. Daalder and James G. Stavridis, "NATO's Victory in Libya," *Foreign Affairs* 91, no. 2 (2012).

[3] Daalder and Stavridis, "NATO's Victory."

[4] Daalder and Stavridis, "NATO's Victory."

intervention. Nevertheless, despite the principle of sovereignty and international law drawn on to object to Western interventionist narratives, the Chinese explanation for its abstention is not overly critical. The abstention, rather than veto, is perhaps indicative of the strength of the R2P narrative of France and the UK and ultimately the US. Chinese media reports focused on the conceptions of multipolar dynamics in the diplomacy and in particular stressed historical tensions between Russia and the US as underlying explanations for their divergent positions.[164] Russia took a more robust and critical stance on UN1973 based on law and sovereignty to oppose intervention out of concerns for instability in the region.[165] In terms of the spectrum of persuasion, the strategic narrative of the UK and France in favor of intervention had limited impact on China, Germany, and Russia. Indeed, the UK and France's attempts to persuade Germany to agree to the UN1973 resulted in a very robust rejection of the UK-French strategic narrative. Where the UK and France were successful was in mobilizing the US government to agree to the intervention by appealing to the US identity as the global leader and supporter of a stable international order.

The US initial leadership-avoidance narrative quickly waned when NATO became the main forum for enforcing the no-fly zone. Ultimately, despite Obama's hesitancy to become embroiled in an overseas military operation, the US could not argue against the way in which France and the UK narrativized the R2P discourse, as it was consistent with US narrative and values. Germany and the US shared similar public views of the emerging crisis until the evening of the vote. Germany's narrative was skeptical of the utility of military force and demonstrated real concerns that there was a growing commitment to military intervention in the Arab Spring. The German government thought that its views were shared by the US, therefore having some powerful support for its position. When Obama changed his mind to support the resolution, Germany was left exposed.

The new media ecology increased the pressure on the UN, and speed of decision making and narrative of imminent threat to Benghazi outpaced democratic consideration of the intervention. Parliamentary scrutiny of the Libya decision was retrospective. Reporting of events puts politicians on the back foot, creating the impression they were unable to respond to events quickly enough. Particularly in the case of Germany the decision was made to abstain, in some part, due to the conception that the German government did not have enough time to methodically consider the risks and opportunities of the intervention (with the underlying criticism of the hot-headed, impulsive Sarkozy). The German government's narrow legal position on intervention meant they were very cautious of creating an interventionist precedent in Africa based on R2P, which would increase expectations on Germany.

The UK and French strategic narratives attempted to underscore a broader narrative of a liberal order in which states have responsibilities to individuals faced with authoritarian machinations. The Chinese and Russian behavior seem to suggest an acquiescence (rather than an acceptance) of the French/

UK narrative, because their preferred narrative of order emphasizes states as primary actors, and sovereignty as a cherished and indivisible foundation of order. The US was caught between its narrative of order that corresponds with that of France and the UK and its historical narrative about entanglements (and protracted war), given Obama's concern to narrate a break from the recent past in US foreign policy.

CONCLUSIONS

Strategic narratives are central to understanding order. They are often used as a means to legitimate order based on material power distribution in the system. Lippmann suggests,

> The way in which the world is imagined determines at any particular moment what men will do. It does not determine what they will achieve. It determines their effort, their feelings, their hopes, not their accomplishments and results.[166]

We have sought to illustrate how states imagine and enact international order through the projection of strategic narratives. As we outlined in the book's introduction, we highlight the role of system narratives, actor narratives, and issues narratives. We understand discourse as static blocks to craft narratives from which concepts can change or be substituted in a strategic narrative. States seek to narrate the order they are in to their advantage. There is a real world independent of us, but narratives shape how we perceive and understand it and those understandings condition behavior. Material conditions matter, to a point. Joseph Nye's contention in his formulation of soft power was that hard power was not enough for the US to continue to shape international order after the Cold War.[167] The new media ecology does not alter material power allocation among powerful states and nonstate actors. But it does both facilitate and complicate the ways in which powerful states are able to shape conceptions of order. Therefore order is the narrated understandings of the material base and the normative frameworks intrinsic to those understandings. In making this argument we draw on both rationalist literature concerning order and constructivist understandings of international relations.

As we have highlighted in this chapter, strategic narratives are means to shape the behavior of actors. Materially powerful states face challenges to project successful narratives.[168] Despite the significant power at their disposal, great powers use narratives to justify policy objectives, such as the decision to deploy military force, as demonstrated in the debates over UN Security Council Resolution 1973. The effect of changes in the material conditions of order in the system has the potential to alter relations between great powers. Unipolarity and its associated strategic narrative of legitimacy, such as *Pax Americana* or *Pax Britannica*, is likely to fade in to a more decentered international order with different conceptions of order.[169] Ikenberry's argument that the American liberal order is being taken on by others suggests that there will be limited fundamental contestation of the current way order is narrated. However, in our study of the Libya crisis, existing great powers do differ on some of the fundamental principles of the current order when it comes to the sanctioning of military force. Liberal interventionism faces opposition from China and Russia, who so far have not embraced the West's commitment to R2P. Policy makers draw on a set of discourses to reinforce narratives, such as R2P in the case of Libya.

By this point the book has offered our theorization of actors and international order. In the next chapter we explore more deeply what happens when narratives clash and what counts as victory. Different IR scholars have addressed a variety of forms of contestation, from short-term trapping of one state by another around a particular issue[170] and numerous studies of framing, to long-term discursive shifts through which actors purposefully seek to define the core terms through which international relations are understood.[171] The next chapter offers a framework to give scholars clear research paths to finding out what is being contested and how. The framework is illustrated using three examples of narrative contestation in the last half century: the narrative contests that emerge during Israel's conflicts with its neighbors, the narrative work involved when a bulk of the world's states and citizens shifted from pro-whaling to anti-whaling in the 1960s and 1970s, and contestation of Iran's nuclear program. We will use these analyses to highlight the how strategic narratives draw upon long-standing discourses, the raw material of news and events, and the role of different types of actors in narrative contests. It concludes by cautioning against the quest for a successful model or template of narrative success.

NOTES

1. Cited in Nicholas J. Rengger, *International Relations, Political Theory, and the Problem of Order: Beyond International Relations Theory?* (London: Routledge, 2000), 1.
2. Abramo F. K. Organski, *World Politics* (New York: Knopf, 1958). For an alternative take, Richard Ned Lebow and Benjamin Valentino, "Lost in Transition: A Critical Analysis of Power Transition Theory," *International Relations* 23, no. 3 (2009), 389–410.
3. Barry Buzan, "The Inaugural Kenneth N. Waltz Annual Lecture: A World Order without Superpowers; Decentred Globalism," *International Relations* 25, no. 1 (2011).
4. Robert D. Putnam, "Diplomacy and Domestic Politics: The Logic of Two-Level Games," *International Organization* 42, no. 3 (1988).
5. Peter Gourevitch, "The Second Image Reversed: The International Sources of Domestic Politics," *International Organization* 32, no. 4 (1978).
6. Martin Albrow, Helmut K. Anheier, Marlies Glasius, Mary Kaldor, and Monroe E. Price, eds., *Global Civil Society 2007/8: Communicative Power*

and Democracy (London: Sage, 2007); Manuel Castells, *Communication Power* (Oxford: Oxford University Press, 2009).

7. Andrew Hoskins and Ben O'Loughlin, *War and Media* (Cambridge: Polity, 2010); Monroe E. Price, *Media and Sovereignty: The Global Information Revolution and Its Challenge to State Power* (Cambridge: MIT Press, 2002); Philip Seib, *New Media and the New Middle East* (Basingstoke: Palgrave Macmillan, 2009); Philip Seib, ed., *Towards a New Public Diplomacy* (Basingstoke: Palgrave Macmillan, 2009).

8. Francis Fukuyama, *The Origins of Political Order: From Prehuman Times to the French Revolution* (London: Profile Books, 2012), 12.

9. Kathleen Hall Jamieson, *Dirty Politics: Deception, Distraction, and Democracy* (Oxford: Oxford University Press, 1992), 41, cited in Colleen E. Kelley, *The Rhetoric of First Lady Hillary Rodham Clinton: Crisis Management Discourse* (London: Praeger, 2001), 26.

10. Lawrence Freedman, "Order and Disorder in the New World," *Foreign Affairs* 71, no. 1 (1991): 37.

11. Hoskins and O'Loughlin, *War and Media*, 11. See also David Runciman, *The Politics of Good Intentions* (Princeton: Princeton University Press, 2006).

12. Robert Kagan, *Paradise and Power: America and Europe in the New World Order* (London: Atlantic Books, 2003), 3.

13. Hans Joachim Morgenthau, "Principles of Propaganda," in *Truth and Power: Essays of a Decade, 1960–1970* (London: Pall Mall, 1970), 320.

14. Morgenthau, *Truth and Power*, 324.

15. Wayne Porter and Mark Mykleby, *A National Strategic Narrative* (Washington, DC: Woodrow Wilson International Center for Scholars, 2011), 14.

16. Ian Manners, "Normative Power Europe: A Contradiction in Terms?" *JCMS: Journal of Common Market Studies* 40, no. 2 (2002); Ian Manners, "The European Union as a Normative Power: A Response to Thomas Diez," *Millennium-Journal of International Studies* 35, no. 1 (2006).

17. Geoffrey Roberts, "History, Theory and the Narrative Turn in IR," *Review of International Studies* 32, no. 4 (2006); George Lawson, "The Eternal Divide? History and International Relations," *European Journal of International Relations* 18, no. 2 (2012): 203–26.

18. Robert M. Cover, "The Supreme Court, 1982 Term—Foreword: Nomos and Narrative," *Harvard Law Review* 97 (1983); Anne Orford, *Reading Humanitarian Intervention: Human Rights and the Use of Force in International Law*, Vol. 30 (Cambridge University Press, 2003). See also Karin M. Fierke, *Diplomatic Interventions: Conflict and Change in a Globalizing World* (Basingstoke: Palgrave Macmillan, 2005), 165–7.

19. Berenskoetter, Felix, "Parameters of a National Biography," *European Journal of International Relations* (2012); Janice Bially Mattern, *Ordering International Politics: Identity, Crisis, and Representational Force* (London: Routledge, 2005); Ciută, Felix, "Narratives of Security: Strategy and Identity in the European Context," in *Discursive Constructions of Identity in European Politics*, ed. Richard Mole (Basingstoke: Palgrave MacMillan, 2007); Jeffrey W. Legro, *Rethinking the World: Great Power Strategies and International Order* (Ithaca: Cornell University Press, 2005); Meghana Nayak and Eric Selbin, *Decentering International Relations* (London: Zed Books, 2010); Eric Selbin, *Revolution, Rebellion, Resistance: The Power of Story* (London: Zed Books, 2009); Hidemi Suganami, "Narratives of War Origins and Endings: A Note on the End of the Cold War," *Millennium* 26 (1997); Hidemi Suganami, "Agents, Structures, Narratives," *European Journal of International Relations* 5, no. 3 (1999); Annick Wibben, *Feminist Security Studies: A Narrative Approach* (London: Routledge, 2011).

20. John S. Dryzek, *Deliberative Global Politics: Discourse and Democracy in a Divided World* (London: Polity, 2006); Maarten A. Hajer, *The Politics of Environmental Discourse* (Oxford: Oxford University Press, 1995); Frank Fischer, *Reframing Public Policy: Discursive Politics and Deliberative Practices* (Oxford: Oxford University Press, 2003).
21. Clifford Geertz, *The Interpretation of Cultures: Selected Essays*, Vol. 5019 (London: Basic Books, 1973).
22. Layne, Christopher. "A Matter of Historical Debate." *Foreign Affairs* 85, no. 6 (2006).
23. Kenneth N. Waltz, *Theory of International Politics* (Reading, MA: Addison-Wesley, 1979). For a contrasting view, Robert W. Cox, "Social Forces, States and World Orders: Beyond International Relations Theory," *Millennium: Journal of International Studies* 10, no. 2 (1981): 126.
24. Michael N. Barnett, *The International Humanitarian Order* (New York: Taylor & Francis, 2010).
25. Kenneth N. Waltz, "The Emerging Structure of International Politics," *International Security* 18, no. 2 (1993): 44.
26. Waltz, "The Emerging Structure of International Politics"; Kenneth. N. Waltz, "Imitations of Multipolarity," in *New World Order: Contrasting Theories*, eds. Birthe Hansen and Bertel Heurlin (Basingstoke: Palgrave, 2000).
27. Andrew J. Bacevich, *American Empire: The Realities and Consequences of US Diplomacy* (Cambridge: Harvard University Press, 2002).
28. Christopher Layne, "The Unipolar Illusion Revisited: The Coming End of the United States' Unipolar Moment," *International Security* 31, no. 2 (2006); Layne, "A Matter of Historical Debate."
29. Joseph S. Nye, Jr., "US Power and Strategy after Iraq," *Foreign Affairs* 82, no. 4 (2003): 60–73. See also Joseph S. Nye, Jr., "The Changing Nature of World Power," *Political Science Quarterly* 105, no. 2 (1990).
30. Nancy Birdsall and Francis Fukuyama, "The Post-Washington Consensus: Development after the Crisis," *Foreign Affairs* 90, no. 2 (2011): 45–53; David P. Calleo, "The Tyranny of False Vision: America's Unipolar Fantasy,"*Survival* 50, no. 5 (2008); Charles Krauthammer, "Decline Is a Choice: The New Liberalism and the End of American Ascendancy," *The Weekly Standard* 15, no. 5 (2009); Charles A. Kupchan, "After Pax Americana: Benign Power, Regional Integration, and the Sources of a Stable Multipolarity," *International Security* 23, no. 2 (1998); Charles A. Kupchan, *The End of the American Era: US Foreign Policy and the Geopolitics of the Twenty-First Century* (New York: Knopf, 2002); Melvyn P. Leffler and Jeffrey W. Legro, eds., *To Lead the World: American Strategy after the Bush Doctrine* (Oxford: Oxford University Press, 2008); Michael Mastanduno, "Preserving the Unipolar Moment: Realist Theories and US Grand Strategy after the Cold War," *International Security* 21, no. 4 (1997); John J. Mearsheimer, *The Tragedy of Great Power Politics* (New York: Norton, 2001); Barry R. Posen and Andrew L. Ross, "Competing Visions for US Grand Strategy," *International Security* 21, no. 3 (1997); Stephan M. Walt, *Taming American Power: The Global Response to U.S. Primacy* (New York: Norton, 2005).
31. Kai He, "Undermining Adversaries: Unipolarity, Threat Perception, and Negative Balancing Strategies after the Cold War," *Security Studies* 21, no. 2 (2012); G. John Ikenberry, "The Rise of China and the Future of the West," *Foreign Affairs* 87, no. 1 (2008); G. John Ikenberry, "A Weaker World," *Prospect* (November 2010); Christopher Layne, "The Global Power Shift from West to East," *The National Interest* 119 (2012): 22; Jolyon Howorth and Anand Menon, "Still Not Pushing Back: Why the European Union

Is Not Balancing the United States," *Journal of Conflict Resolution* 53, no. 5 (2009); Robert A. Pape, "Soft Balancing against the United States," *International Security* 30, no. 1 (2005); Thazha V. Paul, "Soft Balancing in the Age of US Primacy," *International Security* 30, no. 1 (2005).

32. Waltz, "Imitations of Multipolarity," 1.
33. Nye, "US Power and Strategy," 60.
34. Stephen G. Brooks and William C. Wohlforth, *World Out of Balance: International Relations and the Challenge of American Primacy* (Princeton: Princeton University Press, 2008). See *Cambridge Review of International Affairs* 24, no. 2 (2011) for a review symposium of Brooks and Wohlforth's argument. See also William C. Wohlforth, "The Stability of a Unipolar World," *International Security* 24, no. 1 (1999): 5–41.
35. David A. Lake, *Hierarchy in International Relations* (Ithaca, NY: Cornell University Press, 2009); Organski, *World Politics*.
36. Lake, *Hierarchy in International Relations*.
37. Bruce W. Jentleson and Steven Weber, "America's Hard Sell," *Foreign Policy* 1 (2008); Christopher Layne, "The Unipolar Illusion: Why New Great Powers Will Rise," *International Security* 17, no. 4 (1993); Steven Weber and Bruce W. Jentleson, *The End of Arrogance: America in the Global Competition of Ideas* (Cambridge: Harvard University Press, 2010).
38. G. John Ikenberry, *Liberal Leviathan: The Origins, Crisis, and Transformation of the American World Order* (Princeton, NJ: Princeton University Press, 2012). See also G. John Ikenberry, *After Victory: Institutions, Strategic Restraint, and the Rebuilding of Order after Major Wars* (Princeton, NJ: Princeton University Press, 2001); G. John Ikenberry, ed., *America Unrivalled: The Future of the Balance of Power* (Ithaca,NY: Cornell University Press, 2002); G. John Ikenberry, Michael Mastanduno, and William C. Wohlforth, eds., *International Relations Theory and the Consequences of Unipolarity* (Cambridge: Cambridge University Press, 2011).
39. Ikenberry, *Liberal Leviathan*, 3.
40. Ikenberry, *Liberal Leviathan*, 1.
41. Ikenberry, *Liberal Leviathan*, 2.
42. Ikenberry, *Liberal Leviathan*, 1.
43. Ikenberry, *Liberal Leviathan*, 50.
44. Ikenberry, *Liberal Leviathan*, 3.
45. Ikenberry, *Liberal Leviathan*, 32.
46. Ikenberry, *Liberal Leviathan*, 32.
47. Ikenberry, *Liberal Leviathan*, 7.
48. Ikenberry, *Liberal Leviathan*, 300.
49. Robert Gilpin, *War and Change in World Politics* (Cambridge: Cambridge University Press, 1981), 280, 334.
50. Ikenberry, *Liberal Leviathan*, 337.
51. Ikenberry, *Liberal Leviathan*, 351.
52. Arnold Wolfers, *Discord and Collaboration: Essays on International Politics* (Baltimore: Johns Hopkins University Press, 1962).
53. Ikenberry, *Liberal Leviathan*, 164.
54. Ikenberry, *Liberal Leviathan*, 164.
55. *National Security Council Report* 68, 1950, accessed 13 March 2013, https://www.mtholyoke.edu/acad/intrel/nsc-68/nsc68–1.htm; Steven Casey, "Selling NSC-68: The Truman Administration, Public Opinion, and the Politics of Mobilization, 1950–51," *Diplomatic History* 29, no. 4 (2005); Paul Nitze, "The Development of NSC 68," *International Security* 4, no. 4 (1980).
56. Ikenberry, *Liberal Leviathan*, 57–8.
57. Ikenberry, *Liberal Leviathan*, 65.

58. Ikenberry, *Liberal Leviathan*, 12. See also Ian Clark, *Legitimacy in International Society* (Oxford: Oxford University Press, 2005).
59. Ikenberry, *Liberal Leviathan*, 13.
60. Ikenberry, *Liberal Leviathan*, 358.
61. Ikenberry, *Liberal Leviathan*, 62.
62. Ikenberry, *Liberal Leviathan*, 38.
63. Robert Jervis, "Unipolarity: A Structural Perspective," *World Politics* 61, no. 1 (2009).
64. Ikenberry, *Liberal Leviathan*, 147.
65. Ikenberry, *Liberal Leviathan*, 147.
66. Michael J. Hogan, *A Cross of Iron* (Cambridge: Cambridge University Press, 1998).
67. Ikenberry, *Liberal Leviathan*, 183.
68. Ikenberry, *Liberal Leviathan*, 189.
69. Anne-Marie Slaughter, "America's Edge-Power in the Networked Century," *Foreign Affairs* 88 (2009).
70. Ikenberry, *Liberal Leviathan*, 136.
71. Anne-Marie Slaughter, *A New World Order* (Princeton, NJ: Princeton University Press, 2005): 18.
72. Ikenberry, *Liberal Leviathan*, 161.
73. Ikenberry, *Liberal Leviathan*, 190.
74. Hogan, *A Cross of Iron*.
75. John M. Owen, IV, *The Clash of Ideas in World Politics: Transnational Networks, States, and Regime Change, 1510–2010* (Princeton, NJ: Princeton University Press, 2010).
76. Owen, *The Clash of Ideas in World Politics*, 56.
77. Owen, *The Clash of Ideas in World Politics*, 58.
78. Castells, *Communication Power*; Sebastian Conrad and Dominic Sachsenmaier, *Competing Visions of World Order: Global Moments and Movements, 1880s-1930s* (Basingstoke: Palgrave Macmillan, 2007).
79. Fierke, *Diplomatic Interventions*, 166.
80. Nisha Shah, "Beyond Sovereignty and the State of Nature: Metaphorical Readings of Global Order," in *Metaphors of Globalization*, ed. Markus Kornprobst, Vincent Pouliot, Nisha Shah, and Ruben Zaiotti (Basingstoke: Palgrave Macmillan, 2007), 188.
81. Siobhan McEvoy-Levy, *American Exceptionalism and US Foreign Policy* (Basingstoke: Palgrave, 2001): 140–1. The assertion that the "end of history" was a poem or narrative is from James Atlas's interview with Fukuyama, which appeared in the *New York Times Magazine*. James Atlas, "What Is Fukuyama Saying?" *New York Times Magazine*, October 22, 1989.
82. Ulrich Beck, *German Europe*, (London: Polity, 2013), 12.
83. Randall L. Schweller and Xiaoyu Pu, "After Unipolarity: China's Visions of International Order in an Era of US Decline," *International Security* 36, no. 1 (2011): 42–4.
84. Randall and Pu, "After Unipolarity," 46.
85. Randall and Pu, "After Unipolarity," 72.
86. Charlotte Epstein, "Stop Telling Us How to Behave: Socialization or Infantilization?" *International Studies Perspectives* 13, no. 2 (2012); Martha Finnemore, "Legitimacy, Hypocrisy, and the Social Structure of Unipolarity: Why Being a Unipole Isn't All It's Cracked Up to Be," *World Politics* 61, no. 1 (2009); Henry Kissinger, *Diplomacy* (London: Simon & Schuster, 1995), 806, 808; Brent J. Steele, *Defacing Power* (Ann Arbor: University of Michigan Press, 2012).

87. Margaret MacMillan, *Paris 1919: Six Months that Changed the World* (London: Random House, 2007).
88. Dryzek, *Deliberative Global Politics*, 74.
89. Price, *Media and Sovereignty*, 249–50.
90. Michael Ignatieff, "The Diplomatic Life: The Dream of Albanians," *The New Yorker*, January 11, 1999.
91. Janice Bially Mattern, *Ordering International Politics: Identity, Crisis, and Representational Force* (New York: Routledge, 2005), 10.
92. Bially Mattern, *Ordering International Politics*, 12.
93. Hedley Bull, *The Anarchical Society*, 4th ed. (Basingstoke: Palgrave, 2012); Andrew Hurrell, *On Global Order: Power, Values and the Constitution of International Society* (Oxford: Oxford University Press, 2007).
94. Castells, *Communication Power*.
95. G. John Ikenberry, "Liberal Internationalism 3.0: America and the Dilemmas of Liberal World Order," *Perspectives on Politics* 7, no. 1 (2009).
96. Barry Buzan, "Civilisational Realpolitik as the New World Order?" *Survival* 39, no. 1 (1997).
97. Buzan, "A World Order Without Superpowers," 6.
98. Buzan, "A World Order Without Superpowers," 8.
99. Buzan, "A World Order Without Superpowers," 9.
100. Robert Cooper, *The Post-Modern State and the World Order* (New York: Demos, 2000).
101. Kjell Goldmann, *The Logic of Internationalism: Coercion and Accommodation* (London: Routledge, 1994), 46.
102. Marc Lynch, "Why Engage? China and the Logic of Communicative Engagement," *European Journal of International Relations* 8, no. 2 (2002): 197.
103. Lynch, "Why Engage?"; Clinton's speech cited by Lynch was, "Remarks by the President," Mayflower Hotel, Washington, DC, 7 April 1999.
104. W. Lance Bennett and Jarol B. Manheim, "The One-Step Flow of Communication," *Annals of the American Academy of Political and Social Science* 608, no. 1 (2006). For a discussion of the impact of the media on foreign policy, see Derek B. Miller, *Media Pressure on Foreign Policy: The Evolving Theoretical Framework* (Basingstoke: Palgrave Macmillan, 2007).
105. Joshua Cooper Ramo, "The Beijing Consensus," Foreign Policy Centre, 2004, accessed March 13, 2013, at http://fpc.org.uk/fsblob/244.pdf, 28; Joshua Cooper Ramo, *Brand China* (Foreign Policy Centre, London, 2007).
106. Felix Ciută. "Narratives of Security: Strategy and Identity in the European Context." In *Discursive Constructions of Identity in European Politics*, ed. by Richard Mole (Basingstoke: Palgrave MacMillan, 2007).
107. Buzan, "A World Order with Superpowers."
108. Derek Chollet and James M. Goldgeier, *America between the Wars: From 11/9 to 9/11: The Misunderstood Years between the Fall of the Berlin Wall and the Start of the War on Terror* (New York: Public Affairs, 2008).
109. Porter and Mykleby, *A National Strategic Narrative*.
110. Seib, *Towards a New Public Diplomacy*.
111. Orford, *Reading Humanitarian Intervention*.
112. Alister Miskimmon, "German Foreign Policy and the Libya Crisis," *German Politics* 21, no. 4 (2012).
113. Jessica Bucher, Lena Engel, Stephanie Harfensteller, and Hylke Dijkstra,, "Domestic Politics, News Media and Humanitarian Intervention: Why France and Germany Diverged over Libya," *European Security*, published online, 2013.
114. For a summary of the national explanations for voting in the Security Council and the text of UNSCR1973, see United Nations Security Council (2011),

United Nations Security Council SC/10200, 6498th Meeting, available at http://www.un.org/News/Press/docs/2011/sc10200.doc.htm#Resolution.

115. Josh Rogin, "European Governments 'Completely Puzzled' about U.S. Position on Libya," March 16, 2011, accessed August 21, 2011, http:// thecable.foreignpolicy.com/posts/2011/03/16/european_governments_ completely_puzzled_about_us_position_on_libya; Rogin, Josh, "How Obama Turned on a Dime toward War," March 18, 2011, accessed August 21, 2011, at http://thecable.foreignpolicy.com/posts/2011/03/18/how_obama_ turned_on_a_dime_toward_war.

116. *Economist*, "The Welcome Return of French Diplomacy," March 2011, accessed September 1, 2011, at http://www.economist.com/blogs/newsbook/2011/03/ frances_role_libya.

117. Press release on G8 Meeting, Paris, March 15, 2011, available at http://www .g20-g8.com/g8-g20/g8/english/for-the-press/news-releases/meeting-of- foeign-ministers-14–15-march-2011.1048.html; German Foreign Ministry news release: http://www.auswaertiges-amt.de/EN/Aussenpolitik/Globale Fragen/G8/110314_G8_Treffen_Paris_node.html.

118. *EurActiv*, "France and Germany Clash over No Fly Zone," March 15, 2011, accessed September 1, 2011, at http://www.euractiv.com/en/global-europe/ france-germany-clash-libya-fly-zone-news-503090.

119. The French Philosopher Lévy was at the forefront of convincing Sarkozy to act and was an ardent supporter of action against Gadhafi. See for example, Bernard Henri Lévy, "Libya Wins One for Freedom," August 22, 2011, accessed May 1, 2011, at http://www.thedailybeast.com/articles/2011/08/22/ bernard-henri-levy-libya-wins-one-for-freedom.html.

120. Alain Juppé, "Libya"—Speech by Alain Juppée, Minister of Foreign Affairs and European Affairs, to the United Nations Security Council, March 17, 2011, accessed May 22, 2013, at http://www.ambafrance-uk.org/ Alain-Juppe-backs-UN-resolution.

121. Nicolas Sarkozy, "Libya"—Paris Summit for the Support of the Libyan People—Statement by Nicolas Sarkozy, President of the Republic," March 19, 2011, accessed May 22, 2013, at http://www.ambafrance-uk.org/ President-Sarkozy-urges-Gaddafi-to.

122. Erlanger, Steven, "Sarkozy Puts France at Vanguard of West's War Effort," *New York Times*, March 21, 2011, 12.

123. Peter Wittig, "Explanation of Vote by Ambassador Wittig on the Security Council Resolution on Libya," March 17, 2011, accessed September 1, 2011, http://www.new-york-un.diplo.de/Vertretung/newyorkvn/en/__pr/Speeches/ PM__2011/20110317_20Explanation_20of_20vote_20-_20Libya.html? archive=2984642.

124. Simon Tisdall, "Libya: Reaction: Britain and France Appear Ever More Isolated as World Opinion Turns Hostile: China, Russia, Germany, Brazil Voice Objections; NATO Also Divided as Turkey Blocks Agreement," *The Guardian*, March 22, 2011, p. 6.

125. Deutsche Welle, "German Defends Cautious Approach to Libya, Denies Isolation," March 21, 2011, accessed September 1, 2011, at http://www .dw-world.de/dw/article/0,,14926360,00.html.

126. *European Voice*, "French German Libya Rift Deepens," March 25, 2011, accessed August 2011 at http://www.europeanvoice.com/article/2011/march/ french-german-libya-rift-deepens/70661.aspx.

127. Der Spiegel (2011) "Merkel Cabinet agrees AWACS for Afghanistan," March 23, 2011, accessed August 21, 2011, http://www.spiegel.de/interna tional/world/0,1518,752709,00.html.

128. Der Spiegel, "Merkel Cabinet agrees AWACS for Afghanistan."
129. Felix Berenskoetter and Bastian Giegerich, "From NATO to ESDP: A Social Constructivist Analysis of German Strategic Adjustment after the End of the Cold War," *Security Studies* 19, no. 3 (2010).
130. Barry Buzan, Ole Waever, and Jaap De Wilde, *Security: A New Framework for Analysis* (Boulder, CO: Lynne Rienner, 1998).
131. *Bild am Sonntag*, "Krieg in Libyen: Über 60 Prozent der Deutschen befürworten den Angriff," March 20, 2011, accessed August 21, 2011, http://www.bild.de/politik/2011/libyen-krise/aber-mehrheit-lehnt-beteiligung-ab-16933388.bild.html.
132. Alister Miskimmon, "Falling into Line? Kosovo and the Course of German Foreign Policy," *International Affairs* 85, no. 3 (2009): 561–73.
133. Mark L. Grant, "Explanation of Vote," delivered by Sir Mark Lyall Grant, Ambassador and Permanent Representative of the UK Mission to the United Nations, on Security Council Resolution on Libya, March 17, 2011, accessed September 1, 2011, http://ukun.fco.gov.uk/en/news/?view=News&id=568282782.
134. William Hague, Foreign Secretary Comments on UN vote on Libya no-fly zone, March 18, 2011, accessed August 21, 2011, http://ukun.fco.gov.uk/en/news/?view=News&id=568543282.
135. William Hague, Statement to the House of Commons, March 24, 2011, accessed August 21, 2011, http://www.fco.gov.uk/en/news/latest-news/?view=PressS&id = 571853282.
136. William Hague, Statement to the House of Commons on North Africa and the Middle East, House of Commons Official Report, *Parliamentary Debates* (*Hansard*), Vol. 525, no. 139, March 24, 2011: 1113–1130, esp. 1123.
137. Mark L. Grant, "Evidence to House of Commons Defence Select Committee HC905," October 12, 2011, accessed March 1, 2012, http://www.publications.parliament.uk/pa/cm201012/cmselect/cmdfence/950/11101201.htm.
138. Roy D'Andrade, "Schemas and Motivations," in *Human Motives and Cultural Models*, eds. Roy D'Andrade and Claudia Strauss (Cambridge: Cambridge University Press, 1992); Claudia Strauss, "Models and Motives," in *Human Motives and Cultural Models*, eds. Roy D'Andrade and Claudia Strauss (Cambridge: Cambridge University Press, 1992).
139. Barack Obama, "Renewing American Leadership," *Foreign Affairs* (2007); Barack Obama, "2009 Inaugural Presidential Address," January 20, 2009, accessed May 1, 2013, http://avalon.law.yale.edu/21st_century/obama.asp.
140. *Economist* (Lexington), "The Birth of an Obama Doctrine," March 28, 2011, accessed September 1, 2011, http://www.economist.com/blogs/lexington/2011/03/libya_4.
141. Richard McGregor and Daniel Dombey, "Foreign Policy: A Reticent America," *Financial Times*, March 23, 2011, accessed September 1, 2011, http://www.ft.com/cms/s/0/3ddd2d0c-557e-11e0-a2b1-00144feab49a.html#axzz2QtWEz7j3.
142. Michael O'Hanlon, "Winning Ugly in Libya," *Foreign Policy*, March 30, 2011, accessed September 1, 2011, http://www.foreignaffairs.com/articles/67684/michael-ohanlon/winning-ugly-in-libya; Michael O'Hanlon, "Libya and the Obama Doctrine," *Foreign Policy*, August 31, 2011, accessed September 1, 2011, http://www.foreignaffairs.com/articles/68237/michael-ohanlon/libya-and-the-obama-doctrine.
143. Christopher M. Blanchard, "Libya: Unrest and U.S. Policy," CRS Report for Congress 7–5700, accessed August 21, 2011, http://www.fpc.state.gov/documents/organization/159788.pdf.

144. Ryan C. Hendrickson, "Libya and American War Powers: Barak Obama as Commander in Chief," paper presented to the Annual Convention of the International Studies Association, San Diego, April 2–5, 2012.

145. United States Senate (2011) S.Res.85.ATS, 112th Congress, March 1, 2011, accessed May 1, 2013, http://thomas.loc.gov/cgi-bin/query/z?c112:S.RES.85.

146. Ben Feller, "Obama Doctrine on Military Intervention Tested in Libya, *Huffington Post*, March 9, 2011, accessed September 1, 2011, http://www.huff ingtonpost.com/2011/03/09/obama-libya-military-intervention_n_833345 .html.

147. Feller, "Obama Doctrine."

148. John Irish and Tim Hepher, "France Fails to Get G-8 Accord on Libya No Fly Zone," *Reuters*, March 15, 2011, accessed September 1, 2011, http://www .reuters.com/article/2011/03/15/us-g8-libya-idUSTRE72E0BX20110315.

149. Susan Rice, "Remarks by Ambassador Susan E. Rice, U.S. Permanent Representative to the United Nations, in an Explanation of Vote on UN Security Council Resolution 1973," March 17, 2011, accessed September 1, 2011, http://usun.state.gov/briefing/statements/2011/158563.htm.

150. Barack Obama, "Speech to the National Defense University, Washington, D.C., March 28, 2011," accessed May 1, 2013, http://www.whitehouse.gov/ the-press-office/2011/03/28/remarks-president-address-nation-libya.

151. Secretary of Defense Robert Gates quietly ordered two US warships, *USS Kearsarge* and *USS Ponce*, to pass through the Suez Canal in to the Mediterranean on 2 March 2011, ostensibly in case the evacuation of civilians from Libya was needed."2 US Warships Move Closer to Libya through Suez Canal," *Washington* Post, March 2, 2011, accessed May 10, 2013, http://www.washingtonpost.com/wp-dyn/content/article/2011/03/02/ AR2011030201087.html.

152. Obama, "Speech to the National Defense University, Washington, D.C., March 28, 2011."

153. Miskimmon, "German Foreign Policy and the Libya Crisis."

154. Obama, "Speech to the National Defense University, Washington, D.C., March 28, 2011."

155. Obama, "Speech to the National Defense University, Washington, D.C., March 28, 2011."

156. Baodong Li, "Explanation of Vote by Ambassador Li Baodong after Adoption of Security Council Resolution on Libya, March 17, 2011," accessed August 21, 2011, http://www.china-un.org/eng/gdxw/t807544.htm.

157. Li, "Explanation of Vote by Ambassador Li Baodong after Adoption of Security Council Resolution on Libya, March 17, 2011."

158. Vitaly Churkin, "Statement by Mr. Vitaly Churkin, Permanent Representative of the Russian Federation to the United Nations, at the Official UN Security Council Meeting during the Vote on the Resolution on Libya, New York, March 17, 2011," accessed August 21, 2011, http://www.rusembassy.ca/node/546 .

159. "Statement by Mr. Vitaly Churkin, Permanent Representative of the Russian Federation to the United Nations, at the Official UN Security Council Meeting during the Vote on the Resolution on Libya, New York, March 17, 2011."

160. Isabelle Gorst and Neil Buckley, "Medvedev and Putin Clash over Libya," *Financial Times*, March 21, 2011, accessed May 22, 2013, http://www .ft.com/cms/s/0/2e62b08e-53d2–11e0-a01c-00144feab49a.html.

161. Gideon Rachman, "Libya: A Last Hurrah for the West," March 28, 2011, accessed September 1, 2011, http://www.ft.com/cms/s/0/6ed0e3f6–5955– 11e0-bc39–00144feab49a.html#axzz2QtWEz7j3.

162. Benoit Gomis, "Franco-British Defence and Security Treaties: Entente While It Lasts?" Royal Institute for International Affairs/Chatham House, Programme

Paper: ISP PP 2001/01, 2011; Ben Jones, "Franco-British Defence Co-operation: A New Engine for European Defence?" *Occasional Paper No. 88*, European Union Institute for Security Studies, February 2011, accessed April 14, 2011, http://www.iss.europa.eu/uploads/media/op88—Franco-British_military_cooperation—a_new_engine_for_European_defence.pdf; Bruce D. Jones, "Libya and the Responsibilities of Power," *Survival* 53, no. 3 (2011).

163. Public opinion in France, Germany, the UK, and the US fluctuated throughout the spring of 2011. Pew polls indicate a preference for sanctions over NFZ enforcement, March 10–13. Pew Research Centre, "Public Wary of Military Intervention in Libya: Broad Concern that U.S. Military Is Overcommitted," 14 March 2011, accessed 22 May 2013 at http://www.people-press.org/2011/03/14/public-wary-of-military-intervention-in-libya/. A second poll conducted by Pew March 24–27, 2011, indicates reduced opposition to US involvement with overall support remaining static from the March 10–13 poll. Interestingly, 57 percent of respondents did not think the US was taking a leading role in the operation. Pew Research Centre, "Modest Support for Libya Airstrikes, No Clear Goal Seen: *Little Public Interest in Libyan Mission*," March 28, 2011, accessed May 22, 2013 at http://www.people-press.org/2011/03/28/modest-support-for-libya-airstrikes-no-clear-goal-seen/. An Ipsos/Mori poll of April 11, 2011, comparing France, Italy, UK, and US attitudes indicates robust support in France, followed by the US and the UK, with Italians being most skeptical of the military operation. Ipsos/Mori (2011), "Military Action in Libya: Topline Results," April 12, 2011, accessed August 21, 2011 at http://www.ipsos-mori.com/Assets/Docs/Polls/Reuters-Libya-topline-Apr11.PDF. In the longer term after very strong support for the operation, French citizens' support for the operation slipped below 50 percent. IFOP, "Survey of French Views of Libya Crisis from March 2011—June 2011," accessed March 1, 2013, at http://www.ifop.com/media/poll/1558-2-study_file.pdf. By June 2011, a Harris poll conducted for the *Financial Times* shows growing concern over NATO's bombing campaign and an increase in support in France, the UK, Spain, and the US for the deployment of ground troops. James Blitz, "Public Opposes Wider Libya Campaign," *Financial Times*, June 20, 2011, including Harris opinion poll for the *Financial Times*, June 20, 2011, accessed August 21, 2011 at http://www.ft.com/cms/s/0/19f0dc8a-9b5c-11e0-bbc6-00144feabdc0.html#axzz1qPRjAE6X. German public opinion in the run-up to the UN vote indicated support for NATO involvement in Libya (Infratest/diMap, 2011a). Infratest diMap, "Poll on Libya for ARD, March 8–9, 2011," accessed August 21, 2011 at http://www.infratest-dimap.de/uploads/media/dt1103_bericht.pdf. But by September 2011 polling indicates support for the German abstention on UN1973. Infratest/diMap. September 9, 2011, "ARD Infratest Poll," accessed August 21, 2011 at http://www.infratest-dimap.de/uploads/media/dt1109_. The Harris poll for the *FT* indicates strong opposition to NATO operations within Germany. James Blitz, "Public Opposes Wider Libya Campaign," *Financial Times*, June 20, 2011, including Harris opinion poll for the *Financial Times*, June 20, 2011, accessed August 21, 2011 at http://www.ft.com/cms/s/0/19f0dc8a-9b5c-11e0-bbc6-00144feabdc0.html#axzz1qPRjAE6X.

164. Aimei Yang, Anna Klyueva, and Maureen Taylor, "Beyond a Dyadic Approach to Public Diplomacy: Understanding Relationships in Multipolar World," *Public Relations Review* 38, no. 5 (2012).

165. Churkin, "Statement by Mr. Vitaly Churkin, Permanent Representative of the Russian Federation to the United Nations, at the official UN Security Council meeting during the vote on the resolution on Libya, New York, March 17, 2011."

166. Walter Lippmann (1921), *Public Opinion,* accessed May 1, 2013 at http://xroads.virginia.edu/~Hyper2/CDFinal/Lippman/cover.html.
167. Joseph S. Nye, *The Paradox of American Power: Why the World's Only Superpower Can't Go It Alone* (New York: Oxford University Press, 2002).
168. Bially Mattern, *Ordering International Politics*; Finnemore, "Legitimacy"; Steele, *Defacing Power.*
169. Buzan, "A World Order without Superpowers."
170. Ronald R. Krebs and Patrick Thaddeus Jackson, "Twisting Tongues and Twisting Arms: The Power of Political Rhetoric," *European Journal of International Relations* 13, no. 1 (2007).
171. Charlotte Epstein, *The Power of Words in International Relations: Birth of an Anti-Whaling Discourse* (Cambridge, MA: MIT Press, 2008).

4 Contestation

INTRODUCTION

> The fundamental challenge for US policy is to persuade China to define its own national interests in a manner compatible with ours. That's why we are working to encourage China's development as a secure, prosperous and open society as well as its integration as a full and responsible member of the international community.
>
> Madeleine Albright, 1997[1]

> China's current reputation for power benefits from projections about the future. Some young Chinese use these projections to demand a greater share of power now. Feeling stronger, they demand greater accommodation of what they consider their "core interests" in Taiwan, Tibet, and the South China Sea. . . . Extrapolating the wrong long-term projections from short-term cyclical events like the recent financial crisis can lead to policy miscalculations.
>
> Joseph S. Nye, Jr., 2010[2]

In 1997, US Secretary of State Madeleine Albright proposed persuading China that its interests lay in the US-led liberal order by progressively integrating China into its rule-governed architecture. Thirteen years later, Harvard professor Joseph S. Nye, Jr. clearly feared that such integration would be insufficient to constrain Chinese ambitions. Nye's quote points to the importance of narratives. For Nye, if young people in China believed their country was on a path to power then they would start behaving as if it definitely was. To persuade China, by 2010, meant addressing how Chinese people located themselves in the world. We do not deny that states, leaders, and public can have their interests and identities altered by integration into institutional systems. However, the problem Nye identifies is, we believe, a far more important one for explaining long-term change in international relations. How do you get people in other countries to experience the world through your preferred narrative? How do you undermine or change their narratives, and render your narrative plausible to the extent it is commonsensical and not even noticed?

In this chapter we ask what happens when narratives clash—when actors contest each other's projections of international relations. All states in international relations hold a narrative about their own past, present, and future, and that of the system. No state's narrative exists in a vacuum: the ether of international affairs is filled with multiple narratives—competing and overlapping, epochal and issue-specific. In the past decade, public and expert discussion of international affairs has featured master narratives that cut across regions and policy areas to give meaning to the international system. These include the clash of civilizations, the war on terror, and the rise of the BRICS.[3] Political struggles in Syria and Iran have gained much media attention but also became narrative pivots in broader struggles between the US and EU on the one hand and Russia and China on the other, concerning whether we are moving to a world in which state sovereignty is the primary value in international relations or whether international society should put sovereignty to one side and intervene to protect human rights. Russia and China seek the continuation of a Westphalian world; the US and EU feel compelled to enact a shift to a post-Westphalian one.[4] Yet we have also seen more focused issue narratives, for instance narratives that depict climate change as a real threat humanity must respond to, versus narratives of climate change as an issue concocted by scientists and untrustworthy elites to justify restraint on economic activities, and the global finance crisis as a narrative about a unique conflation of factors or about recurring crises of market capitalism. These narratives give meaning to events and, naturally enough, all actors wish their preferred meaning to be held by others. This explains why so many issues have come to be cast as a battle of narratives.

The aim of this chapter is to help the reader understand how narrative contestation works in international relations. We propose an analytical framework that distinguishes system narratives, identity narratives, and issue-specific narratives. NATO intervention in Afghanistan since 2001 is a good example. At the issue-specific level, NATO members such as the UK, Canada, the Netherlands, and Denmark have each tried to convince their publics that victory (however defined) is achievable in Afghanistan and that progress toward victory is being made.[5] Each has faced domestic dissent and varying degrees of contestation of their Afghanistan narratives. This contestation has been triggered by facts on the ground that become media reports that visually contradict the narrative of progress, but also because of reasoned political claims that contest the internal logic of the policy or its likelihood of achieving its goals. These contests reveal assumptions about each state's self-identity. For example, the Canadian government's statement of its goals in Afghanistan expresses a narrative about what Canada is and does.[6] Yet these contests also reveal broader assumptions about how the international system should work: about the value of sovereignty or human rights, the responsibility of states to take action to preserve others' security, the legitimacy of military intervention, and the role of alliances and importance of cooperation. NATO members require strategic narratives about the Afghan conflict but these must be embedded with, and supported by, broader strategic narratives about how the international system functions to ensure security.

As we set out in the book's introduction, strategic narratives have a two-fold power effect. Strategic narratives are an instrument of power in the traditional Weberian or *behavioral* sense of A getting B to do what B otherwise would not. We are interested in identifying the role strategic narratives play in shaping behavior in an observable way. If the strategic narrative of your state is convincing, allies will follow your policy lead and commit resources to solving a shared problem, publics will reelect your party because they believe your foreign policies should continue, and enemies will recognize how your narrative is convincing others and consider changing course themselves. Strategic narratives are also an instrument of power by *constituting* the experience of international affairs. Strategic narratives are central to the identity of its actors and the meaning of the system. If states believe that a solution to climate change is best achieved by following a policy path that acquires sense through your strategic narrative, then they will come to identify themselves as part of the solution, as states-who-are-ending-climate-change. Their policies will thereafter follow from this identity. Hence, the processes of behavioral and constitutive power work together. If the narrative of your state comes to constitute an important part of the identity of another state, this will shape its behavior. Alternatively, if your state convinced another state to commit to specific policies and actions on a consistent basis, perhaps ensuring this is institutionalized through an international regime, then the other state may come to take on the identity of a state that carries out such policies naturally, as an expression of their values. We see this with the whaling case study below.

What counts as victory in the battle of the narratives? Is it when your rival's narrative disappears?[7] Can there be an absence of any shared narrative of the international system, or just the replacement of a formerly shared or embedded narrative with another? Narrative would disappear altogether if actors no longer experience the world in terms of narrativity, and this is impossible because narrative is central to how humans experience the world (see the introduction to this volume). We can only ask what it would mean for a specific narrative to disappear. A narrative disappears when actors no longer interpret the world in the terms of that narrative, that is, the meaning of the past, present, and future contained in that narrative no longer holds. The obstacles, dilemmas, and potential solutions and resolutions are not thought of through the prism of the narrative, and the range of actors/characters and environments the actor knows are not defined through the prism of the narrative.

Take, for example, the "rising China" narrative. This depicts a state of affairs in which China has woken from its slumber and will become an objectively stronger and more significant character in the future of international affairs; that this presence will unsettle the balance of power, create tensions with other leading characters, and that the environment as a whole will be different. The narrative even poses a potential unhappy ending: if the US and China view each other as zero-sum antagonists and eventually enemies, then there is a possibility of conflict between them.[8] As we saw in earlier chapters, China presents itself in an ambiguous way. It is perceived alternately as an aspiring normal great power to balance others or as a rising hegemon. Either way, what are the conditions of the rising China narrative disappearing? First, this would mean that all relevant actors experience the present world in entirely different terms and hold entirely different visions of the future. Second, it would mean that the objective conditions that make that narrative plausible disappear; for example, if the US and EU economies bounced back strongly, China's economy slowed down, and suddenly the share of world GDP of the US and EU started increasing again. Third, that narrative would begin to disappear if powerful narrators, principally China itself, or the US as its potential foe, constructed an alternative and plausible narrative about changes in international relations, a different story of power transition, that accommodated the same shared facts and understandings of how international relations works but puts them within a different projection of past, present, and future. Finally, the rising China narrative could disappear if the shared space of communication that allows that shared narrative disappeared; for instance, if a radical fragmentation of the global media ecology occurred, such that different regions and communities receive different information and began to experience the world in different terms—to live in different worlds, so to speak.

What these considerations make clear is that strategic narrative contestation may not simply be a matter of the elimination or subjugation of a rival's narrative, but the destruction of the conditions that make alternative narratives plausible, communicable, and intelligible. However, it may be useful to keep opposing narratives alive in order to use the differences to legitimize your own narrative. The credibility of the strategic narratives of the US and USSR during the Cold War was enhanced by the opportunity to compare, contrast, and denigrate the other's narrative.

By this point the book has offered our theorization of actors and international order. In this chapter we ask what happens when narratives clash and what counts as victory. Different international relations (IR) scholars have addressed a variety of forms of contestation, from short-term trapping of one state by another around a particular issue and numerous studies of framing, to long-term discursive shifts through which actors purposefully seek to define the core terms through which international relations are understood. This chapter offers a framework to give scholars clear research paths to finding out what is being contested and how. The framework is illustrated using three examples of narrative contestation in the last half century. First, we draw upon Ben Mor's work on the narrative contests that emerge during Israel's conflicts with its neighbors. Mor does an excellent job of tracking how all sides make tactical use of media as conflict events unfold, trying to generate support and legitimacy both from their home constituencies and key international allies. We reinterpret Mor's body of work to show how those political and military leaders are at the same time trying to sustain more overarching strategic narratives about their nation, its identity, and its struggles with malevolent or untrustworthy neighbors. Second, we draw on Charlotte Epstein's analysis of global environmental politics and the persuasion involved when a bulk of the world's states and citizens shifted from pro-whaling to anti-whaling positions in the 1960s and 1970s. Epstein's studies are exemplary in addressing the interplay of narratives and the discourses actors draw upon when crafting those narratives. While language structured actors' identity and understanding of political possibility, naturalizing a certain status quo in which whaling was a normal industrial practice, activists worked out how to exert agency within those conditions to shift those linguistic and conceptual parameters, create a new shared understanding of whales and whaling, and achieve lasting policy change. This is an instance of success in the world of strategic narrative, and we draw out the way in which activists narrativized the issue to create new expectations about how humans should treat whales. Finally, we offer our own analysis of US and EU efforts to limit Iran's nuclear program. We show how Iran has managed to outmaneuver their opponents by shifting from scientific and legal to geopolitical and theological discursive foundations just when they appear pinned down to an agreement. The Iran case again shows the role of skill and agency, the tactical use of media ecologies to engage public opinion, and how national actors are severely constrained in the wriggle room they have to depart from their nation's traditional narrative and craft a new position. After these three cases, we conclude the chapter by cautioning against the quest for a successful model or template of narrative success.

THE SPECTRUM OF PERSUASION

Strategic narratives are a means for political actors to construct a shared meaning of the past, present, and future of international politics to shape the behavior of domestic and international actors. They can be used to achieve behavioral change but also to constitute the identity of actors and the system. Serious scholars of international relations will immediately point to the difficulty of synthesizing rationalist, constructivist, and poststructuralist approaches that depend upon distinct ontologies and epistemologies. Each has a different conception of the actor, structures, and power, and these bear upon how communication and persuasion are theorized. This can be understood in terms of a spectrum from thin to thick approaches to persuasion—set out in Table 4.1 on next page. The four main approaches to persuasion in IR are those used in Brent Steele's[9] approaches to discourse: rationalist, communicative, reflexive, and poststructural. Steele himself selects one—reflexive—and produces a study of US foreign policy and identity from that perspective. Our purpose here is to inform readers about the

Table 4.1 The Spectrum of Persuasion

Spectrum	Approach	Ontology of IR	Role of Communication	Role of Persuasion	Example Studies
Very thin	Rationalism	Interactions between actors with given preferences within a given structure of anarchy	Strategic. Signaling intentions or "cheap talk" used to manipulate impressions	Secondary to material inducement (coercion, bargaining). But possible: by trapping others into committing to action through rhetorical skill or by producing a road map or blueprint which others agree to commit to.	Lake on hierarchy; Liberal constructivist studies of norms; Krebs and Jackson on rhetorical coercion; Jervis on signaling; Ringsmose and Borgensen on NATO
Thin	Communicative action	Interactions between actors with given identities create intersubjective understandings of the system and issues	Exchange of claims between actors who are equals at the debating table	Winning arguments can create new consensus and reshape how others see the world.	Risse, Lynch on US-China relations
Thick	Reflexive	Actors whose identities are mutually implicated and whose identities and actions generate responses among others	Strategic in moments when actors target the contradictions and anxieties in others' identities and self-image	Getting others to change behavior by publicizing their faults	Bially-Mattern on the Suez crisis, Steele on the aesthetics of insecurity; Price on US-Iran soft war, Mor on Israel's impression management
Very thick	Poststructuralism	Discourse (power-knowledge relations) manifest in practices (linguistic and material)	Fundamental. Stable discourses define what counts as valid and normal talk and action. Actors enact discourse.	All actors are born into and produced through discourse. But benefits are uneven; those in margins / interstices may resist and contest.	Epstein on whaling, Hansen on security, Holland on US foreign policy

possibility of picking and choosing from this menu depending on their research questions—on what they want to explain. At one end of the spectrum are thin approaches that take the identity of actors and the system as given and seek to explain how those actors manipulate each other's behavior using material incentives or rhetorical entrapment. Less thin approaches such as studies of communicative action acknowledge that these interactions can alter actors' preferences and identities over time, making for a more meaningful sense of persuasion being achieved. Reflexive approaches are thicker still, focusing on the continual impression management that actors engage in to bolster their own identity and undermine others, again in order to achieve power effects over others. At the thick end of the spectrum are poststructural approaches that ask whether a hegemonic state constructed the narrative of the entire international system that others take for granted and work within, since that process might strongly condition how the interaction studies by thinner approaches play out. Poststructural analysis is concerned that the powerful state has won before the game begins by normalizing their strategic narrative to the degree that alternative meanings of international relations are not thinkable.

For example, Krebs and Jackson[10] take a thin approach to studying how state A exerts power through language, dismantling state B's arguments so as to force B into policy positions that B would not otherwise support. The focus is on "framing competitions" around particular issues—"specific bounded episodes of contestation."[11] Krebs and Jackson argue that there is no need to inquire as to the intentions or beliefs held by the leaders of A and B, since we can explain the outcome by analyzing their public rhetorical interactions. Methodologically, it is very difficult to access the actual thoughts of leaders,[12] whose modes of reasoning may simply reflect their culture, and whose language may be deceitful. From this perspective, demonstrating that an actor is persuaded is impossible and unnecessary.[13] However, those at the thicker end of the spectrum of persuasion would ask: who shapes leaders' cultural assumptions and commonsensical beliefs in the first place? How do actors take on and come to consent to new norms? These questions are outside the framing competitions Krebs and Jackson seek to explain, but for those interested in the power of language, such questions may be the starting point. Equally, scholars taking an approach similar to Krebs and Jackson may draw upon the communicative, reflexive, or poststructural studies that explain why certain phrases, concepts, or historical events take on a central meaning to specific actors. Drawing on such studies, they may investigate how state A uses rhetoric to exploit these meanings, to perhaps gain media attention and move public opinion in state B, and thereby trap state B's leaders into a certain decision.

Patrick Jackson has offered a thicker analysis of identity narratives.[14] After World War II the idea of Western civilization played a critical role in binding transatlantic states to each other, he argues. The understanding of being part of a community of shared identity and interests meant that forming the NATO alliance became common sense. In deliberations, certain actors used this rhetorical commonplace in a strategic way to sway national leaders who held doubts. Ultimately, however, Jackson argues that the feeling of being part of the West and its narrative was "causally significant," vis-à-vis other factors. As poststructural scholars would point out, too,[15] what was at stake for Jackson were the "boundaries in question . . . not merely physical or geographical, but social and meaningful: boundaries are limitations on acceptable actions."[16] Without that narrative, without that understanding of moving forward together in international politics, and without the boundaries of civilization and its members that the narrative established, the leading states would have found a different path. Such an account raises questions, however. At the thick end of analysis: How was the narrative of Western civilization established in the first place; through what power relations, over what time frame, and what other narratives and possibilities were silenced along the way? And at the thinner end: What scope did actors have to recraft the narrative of Western civilization to the context in the late 1940s? Since the Cold War ended, how have narratives of the West, of civilization, or even of Western civilization, been strategically deployed or contested? Amid claims about a clash of civilizations and war on terror, to whom do civilizational narratives make international relations meaningful and certain boundaries given, and how does this affect their behavior?

We must study the establishment of these boundaries and identities through which constitutive power takes effect, whilst allowing for the analytical insight that these constitutive effects enable the organization of actors and agency who can exercise behavioral power. In international relations, actors use their agency, within specific situations and historical relationships, to entrench the meaning of these boundaries and identities in order to steer other actors toward certain behavior.

To fully explain how strategic narratives function in international relations would entail paying attention not just to all the processes each approach concentrates on, but how these processes interact and shape each other. This is the structurationist problem of identifying how the thick sets the terms for the thin, and the thin interactions work upon and gradually reform the thick. But it also entails attention to the multiple temporalities through which these processes unfold and to which these approaches pay attention. In effect, then, we are proposing a recursive theory of persuasion, a set of loops in which the researcher must choose when and where to make cuts.

How does our theory of strategic narratives fit into broader theories of international relations? At first glance it is an agential constructivism. It is constructivist because we propose that actors experience and understand anarchy, hierarchy, order, and events through lenses and prisms rather than perceive them directly as reality unmediated by their ideas and prior experiences. If anarchy is what states make of it, then what they make of it depends on the narratives they experience reality through. It is agential because we argue that international relations involve struggles to determine which narratives actors experience the world through. Others might refer to this as a struggle for hegemony or ideational dominance. The point is that there *is* a political struggle, by actors seeking to achieve as great a degree of consensus around their narrative as possible. Actors use their agentic capacities[17]—the organization of power relations within and vis-à-vis other actors—to try to project their narrative and control international communication in a way that establishes their narrative as the commonsense understanding of the past, present, and future of international relations. As set out in Chapter 2, "Actors in Strategic Narratives," we wish to begin the analysis of strategic narratives with actors.

One object of narrative struggle is the understanding actors hold of the international system—its history, how it works, and how it is likely to develop. As scholars across the whole spectrum of persuasion acknowledge, there has to be some shared understanding for actors to be able to hold meaningful conversations. States and their leaders are born into an international system and recognize hierarchy, law, and certain norms, and it is this shared basic recognition that allows actors to contest the prevailing hierarchy, law, and norms.[18] For the rationalist and communicative scholars, these are the structural conditions for competition and argumentation to occur. These understandings may be embedded in institutions,[19] resulting in a given arena within which interactions are played out. Reflexive and poststructural scholars might point to shared experiences, crises, and feelings of threat or hope that are part of these conditions. We argue that these underlying understandings and experiences take narrative form; there is always some shared narrative about humanity and the role, status, identity, and power of different states within it. While rationalist and communicative scholars take these as the preconditions for negotiation,[20] we argue that these preconditions are subject to contestation; states project strategic narratives of the system in an attempt to structure understandings of hierarchy, law, and norms before any interaction has begun. Their scope to do this is limited, they work upon existing narratives which may be deeply held, and their narrative is subjected to contestation and possibly contradiction by events. Nevertheless, states—and great powers in particular—continually work to project and embed their system narrative.

As a result, winning any battle of narratives is not easy. As we saw in Chapter 2, whether strategic narratives are aimed at systemic, identity, or issue levels, there are multiple constituencies: rival and allied states, international organizations, nongovernmental organizations (NGOs), state and independent media, lobby groups, home publics, overseas publics, even diasporic publics who can have a presence both at home and overseas at the same time. As we argued in Chapter 1, "Introduction," and will argue in Chapter 5, "Information Infrastructure," there is a need to win debate within the global media-public sphere *and* control what voices are heard and by whom in that global media-public sphere. In other words, states seeking to gain consensus for their strategic narrative must exploit the infrastructure of the day, but also compete to shape the infrastructure itself. The United States projects a narrative about Internet freedom as something the world is and should be moving toward, but it also takes concrete action to try to make this happen by encouraging companies and activists to distribute technology overseas that keeps the Internet "free." Meanwhile China projects a narrative about sovereignty and states' rights in the realm of information and communication and similarly enacts policies to make this happen. They contest each other's narratives while materially contesting the media ecology within which that narrative contest occurs.

In the next section we break down a number of aspects of narrative contestation. What is it about a narrative that is contested? Is it its content, its author, or the actors delivering it?

ASPECTS OF NARRATIVE CONTESTATION

In Table 4.2, we sketch out the different ways in which narratives can be convincing and the fields in which they are contested. *Convincing* is a catch-all term here, because we are concerned not just with whether the content of the narrative is convincing, appealing, or compelling, but whether its projection, formation, and reception have been conducted in a way that does not strike the audience as dubious. We also recognize that different strategies and communication features may be more or less convincing depending on a variety of factors, including audience makeup and individuals' characteristics. The political communication literature is replete with works on contingent effects.

Note that these aspects remain in the abstract before strategy has begun to be applied. Once events unfold, then all of these aspects get complicated, as we see in the case studies.

Content

A narrative must contain informational content that captures an audience's attention and be clearly understood to be convincing. Most communications practitioners learn that relevance, usefulness, and interest are extremely important characteristics for effective communication.[21] Information that is perceived to serve a purpose—that is useful and relevant in some way—can elicit attention. For example, in the period immediately following a crisis, a narrative that describes what has happened and why can be quite convincing. That is exactly the information that the audience will be looking for. This suggests why a rally-'round-the-flag response makes sense.[22] A leader's narrative is convincing and rallies support for that leader. Likewise if an audience sees information as interesting or compelling, more attention will be paid to that information. Certain types of information can increase

Table 4.2 Aspects of Narrative Contestation

What aspect of the Narrative is Contested?	Convincing	Unconvincing
Informational content	Exciting, salient, relevant, useful, interesting, clear and intelligible, repeatable, resonant	Boring, irrelevant, confusing, immediately forgotten, dissonant with values or experience
Emotional content	Focus on feelings, lived experience, realistic emotions depicted	Overly rational, overly sentimental or maudlin
Epistemology	Based on a solid grounding of how valid knowledge about the world is arrived at	Based on spurious or uncertain grounds
Degree of ambiguity	Open enough for a variety of audiences to find their values and interests reflected in the narrative, but closed enough for them to believe the narrative is strong, consistent, and firmly grounded	So open that anyone could support it and thus it loses any meaning or purchase, or so closed that it excludes important support or allies or even appears dogmatic and irrational
Relation to action	Consistent with how events in the world are thought to be happening	Contradicted by what is thought to be happening
Process of formation	Arrived at by representatives through clear and legitimate processes; the representatives understand, articulate and take into account the nation's values, interests, and aspirations	Arrived at by unrepresentative and out-of-touch or self-interested figures through opaque or illegitimate processes
Process of projection	Narrated by credible and trustworthy voices through appropriate channels	Narrated by figures who lack trust and credibility and projected through dubious or inappropriate channels, for instance, propaganda
Process of reception	The narrator allows audience to form their own understanding and impression of the narrative, listens to responses, shows serious consideration of those responses through language or policy action	The narrator controls the reception to a stifling degree that is obvious to audiences, leading to them switching off and thereafter holding the narrator and narrative in lower esteem

the probability that informational content is considered to be interesting, including the inclusion of conflict or struggle, proximity to the receiver's experience or geographic location, or magnitude. Much of the literature in communications and public relations speaks to how the message, or informational content, can affect the degree to which a narrative is convincing. This also suggests that information that does not conform to these characteristics is less likely to be convincing. Related to this is Hallin's concept of a sphere of deviance,[23] which we suggest relates to information that is outside of an acceptable narrative.

Emotional Content

It is through narrative that we can evaluate events and conduct. Being unable to tell narratives therefore diminishes social and political life because it limits scope for moral judgment about events.[24] Narratives do not just present information to us about a problem, a cast of actors, a causal transformation required to overcome the problem, and a desired end state. Narratives ask us to judge the nature and gravity of the problem, the character of the actors involved, and what kind of future would be preferable. Narratives thus engage us on an emotional level, bringing out hope or disappointment, anger or joy.[25]

Media ecologies enable audiences to engage with the emotional charge of narratives. A real-time ecology of images and video footage could be said to realize McLuhan's idea of a global village, argues W. J. T. Mitchell, including a dark side: the tribal drums of the neighboring village can be heard, announcing enmity and war.[26] Emotive interactions can easily be triggered. During the war on terror of the 2000s, episodes such as US President Bush talking of crusades, the Danish cartoon depictions of the Prophet Muhammad, and images of torture and mutilation of bodies could all be used to enhance the charge of strategic narratives. Symbolism was also used to characterize each side. Communication does not have to involve the exchange of words; it can involve the exchange of heads: US soldiers covered the head of Saddam Hussein's statue with a US flag, and invaded Saddam Hussein's actual head by publicizing photos of him being examined dentally; the US hooded its victims in Abu Ghraib. In exchange, Al-Qaeda took the heads of US civilians by encouraging decapitation videos. While this was partly the reenactment of ancient trophy rituals, these interactions also had an eye for an eye, a head for a head, logic[27] that worked through emotion rather than truth-seeking claims. Of course, these exchanges may involve visual symbols but they are interpreted through language. They are fitted into narratives, as we argued in Chapter 2. Al-Qaeda operatives were particularly adept at this.

It could be argued that Al-Qaeda was expert at managing the emotional content of narratives. The mutilation of US contractors in Iraq played on US anxieties about being seen to enforce its power and led to the US destruction of Faluja, a tactical error that lent credence to Al-Qaeda's narrative depiction of the US as a brutal aggressor willing to kill civilians. Indeed, the interaction of symbols in an age of social media and virality means an episode can easily spiral out of control and create unintended consequences. For Al-Qaeda, with asymmetric power lack, such chaos may have been to its benefit. Consequently, there will be contexts in which it is strategically advantageous for some actors to initiate emotional, primal interactions in order to reinforce their narrative.

Epistemology

A narrative presents a version of the world that audiences may treat with skepticism even if they trust the author or projector of the narrative. The interpretation of a narrative depends on the epistemology audiences hold. Epistemology refers to a theory of how we know the world. We may know how things work through divine revelation from an extra-human deity, through trial and error scientific experiments, or by some other theory of what counts as knowledge. Narratives draw upon discourses about economics, religion, science, law, and so forth, each of which presents a body of knowledge and way of knowing the world. Part of the skill of using strategic narratives is plotting events in a way that can be justified by several discourses, as we argued in the book's introduction. In the case study on Iran's nuclear program later in this chapter we find political leaders drawing on several epistemologies depending on who they are addressing, and in our analysis of Obama's Cairo speech in Chapter 5 it is also evident that the US president drew upon several forms of truth.

Degree of Ambiguity

While language inevitably contains a degree of ambiguity, given that words can mean different things to speaker and addressee, ambiguity can be used intentionally in politics so that audiences can find a meaning in a political idea or narrative that they prefer to find.[28] In Chapter 3, for example, we saw that China has preferred to present an ambiguous identity and narrative to the West about its rise.

Narratives have to be sufficiently flexible to allow some redescription so that when events threaten to contradict the narrative, that narrative can be seen to be unaffected. For example, political and military leaders can redefine what counts as victory if the original aims were sufficiently ambiguous. In 2006 the UK's Secretary of Defense John Reid said, "We would be perfectly happy to leave in three years and without firing one shot," speaking about the UK's aims in Afghanistan. Ringsmose and Børgensen[29] note that "as conditions on the ground changed to the worse, the narrative changed as well. While still arguing that the military action did have suppressive effects on Al-Qaeda's ability to operate in the region, reaching success was now termed as achievable, although not in the near future." The UK's purpose had not changed—to achieve national security by diminishing the capacity of jihadists to form and plan attacks from Afghanistan on the UK—but the time frame was presented more ambiguously. This is reminiscent of the US in Vietnam and the USSR in Afghanistan, where the decisions to withdraw did not coincide with the achievement of political objectives, but with the determination that staying was too costly.[30] Instead, in both cases, leaders claimed that their states had acted honorably, and stressed the responsibility of allies to act (through Vietnamization and Afghan national reconciliation).

Hence, leaders must strike a balance, constructing a narrative that appears direct and coherent but that contains sufficient ambiguity to allow it to absorb contradictory events and opinions.

Relation between Narrative and Action

A narrative must appear consistent with events as they are known by the narrative's audiences. The issues of ambiguity and epistemology have already shown this is not straightforward. Any disjuncture between narrative claims about how the world is, and direct experience of the world or expectations about how the world should work, can lead to charges of hypocrisy being leveled against the narrator. This in turn will reduce the narrator's credibility and trustworthiness and make audiences less likely to engage with them in the future. Related to this is timeliness. When political actors take the initiative to present information ahead of their rivals there is a great chance of winning the audience's confidence.[31] If political actors do not present information in a timely fashion, they may be forced to counter other narratives about that information.

PROCESS OF FORMATION

International relations scholars have looked at the formation and evolution of great powers' ideas about themselves and the international system. Jeffrey Legro has explained whether these states identify their relation to the system as one of integration, revision, or separation from the system's values and operations.[32] Vivien Schmidt has explained the formation and projection of "coordinative discourses" that are generated within political elites, which serve to provide a common language or narrative through which policy stakeholders can come to agreement in order to construct a policy program.[33] Such coordinative discourses differ in strategic purpose from what she calls "communicative discourse," a tool to persuade publics of the necessity of policies developed at the coordinative stage.

Changing media technologies appear to be opening up, or promise to open up, the formation of strategic narratives. What was once an elite process can now begin to accommodate mass authorship. Social science and online tools can be used to solicit and consult, to trial and test narratives, and at least create an impression of consultation. In the next chapter we see how the BBC World Service ran a participatory experiment in which it invited audiences to contribute to the production of each show by deciding upon guests, the questions they were asked, and the topics of conversation. The BBC realized that changing media ecologies can allow more transparency and democratic participation in the design of a mass media broadcast and tried to embrace the slight risk of chaos that comes with audience involvement.

THE PROCESS OF PROJECTION

Who projects the narrative, represents the narrative, and is the guarantor of its credibility? Often, the answers to these questions depend on the configuration of political institutions. National leaders' ability to talk about change and enact change depends on executive autonomy and the structure of the state.[34] We would go further, however. This capacity is transparent to other states: they can recognize under what circumstances a rival state's leader will be in a position to offer a new or challenging strategic narrative. Iran's president will be able to call upon political scientists who can explain under what circumstances an American president can make certain narrative moves. For instance, the ability of US presidents to talk up their willingness to intervene militarily around the world depends upon whether they have support from the US Congress and public opinion, all of which is reported daily by US and international news media and thus entirely transparent to Iran or other possible targets of US rhetorical or even kinetic force.[35]

Public diplomacy practitioners in the last decade have sought to conduct joint projection of strategic narratives through cooperative initiatives with business, NGOs, and cultural and sporting institutions. While this can present the appearance of cohesion and amplify the narrative in productive ways, it can create dilemmas for those participants. Take, for example, the role of NGOs in NATO's actions in Afghanistan. Both NGOs and international organizations are part of a multi-actor joined-up network that political leaders have tried to build. In Afghanistan, NATO has found that it must work with NGOs but also international organizations such as the UN, EU, and World Bank in peace-building activities, all of whom try not only to react to crises but manage security proactively.[36] NATO must work with these organizations to bring narrative clarity for home, international, and Afghan audiences. However, it is unclear whether the central, anchoring concept that underpins NATO's narrative about its mission is peace building, nation building, or reconstruction. Each entails slightly different meanings but also different practices on the ground; the conceptual overlap of these terms hints at the possibility of confusion both for those trying to form a coherent narrative and for audiences for whom these terms might mean different things. Thus,

NGOs are part of a multi-actor network that poses a challenge to leading political organizations like NATO. NATO must somehow persuade, cajole, and generally help organize this network to act as a conduit for its single narrative.

NGOs are persuasive not simply because of their power as actors in isolation. They have persuasive capacity because their reputation has emotional purchase. Monroe Price argues that the presence of NGOs inspires anxiety in authoritarian governments or hope among minorities and dissenters, creating expectations of success.[37] There is little NGOs can particularly do about that; it is a question of projection by others, due to the expectations that experience has created about NGOs continuing to create change in the future. Their effect is therefore performative. Their presence makes a situation different, creates a step-change, and triggers responses. In terms of contestation, the role they play is therefore complex: not just about the arguments they advance, but about their sheer presence and symbolic value.

THE PROCESS OF RECEPTION

The process of reception of a strategic narrative is subject to contestation because there is competition to determine who has a chance to receive the narrative. In the next chapter we look at the importance of information infrastructure for shaping who becomes an audience and whose voices are heard in media ecologies. For now, Price's analysis of NATO in Afghanistan is illustrative. When we look at weak states and the competition between overseas militaries (US Department of Defense, NATO), overseas aid organizations (USAID, Department for International Development) and the local state, for example Somalia or Afghanistan, then each has different capacities to influence the information infrastructure in such a way as to affect the circuits of political information flows and the way influence operates. The local state can oversee the introduction of mobile phone services and satellite signals and the location of Internet cafes. The US Department of Defense introduced a radio station called Radio-in-a-Box, working with Afghan generals to help them disseminate information and use music to engage local populations as well as Afghan soldiers. As we argue in the next chapter, political actors will try to control both conversations in the media ecology and the infrastructure of the media ecology that conditions who gets to participate in those conversations at all.

In summary, analysis of narrative contestation must consider which of these aspects of narrative contestation are relevant to explaining the case in question. Each of these aspects of narrative contestation is relational: how convincing any state's narrative is depends on whether other states' narratives are more or less compelling in some way.

IS WINNING ABOUT CREATING A SHARED UNDERSTANDING? THE IMPORTANCE OF RECEPTION

We began this chapter with quotes from Madeleine Albright and Joe Nye about the rise of China. Albright argued that China could be integrated into international institutions. By altering its behavior on certain issues, it would become socialized. Here, the role of strategic narratives in winning the narrative battle would be finding rhetoric to compel or embarrass China into joining those international institutions. Whether the Chinese leadership is truly convinced of the virtues of that order is not necessary to explaining their decision to join. In the spectrum of persuasion, Albright was operating at the thin end of rationalism, but open to allowing socialization to proceed as theorists of communicative action would expect. Writing some years later, Nye was concerned not just with how Chinese people were acting and the demands they were making in international affairs, but about how they think about their country's role in the international system. Nye's analysis falls at the thicker end of the spectrum, since he was trying to explain how the experience of a rising China narrative was constituting the identity and interests of young Chinese people. To achieve victory here would entail, in Janice Bially-Mattern's words, getting them to "live the experience of [their] identity" through a different narrative,[38] one in which China's rise would not imply them making such demands.

While states seek to maximize interests at all times, how they do this depends on the meaning of situations for them. Rational choice theory does not explain how states choose at all because of the intrinsic uncertainty of means and ends in complex international affairs.[39] Certainly the tools of foreign policy analysis allow leaders to have some grasp of the likely costs and benefits of action and the structural constraints and opportunities they face.[40] However, these analytical tools are imperfect. Leaders also rely on their sense of what they're trying to do, and their expectations of what is likely to happen based on past events and the character or reputation of other states, and whether the foreseeable outcomes are consistent with their own aims and identity. How does this happen? Leaders' subjective experience of international affairs is structured by narratives. Their understandings of the past, present, and imagined futures of their state and the international system are not based on objective facts but on the experience living in and governing through ongoing historical trajectories and committing to realizing certain trajectories—committing privately and publicly.[41] This raises the question: Is winning the narrative battle in international relations a matter of getting other states to experience the world in terms of the same narrative as one's own?

For example, national leaders in postwar Europe committed to a narrative of ever-closer union and of sharing risks and opportunities. Jennifer Mitzen argues that what is important is that the European states publicly expressed their commitment to this narrative. They created venues to reaffirm this, established documents to codify it, and developed institutions and policies that enabled them to realize the narrative in practice. European states formed a shared grand strategy around a specific narrative and this had behavioral, disciplining effects. Buy-in created shared expectations of appropriate behavior and expression. After a while, those leaders and the generations of leaders and publics that followed them experienced their continent's history through that narrative. That narrative defined the parameters of what policies were thinkable. Similarly, since World War II American leaders have committed themselves to realizing a narrative about America's role in the world; any new events that emerge are understood in terms of fulfilling or disrupting that narrative. It is the same for China, India, or any country.

The importance of creating a shared understanding that overcomes these divergent narratives is particularly vital in postwar situations. A shared narrative is a condition for the building of a new nation-state that incorporates social groups that had become violent enemies. Lara Nettelfield[42] conducted firsthand research in the former Yugoslavia to examine the stories people told about the Bosnian war (1992–5). She was interested in the way elite narratives from the International Criminal Tribunal for Yugoslavia (ICTY) interacted with local narratives. She argues that the working through and contestation of narratives in postconflict societies is an important part of the transition to a stable or democratic order. She was able to reach this finding by putting into practice a methodology that allowed her to trace the circulation of narratives among elites and publics. Nettelfield carried out ethnography with women's groups, the first survey of former soldiers in the war, narrative analysis of interviews with local people and community leaders, and interviews and analysis of policy documents from NGOs working in the region at the time. She draws on Martha Minow,[43] who argued narratives "are crucial in constructing a sense of self in the face of traditions that have crumbled and human hopes that risk being forgotten."

In the former Yugoslavia, Nettelfield found that most citizens held relatively fixed narratives but some were open to making admissions or reflect about crimes by their ethnic group during the war. The role of the International Criminal Tribunal for the former Yugoslavia (ICTY) was important here because it brought evidence into the public domain, held individuals to account from all sides, and its actions enabled more open conversation among publics "about the nature of the new Bosnian state, what the political community would look like, and how people would relate to one another. These discussions were good for the democratization process," she argues.[44] For a time at least, more extreme nationalist sentiments on different sides were undermined. Many Serbs supported a narrative that the war was only a civil war or conflict in which all sides suffered and so all sides should be regarded as victims, including themselves. In contrast, the narrative held by many Bosnians was that they had been the main victims, that there had been 200–250,000 deaths and Serbs should be held primarily to account. The ICTY trials, and the work of human rights groups encouraged by the creation of a judicial process, generated evidence that made these more extreme Serb and Bosnian narratives untenable. More Serbs than Bosnians were indeed responsible for more war crimes. However, the total number of casualties was closer to 100,000 than the 200,000-plus that had become part of Bosnian received wisdom.[45] What is interesting about Nettelfield's study of ordinary people's narratives of the war is that it shows not only narratives about what happened in the war but also the need to narrativize the role of law and courts in Bosnia, then and in the future. Hence, an elite- and international community-driven process changed the quality or tenor of narratives in Bosnia, introducing a legal discourse that had to be woven into any narrative of the war. It became understood to be a necessity to account for the rule of law and legal accountability. If we equate democracy with the rule of law, Nettelfield argues, then it can be claimed that the ICTY's presence had a democratizing effect. The process might not have created a shared narrative of what happened, but it did create a shared discursive foundation characterized by a focus on law and accountability.

Ultimately, is a shared narrative necessary? Can people just agree on facts, even if they then interpret them differently and construct different narratives? The ICTY's job was to establish the truth of what happened during the war. Its role was not to provide an overarching narrative that all sides could buy into, but to produce an evidence-based account of the actions of certain individuals charged with criminal acts. Each individual case might offer a micronarrative, but the possibility of the formation of an overarching narrative was a more emergent, open process.

In the remainder of this chapter, we analyze three case studies in order to illustrate the points made above. We highlight the role of system narratives versus issue and identity narratives. We explore how narratives draw upon preexisting discourses and how contestation involves using media ecologies in innovative and skillful ways. In the cases of Israel's conflicts with its neighbors and efforts by the US and EU to limit Iran's nuclear program, we see how difficult it is to construct shared narratives. However, the case of the emergence of an anti-whaling narrative in environmental politics shows how it is possible to win an argument and get other actors to behave in your preferred way on an issue.

CASE STUDY 1: ISRAEL AND ITS NEIGHBORS: REPRODUCING THE DAVID AND GOLIATH NARRATIVE

The play of strategic narratives in the Israel-Palestine conflict and Israel's struggles with its other neighbors is of great significance because of the importance of these conflicts to affairs in the Middle East and globally. Given the level of global public attention these conflicts attract, they are useful for understanding the potentials and pitfalls of using media to narrate events in a strategic way. Israel and its antagonists seek to project narratives that enhance their legitimacy and credibility and boost their domestic and international support. They project narratives that convey their interests and identities, but as conflicts are triggered, so these become opportunities also to challenge each other's narratives. The scholar Ben Mor has produced a body of studies exploring how Israel has tried to control its appearance and the narrative used to interpret events in the conflict. What becomes clear is that Israel has great difficulty overcoming a "David versus Goliath" narrative. Given its material advantages over its neighbors, and its support from the world's leading military power, the US, it has a disproportionate advantage in any kinetic contest. However, this does not render Israel invulnerable to attacks on its identity and moral character, attacks that are conducted often through the media ecology. Indeed, for Mor, these conflicts play out in a context in which contestation of images is central to international relations today. This is because of the communications infrastructure we survey in the following chapter. Real-time reporting, the global reach of media, and the preeminence of moving images and hence television and the Internet, all constitute the conditions for relations between states. The volume, speed, and diversity of sources in the new media ecology creates perpetual "risk of credibility loss" for states and their militaries.[46] In the case of Israel, there is also the perpetual risk of shame.[47] Given Israel's overwhelming hard power advantages over the Palestinians, for instance, Israel faces humiliation if it fails to achieve complete military success whenever conflict breaks out. It also faces shame if it is seen to use disproportionate force and risks harming Palestinian civilians. Hence, Israel's abilities to control perceptions of its actions are precarious.

How does Israel pursue its long-term grand strategy within this context of precarious image management? Grand strategy refers to doctrine whose implementation allows a state to achieve long-term goals such as national security.[48] In the short-to-medium term the state may face wars in which it needs to formulate a coherent chain of strategy, operations, and tactics. For Mor, the information infrastructure exposes grand strategy and its instantiation as localized strategy, operations, and tactics. Operations and tactics are transparent before media and citizen journalism; political and military leaders articulate strategy before cameras, their claims intensely scrutinized. People in conflict zones possess mobile camera phones; footage can emerge in unforeseeable ways. Hence, the materialization of grand strategy is more transparent in the new media ecology.

This transparency and visibility means the operationalization of grand strategy must be accompanied by a relentless will to explain.[49] Public diplomacy is required to explain the grand strategy and fit it into a strategic narrative. In the aftermath of immediate events, press teams must offer rapid responses to journalists in multiple languages.[50] Propaganda can be used, but a state using propaganda runs the risk of being seen to use propaganda. Alternatively, the state could integrate public diplomacy with its military, kinetic actions. For instance, in the 1991 Gulf War, the coalition bombing of Baghdad using precision weaponry was not the most effective military strategy but it offered more positive scope for public diplomacy and thus made for a better grand strategy overall. Similarly, Mor explains, Israel sometimes chooses not to use tanks and helicopters because they "photograph badly," in the words of the Israeli Defense Force (IDF) Major General Moshe Ya'alon.[51] Meanwhile, the success of these public communications does not depend on the state communicating, but also on the actions and communications of the state it is in conflict with.

These tensions can be understood by looking at several events in the conflict. This case is useful in highlighting:

• what it means to be strategic
• how strategy mediation is inflected through media ecologies
• how credibility is maintained, and the need for credible narrators
• the relation of actions to narrative, or the "say-do" gap[52]
• the unavoidable relationality of narrative work and the need to adapt one's narrative to emphasize one's strengths and the "intolerable ambiguities" of the opponent's identity and narrative[53]

On March 29, 2002, Israel launched Operation Defensive Shield in response to a suicide bomb attack on a hotel in Netanya. The military operation featured three "flashpoints . . . the Ramallah compound of Palestinian Authority (PA) Chairman Yassir Arafat . . . the Church of Nativity in Bethlehem, which, along with hostages, was taken over by Palestinian gunmen on April 4 and subsequently subjected to an IDF siege . . . and the Jenin refugee camp, which the IDF entered in pursuit of terrorists on April 3 and that became the site of a fierce battle and an alleged massacre."[54] The Israeli cabinet announced the aim was "to defeat the infrastructure of Palestinian terror in all its parts and components" but not to destroy the Palestinian Authority or Yassir Arafat, even though it appeared they had built that infrastructure. The ambiguity of this goal was intensified when a TV pundit noted that most terrorist attacks were the responsibility of the Islamic Jihad and Hamas, not the Palestinian Authority. This lack of clarity was because of a contradiction in the preferences of the Israeli government's key constituents. The Israeli public wanted a vigorous counter-terrorist policy. The US—Israel's leading ally—wanted a viable Palestinian leadership for Israel to negotiate with. Hence, the US wanted the Palestinian Authority to remain in place.

In the absence of a clear Israeli strategy, military logics took precedence, leading to the three flashpoints above. Images circulated on international television of Israeli bulldozers razing Palestinian homes. In response, the Israeli Minister of Defense called for media censorship in combat areas, and a competition developed between Palestinians, Israelis, and various external NGOs and the UN to establish the definitive narrative of what had happened—including whether a massacre at Jenin had taken place at all.[55] However, Israel's communication was ambiguous: it denied the Jenin massacre but claimed that it had no choice but to defend itself using tactics that included operating "in densely populated areas" and claimed that "armed terrorists" were using the Jenin refugee camp as "a battleground against Israeli forces."[56]

Despite starting this episode as the victim of a terrorist attack who had been provoked into a defensive response, Israel managed to amplify the David and Goliath narrative and project to the world images of it using—in the mass-mediated norms of international society—disproportionate and unjustifiable force. Mor argues Israel should have thought first of "what shoots well" not literally but in terms of media visuality and public diplomacy.[57] Israel should have allowed grand strategy to guide its military force—the best "adaptive response to a media-saturated environment and to the diffusion of democratic norms."[58] However, it lacked a clear grand strategy because its own goals and those of its US backer differed. This made it impossible to construct a coherent strategic narrative and then plan events to realize and visually demonstrate that narrative.

A few months later, Israel appeared to have learned a lesson. On July 12, 2006, the Lebanon-based group Hezbollah crossed into Israel and attacked an Israeli Defense Force (IDF) unit. Two Israeli soldiers were taken hostage, three were killed, and Hezbollah fired rockets into Israeli civilian areas. The military tactics Israel deployed in the weeks that followed were chosen less for operational value than for media value.[59] After the Jenin episode, Israel was focused on how its actions appeared to global public opinion. On July 17, 2006, Prime Minister Ehud Olmert's media adviser claimed Israel was "winning the international battle for public opinion"—his evidence was that 80 percent of viewers in a poll conducted by UK television station Sky News found Israel's attacks on Lebanon justified.[60] Israel was keen to represent its own character and that of Lebanon and Hezbollah in order to delegitimize the latter. Israel presented itself as a reluctant warrior having no choice but to respond, and blamed Lebanon for not controlling Hezbollah.

However, Israel was in danger of appearing humiliated. Hamas had kidnapped an Israeli soldier a month earlier and Israel's rescue attempt had only caused more Israeli troop casualties. As Mor recounts, when Hezbollah kidnapped the Israeli soldiers on July 12, its secretary general, Hassan Nasrallah, held a press conference in Beirut in which he mocked the Israeli military leaders. The IDF's reputation had been tarnished by various local defeats that year, and Israel's military strategy of containment appeared ineffective. The July 12 attacks and what became known as the Second Lebanon War became an opportunity for Israeli military and civilian leaders to repair their image and restore credibility among their domestic publics, while at the same time responding in a manner that would not upset international public opinion. What Mor does not explore is how a counter-narrative of humiliation comes about, which domestic groups promote it, and why it might make sense or have an emotional pull to Israeli audiences.

The status of this conflict became critical. While some Israeli leaders were shy of calling it a war, media and public opinion supported the term war. This meant the IDF had to produce a "picture of victory."[61]Enemy casualties were displayed in domestic media and Hezbollah was described by the Israeli government as the "spearhead of the Iranian army."[62]

Israel's self-presentation was disrupted when Israeli air forces hit the Lebanese village of Qana on July 30, 2006, killing 28 people, 16 of them children. European leaders criticized Israel's tactics as excessive and the US had to veto a UN Security Council resolution condemning Israel's actions. With the origins of the conflict now two weeks past, the narrative could have easily slipped away from Israel. It argued that Hezbollah fired from civilian buildings, that Israel had no intention to kill civilians, and that it had sent flyers and phoned ahead, two hours before strikes, to warn villagers that there was a risk of bombing. The IDF even displayed some of the flyers in the hope journalists might use these to lend credibility to its rhetoric. As Mor argues, Israel tried to reinforce the original narrative concerning Lebanon's failure to control Hezbollah.[63] On July 30 the IDF released video footage apparently showing Hezbollah rockets being fired from Qana.[64]

However, outrage in international opinion ran parallel to domestic disenchantment. Israeli public support for the war dropped from 80 percent in July to 40 percent in mid-August, when, Mor notes, a ceasefire was eventually agreed.[65] Amnesty International and Human Rights Watch, two NGOs independent of either party to the conflict, sought to establish evidence of what happened for themselves. They sent their own teams of researchers to Qana, interviewed witnesses, and reviewed information from hospitals and governments. These acts projected the tacit message that Israel could not itself verify the effects of its own actions; or, Israel could try, but an independent, impartial NGO would offer a more credible evaluation. Human Rights Watch found no evidence Hezbollah was using human shields in Qana. To Israel's assertion that it had warned Qana residents to flee, Human Rights Watch said that all roads into Qana had already been destroyed by Israeli bombing; not only did that make escape impossible, but it also made it very unlikely Hezbollah would have been able to transport a rocket launcher to Qana.

In sum, Israel's attempts to fit events into its preferred narrative continued to fail. While it had a clearer strategy than in 2002, the 2006 conflict with Hezbollah illustrated the variety of actors who could contribute to the emerging narratives and find evidence and images contradicting Israel's own narrative. Israel had another opportunity to restore its self-identity and its international reputation in December 2008 when it launched Operation Cast Lead against Hamas in Gaza, a conflict that lasted until January 18, 2009. Public support in Israel was sustained until the conflict's end, and columnists in *Haaretz* newspaper declared it "a corrective experience."[66] However, the political disputes underpinning tensions between Israel and its neighbors show no signs of abating in the long term, so what lessons can we draw from Mor's studies?

An important thread running through Mor's analysis of Israel's strategic narrative and its conflicts is the need for Israel to act within culturally acceptable norms of behavior within international society and to furnish proof about its behavior to international society. That proof must meet shared standards or expectations of what counts as evidence. On the first point, and as we have seen in the examples above, Israel has had to make reference to democratic norms and respond using force in a way considered responsible and proportionate by other states. Effective strategic narratives work with the grain of international norms and ideally are seen to support and enforce those norms. Norms of appropriate behavior and expression are "the medium by which [states] seek to exert influence," Mor writes.[67]

On the second point, concerning knowing how to convince international opinion by presenting a certain kind of evidence, Mor writes:

One unknown about the communications revolution is whether the unprecedented intensification of cross-cultural interaction that it has fostered will ultimately generate shared global norms on the meaning of proof and the criteria of evidence (analogous to the status of court proceedings). However, familiarity with accepted criteria permits even those who are not (or not fully) socialized to "play along" strategically.[68]

In politics, the point is not to definitively meet these standards but to convince others that you do. Mor goes as far as arguing that it is an imperative agenda for IR scholars to set about explaining how states and other actors do "credibility talk": how they go about trying to give this impression, creating this credibility, and whether others recognize it, are convinced, and cooperate with them accordingly.[69] Interactions in international affairs are less about truth seeking than achieving the appearance of seeking truth (although, it is surely easier to appear to be truth seeking if one *is* truth seeking). Projecting the image of one who seeks and values the truth establishes one as a credible actor whose motives can be trusted and, others hope, one whose actions can then be predicted with some certainty. In international affairs, a state's character is being evaluated constantly through its myriad actions. Any actor will need a consistent approach to its performance of credibility. How states project the image of truth seeking is an interesting question, and we would expect them to learn new repertoires and new ways to project this appearance as the media ecology changes year by year.

A third issue concerns whether the increased transparency of the new media ecology makes violence more or less likely. In his earlier analysis, Mor suggested that "the metaphorical meaning of 'what shoots well'" may override its literal meaning.[70] This implies that transparency will reduce violence, for the use of military force will be dictated by grand strategy and public diplomacy objectives. Does the information infrastructure bring moral and humanitarian benefits? On the other hand, Mor elsewhere argues that media transparency acts to "'raise the curtain,' allowing the audience to observe the actors and the events on stage" to a greater degree.[71] Increased transparency offers scope for leaders to make grand gestures and stage dramatic performances. If those leaders seek to repair humiliation or demonstrate strong will, does this make violence more likely? The normative implications of transparency and its new regimes of visibility and attention require further scrutiny.[72]

Ultimately, we would argue that the effects of image management are likely to be small when narratives around an issue are as entrenched as they are for the Israel-Palestine dispute. It is not only a matter of what audiences *do* see, but *how* they see it and interpret it. We know from decades of research in political communication that audiences interpret through relatively stable prisms or worldviews. Here, the relationship between images and narratives becomes more nuanced than many working in strategic communications appreciate. First, images cannot necessarily be considered as primary in audiences' interpretation of events, despite evidence from neuroscience suggesting that our impression and memory of events is largely visual. During the war on terror, many news stories that generated great public debate or even outrage did not include a photographic or other visual representation of the controversial phenomenon in question. The *very notion* that US interrogators had flushed copies of the Koran down toilets at Guantanamo Bay in May 2005 was sufficient to spark riots and killings in Afghanistan.[73] No images were necessary. Audiences seek any whisper, rumor, or other data that confirms the narrative they hold about international politics.

On that basis, O'Loughlin has argued that those seeking to manage and control media content related to war must take into account that it is not the immediate impact of media content that shocks, but *what that content represents*.[74] After a three-year study of audience responses to security news, he found that news content generates the most intense responses when audiences felt a story signified something more profound. It was not audiences' squeamishness at witnessing images of US soldiers being dragged through the streets of Mogadishu in 1993 that mattered, but that audiences might feel these images signified unnecessary deaths, mistaken foreign policy, or incompetent leadership. War images force some audience members to reconsider their understanding of the intervention and, henceforth, the level of casualties they would tolerate.[75] Predicting the effect of media images requires attention to the more complex relation between specific images and the underlying beliefs and narratives held to by particular audiences. If, as Sontag argues, some images resonate "because *they were invested with the meaning of larger struggles*"[76] then we need to know the prior narratives audiences interpret incoming images through.

Strategic narrative work by Israeli, Palestinian, or Hezbollah communication officials involves weaving together long-standing icons and long-held beliefs with real-time events and crisis footage. This must be done in ways that contest both the immediate events and the long-term narratives through which these are perceived and understood. Working to this dual temporality, they should expect to achieve differential levels and kinds of impact upon public opinion in home audiences, the antagonist state's domestic public, the publics of allies and other players, and that diffuse category of international, or global, public opinion.

In the case of Israel, Mor's studies show Israel learning how to adapt its military responses to ensure its image in international media is consistent with the identity and character it wishes global public opinion to hold about itself. Each new crisis offers the opportunity to reinforce Israel's long-term strategic narrative about its role in the region and its historical trajectory, and depict its neighbor-antagonists as the cause of problems, problems which its strong but essentially cooperative character allows it to overcome. Yet each crisis also offers risks in which Israel can lose control of its image and even reinforce negative stereotypes. Disjunctures can emerge between its strategy and tactics, between action and rhetoric, and between aims and outcomes. Managing the media presentation of these dynamics takes great skill and awareness of how the new media ecology works.

The David versus Goliath narrative points to more general narrative character types that cut across stories and ages. In the next example, we see how the David and Goliath identities were used in the shift from whaling to anti-whaling policies in the global economy during the twentieth century.

CASE STUDY 2: WHY DID WHALING BECOME EVIL?

One of the most remarkable examples of international society shifting from one narrative to another in the twentieth century was the shift from whaling being a normal, industrial matter to an evil practice. By the 1960s, when whaling not only became normatively unpalatable to international society but was also uneconomical and yielded no material benefit, Japan, Norway, and a minority of other countries continued to practice whaling but positioned themselves as in a position of resistance. Their identity narrative as whaling states, for whom whaling was part of local tradition, was imperiled by a new policy narrative that framed their identity as illegitimate. The policy narrative had turned upside down. In her definitive study of this narrative shift, Epstein puts it bluntly: How did we go "from a world where killing whales was widespread and unquestioned to one where it is morally wrong and those who continue to do it are frowned upon"?[77]

The answer lies in the way anti-whaling activists took preexisting discourses about international politics and the environment and crafted them into an appealing narrative about whales. That narrative delegitimized whaling. The first discourse was a Cold War discourse on capitalism and democracy. In a breakthrough film in 1974 that caught media attention in the West, the anti-whaling NGO Greenpeace filmed one of their activists standing on a whale protecting it from Russian whalers. It was crucial that Greenpeace challenged a Russian whaling ship and returned to San Francisco Harbor just as World War II veterans had, and that they depicted themselves as rugged individuals disrupting the Soviet industrial juggernaut.[78] Indeed, this activist David stood up to the Soviet Goliath and, using the asymmetric power of communications media, would eventually slay him. The second discourse concerned saving the planet. A discourse of endangered species had already taken hold in the 1960s. Epstein argues that the spread of color television and the regularity of visual environmental crises reinforced a general shift to McLuhan's ideas of the global village and put the environment into public discourse as a term whose meaning was up for contestation. It was unclear what "the environment" meant, Epstein writes, beyond "'that thing' that was being threatened by human activity."[79]

Nevertheless, this was an opportunity for activists, and one that required using the media ecology of the time. Epstein's interviews show how the activists wanted to turn global audiences into witnesses and into consumers; witnesses of the plight of the whale, which required regular news reports on whales suffering, and consumers of NGO subscriptions, whale-watching tours, and news reports about whales.[80] Greenpeace even had to take on a surveillance or monitoring function as ecodetectives to film any infractions of whaling rules by vessels at sea, and then get these films to media organizations and convince them the films were newsworthy. In the Israel case above, we saw Amnesty International and Human Rights Watch taking on a similar monitoring function, seeking to provide verification of material facts and feed them into the media ecology to attract public attention. Understanding that visual excitement and conflict make a film newsworthy, the UK program director of Greenpeace, Chris Rose, told Epstein their campaign was "more an imageology than an ideology."[81] This suggests how the activists tried to use the media ecology and media practices to create subjectivities. Once in those subject positions, people would accept the narrative as commonsensical and the solutions it proposed as justified.

Greenpeace and other NGOs managed to construct a narrative that suggested that by saving the whale, the West would be saving the planet. The narrative located blame and provided a route to action. Every small act would contribute to that global solution. Epstein argues that this process of stitching the discourses into that narrative was highly contingent and could have failed. Instead, however, a new coalition was formed of anti-whaling states, who could portray themselves as doing *something* about the environment (loosely defined). From then on, to the extent that they understood themselves through this narrative, right-thinking states would seek to be seen to be custodians of the planet and right-thinking citizens would take care of their environment.

In 1982 there was a worldwide suspension of commercial whaling. Epstein describes this as a "moment of victory,"[82] since the embedding of the narrative in the identity and social order of states meant the anti-whaling groups had achieved their strategic aim. Ideas had served rational goals. Ironically, when the science of marine life improved through the 1980s and

1990s and it became clear that sustained exploitation of many types of whales would not threaten their existence, policy makers and anti-whaling activists ignored this new scientific advice.

The whaling case study demonstrates an important mechanism in narrative contestation: the use of existing discourses to craft a narrative. Those discourses make certain narratives possible, but there is a skill in how actors stitch them together. The BRICs narrative discussed in Chapter 3, "Strategic Narratives of International Order," depends on a geopolitical discourse of international order as competitive and hierarchal and an economic discourse in which economic growth is taken as an indicator of progress. Epstein argues that studies that miss how such discourses condition possible action are agent-centric and conflate power with agency; discourses create the very subject-positions that actors fill and through which they can ever exert agency in the first place.[83] However, her study also shows how anti-whaling groups, once discourses enabled them to acquire positions to speak and be heard, then *did* exert agency and achieve their aims. Power is both generated by structures and, once organized through authoritative subject positions or roles, exerted by actors. We must account for *both* constitutive *and* behavioral power. For there is no doubt that the combination of anti-whaling actors working through discursive structures and wielding an anti-whaling narrative exerted power over Japan, Norway, and other states, since these outcasts felt compelled to present themselves as resisting. The whaling case study illustrates very clearly that in the projection of strategic narratives there is no pure agency or pure structure, but a set of complex and intersecting mechanisms.

The whaling case also shows how narrativity can be given to an issue. If, once upon a time in the early twentieth century, Western states were engaged in industrial whaling, this was absent from public discussion of the issue by the 1990s. The narrative begins in 1982 with a world made up on an anti-whaling system, the problem of having to change the minds of a few anti-whaling rogue states, and the potential resolution of a universal end to whaling and humanity in harmony with nature. While we might write *rogue states* here with tongue in cheek, this points to a second narrative quality, characterization. Epstein's study shows how actors attempted to typecast states, and how some of those states tried to resist and challenge those characterizations. Finally, the activists were successful in creating an urgent tone and global scale to the narrative.

CASE STUDY 3: IRAN'S NUCLEAR PROGRAM

The case of Iran's nuclear program is a classic example of the importance of states trying to win the war, or battle, of narratives[84] on an issue in which a range of types of actors are involved in the contest, a situation becoming increasingly common, as argued in Chapter 2. Since talks began in the early

2000s, the EU, US, and Iran have failed to reach agreement on the future of Iran's nuclear program. Each actor has projected a strategic narrative about the international system and the place of Iran's nuclear program within that. When these narratives align, agreement is possible because each side is able to understand the issue in the same terms as the others. At least in their use of language, they situate the issue through the terms of the other's narrative. However, this happens very rarely. Why? The first reason is that a state's strategic narrative is deeply embedded and not prone to change, constraining what a state's leader can propose. A second reason is that strategic narratives draw upon numerous discourses within which an issue can be tested. For example, narratives about Iran's nuclear program shift across scientific, legal, sovereignty, and theology-based discourses. While skillful leaders can pin down debate to one basis for agreement—keep debate in the space of a single discourse—Iranian leaders have been highly adept at shifting from one discourse to another to prevent agreement. Once we break down these strategic narrative processes, we can explain how Iran has outmaneuvered the US and EU to continue its nuclear program.

Each of the key actors—Iran, the European Union 3 (France, Germany, and the United Kingdom, along with High Representative of the Union for Foreign Affairs and Security Policy Javier Solana (until 2009 when Baroness Catherine Ashton assumed the post), the International Atomic Energy Agency (IAEA)), and the United States—draw on different sets of understandings and justifications for their diplomacy on Iran's nuclear program. These rarely coalesce around a single view of the issues at stake. This is because each actor's interpretation of the issue is framed by the strategic narratives each projects about the international system and how international relations are conducted.[85] Put simply, the nuclear issue becomes entwined within long-term narratives about the past, present, and future of international relations that each actor communicates to its home audiences and international rivals. For the European Union (EU) and IAEA, Iran's nuclear program is part of the painstaking construction of multilateral, rule-governed order. For the US, it is about maintaining a power structure in the Middle East region, while for Iran the meaning of its nuclear program is tied to challenging that structure and those who seek to uphold it. Since each actor interprets the issue in terms of different narratives, it is very difficult for them to agree on what it is they are disagreeing about in the first place. It is difficult to overcome these disjunctures through truth-seeking discourse because such positions are based on affective associations: multilateral cooperation, science-led progress, global leadership, regional hegemony and being a nuclear state all entail questions of status, identity, and political symbolism.[86]

These system narratives must be broken down into their component parts if we are to understand how dialogue has proceeded. We must break down actors' narratives into discrete justifications of positions at different moments. This is because, as with episodes in Israel's conflicts and the anti-whaling struggle, it is in these specific acts that we see how the epistemic bases of larger narrative structures are sustained or revised. We find the actors shifting the terms of debate from international law to theology to science to sovereignty, a maddening kaleidoscope of terms of debate that Iran has been particularly astute in navigating. There are also issue-specific narratives and contexts that Iran has drawn upon in its engagements with the EU, US, and IAEA. The dispute over the Iran nuclear program takes place in the context of other countries' nuclear programs. Nuclear proliferation, despite the Treaty on the Non-Proliferation of Nuclear Weapons (Non-Proliferation Treaty or NPT), has been witnessed in India, Israel, and Pakistan. Iran claims it has been treated unfairly and that double standards are at play. The major players in this study, the EU3 and the US, are nuclear actors—although Germany stands out as being committed to not developing nuclear weapons technology, and indeed has recently committed to phasing out domestic nuclear energy production in the wake of the 2011 Fukushima disaster in Japan. There have also been differences in opinion on the aims and means of international action. Differences have been evident over what balance of diplomacy and coercion is appropriate, and what the consequences should be if Iran does not comply with US or EU3 aims.

The Iran nuclear issue is extremely intricate due to the highly interwoven nature of negotiations with numerous state and nonstate actors and the complexities of politics of the United Nations Security Council. The role of the US in this issue is interesting, as Washington and Tehran have not had formal relations since the Iranian revolution in 1979. Then-*Newsweek* journalist Fareed Zakaria summed up Iran's view of the diplomatic standoff in the following terms:

> Consider what the world looks like to Iran. It is surrounded by nuclear powers (Russia, China, India, Pakistan, Israel), and across two of its borders sit tens of thousands of U.S. troops (in Iraq and Afghanistan). The President of the United States has repeatedly made clear that he regards the regime in Tehran as illegitimate, wishes to overthrow it, and funds various groups whose aims are similar. If you were in Tehran, would you feel like giving up your nuclear program? Insisting on both policy change and regime change, we have gotten neither.[87]

The EU3 (France, Germany, the United Kingdom and the High Representative of the Union for Foreign Affairs and Security Policy) established a role for itself as an interlocutor in negotiations. Our analysis covers the period in which the EU3 took the lead in negotiations, before a period from 2005–10 when the issue became highly politicized and any basis for agreement became disputed. We end the analysis in 2010, by which time the IAEA had grown so exasperated that its Director General publicly called for an end to the choreography or what he called "kabuki dance."[88]

Our study analyzes four phases or cycles of interactions. In the first cycle, 2002–4, the EU and Iran reached an agreement in Paris with the IAEA. It helped the EU that it could project its policy positions and its identity as clearly distinct from the United States. In his State of the Union address in January 2002, US President Bush labeled Iran, Iraq, and North Korea an "axis of evil" of "regimes who sponsor terror" through threats of weapons of mass destruction and by supporting terrorists.[89] The European Union's own European Security Strategy of 2003 distanced itself from this and presented a different narrative about the international system. Much has been written on the differences between the US 2002 National Security Strategy (NSS) and European Security Strategy (ESS)—both quite different documents with different aims, despite their similar sounding titles.[90] While the ESS appeared to represent the beginnings of a more assertive and self-confident EU in foreign and security policy, it was distinctive in its comprehensive view of security and preference for civilian solutions to security challenges, not military intervention.

The US had accused Iran of running a covert weapons program, and a prominent Iranian dissident group had leaked information about nuclear facilities unknown to the IAEA. In June 2003 IAEA chief Mohamed ElBaradei declared Iran had kept certain nuclear materials and activities secret and thus deceived the agency.[91]

On October 21, 2003, Iran agreed to suspend its enrichment plans, cooperate with the IAEA, and sign and implement the Additional Protocol.[92] This was a rare moment of narrative convergence because Iran, the IAEA, and the EU3 took into account each other's claims and produce an agreement that took into account each other's aspirations. The EU3 acknowledged Iran's right to develop nuclear energy for peaceful purposes as a sovereign state signed up to the NPT and took into account Iran's need for more modern technology. Iran acknowledged the multilateral, law-governed order sought by the EU3 and IAEA by signing up to the Additional Protocol as a "confidence-building measure." Notably, the joint statement suggested "the Additional Protocol is in no way intended to undermine the sovereignty, *national dignity* or national security of its State Parties."[93] The EU3 were willing to tacitly acknowledge that other actors might not recognize Iran's dignity—for instance, the US, which categorized Iran as a rogue state.[94]

Several years later, in 2007, when the US published its National Intelligence Estimate (NIE), the question of why Iran agreed to a deal in October 2003 seemed uncertain. It was simply "in response to international pressure"—pressure that included economic sanctions as well as diplomatic efforts.[95] Nevertheless, sanctions were not unique to that period. What was unique was narrative convergence on a particular set of grounds: these were the technical and legal terms of the IAEA and EU3 and the grounds of sovereignty and recognition sought by Iran.

On February 24, 2004, an IAEA report stated that Iran had been misleading in the October agreement with the EU3 and IAEA. Iran had suggested it presented all nuclear materials for inspection, but omitted reference to centrifuge designs and research—"a matter of serious concern."[96] Iran replied on March 5, 2004, using the same technical-legal register. It stated that it had informed that IAEA that it was conducting research and development on centrifuges and that it had intended to tell the IAEA about these *specific* developments "within the timeline established by the IAEA."[97]

These technical disputes in a scientific-legal order had reached an impasse. Both Iran and the US tried to shift the discourse from science and international law to more political terms. In June 2004 Iran Foreign Minister Kamal Kharrazi told a press conference, "Iran has a high technical capability and has to be recognized by the international community as a member of the nuclear club. This is an irreversible path."[98] This made clear Iran's intentions.

Members of the E3 were conciliatory and willing to engage with the political history that concerned Iran. Hanau Santini notes that UK Foreign Secretary Jack Straw "formulated an elaborate cultural diplomatic discourse . . . with Iran, where one recognizes the responsibilities and mistakes of both sides."[99] In July 2004 Straw said:

> Part of the problem that we have in terms of our relations with Iran go back to our domination of that region. We had been instrumental in putting the Shah's father on the throne and many aspects of the Shah's regime were brutal, repressive, sought to strike out Iran's past and also its Islamic heritage and its Islamic beliefs. So those things are associated in many Iranians' minds with the United Kingdom. I happen to believe that the approach that we in the United Kingdom Government have adopted in recent years is the correct approach. Iran is a very important country, it is the dominant player in the region so you can't ignore it and I think that the approach that we have adopted and I'm working very closely with France and Germany particularly on the nuclear dossier is the correct approach.[100]

On October 21, 2004, the E3 offered a new agreement to Iran. The EU would provide civilian nuclear technology to Iran in exchange for Iran terminating its uranium enrichment program forever. Iran protested that it still had a right to enrich materials, but it agreed to freeze that enrichment in the Paris Agreement of November 14. In the agreement, the "E3/EU recognize Iran's rights under the NPT . . . without discrimination."[101] The EU would also support Iran joining the World Trade Organization (WTO), and Iran promised to "combat terrorism, including the activities of Al-Qaeda." The shared narrative embodied in the Paris Agreement worked across several discourses then: primarily the legal-technical, but also those of sovereignty and security. The EU offered Iran recognition as a sovereign state that could potentially join others in the World Trade Organization, while Iran was willing to recognize the EU's concerns about terrorism.

Iran's failure to comply with the terms of the Paris agreement ushered in a second cycle. In 2005, Iranian President Ahmadinejad and US Secretary of State Condoleezza Rice made dramatic speeches at the UN, taking the issue into a political order and away from legal-scientific order. The EU presented itself as let down by Iran, and as aligning with the US in raising the prospect of action against Iran.

In August 2005 Iran rejected the European Union offer of incentives in exchange for guarantees it would not pursue nuclear weaponry. Tehran announced it had resumed uranium conversion at Isfahan. Iran opted out of the Paris Agreement because the agreement entailed permanent cessation of enrichment. EU3 offers of economic and civilian power incentives were derided by Iran as "very insulting and humiliating."[102] Permanent cessation would violate Iran's rights under the NPT to develop nuclear energy. The IAEA called on Iran to "return to the negotiating process" and the EU3 continued with their narrative of multilateralism.[103] But Iran had moved on. Ahmadinejad had taken the presidency and presented Iran's nuclear program using theological and justice-based orders of justification not present in EU3 or IAEA documents, thereby putting the issue in an entirely different context and long-term narrative. On September 17, 2005, Ahmadinejad made a speech to the UN.[104] The speech was rich in its scope and the complexity with which he articulated different orders as these were woven into a coherent strategic narrative.

In his speech to the UN, Ahmadinejad argued that the only hope for international peace was an order built on "the two pillars of justice and spirituality." Humans in the West had departed from these because of a lack of religious faith stemming from the primacy of enlightenment thinking and scientific knowledge and exclusion of "Divine knowledge" or "knowledge based on revelation." This was shifting, however: "With the passing of the era of agnostic philosophies, today humanity is once again joined in celebrating monotheism and belief in the Creator as the originator of existence." In contrast to the linear temporalities we find with US and EU3 speeches, oriented toward narratives of solving immediate problems, Ahmadinejad offered a cyclical history, a return to "an auspicious beginning" in which faith is rediscovered. The "ending" of the narrative, he suggested, would occur when a messianic figure arrived, "the emergence of a perfect human being [who would] lead the world to justice and absolute peace." By returning the international system to principles of spirituality and justice, Iran was helping to establish the conditions for this perfect being to arrive, God's "last repository."

Ranging across theological, sovereignty, and legal/technical discourses, Ahmadinejad presented Iran within an equivalence of "all peoples and nations" but argued that Iran had been denied this equivalence, signaling a lack of justice. This demonstrated the immoral or hypocritical position of the US and EU3—their lack of spirituality. In short, he responded to their strategic narratives, in which Iran was positioned as at fault or guilty, by shifting the blame within the same discourses they used for justification, but using additional theological and justice-based discourses to reinforce his argument and produce a more comprehensive narrative.

A process of competitive renarration of the issue followed in the coming months, as Iran, the US, IAEA, and EU3 responded to each others' narratives but shifted the emphasis. For instance, on January 13, 2006, the EU renarrated the account given by Iran. Where Iranian communiqués of this period began their narrative by restating the original NPT principles, the EU3 began with Iran's deception of the international community unmasked in 2003. While the EU3 could have immediately gone to the UNSC, it took a diplomatic approach, to give the fallen Iran a chance to redeem itself: "Given Iran's documented record of concealment and deception, the need for Iran to build confidence has been and continues to be the heart of the matter."[105] However, by returning to uranium enrichment in the summer of 2005 Iran had let down the EU again. Ever since Iran was referred to the UNSC there had been "disturbing questions about Iran's links with the AQ Khan network, which helped build Libya and North Korea's clandestine military nuclear programs." Nonetheless, the EU3 had been prepared to go the extra mile and had offered additional talks, but Iran had rejected their good faith. "The Iranian government now seems intent on turning its back on better relations," the EU3 wrote, harming its economic, political, and technological progress. Faced with this impasse, the E3/EU felt it had no choice but to call in a higher authority: "We believe the time has now come for the Security Council to become involved."

The EU3's narrative of "good faith" betrayed by Iran's truculence was misguided in a number of ways. It ignored the domestic pressures on Ahmadinejad. It ignored the hypocrisies in its own position and the fact that the implementation of the NPT was uneven around the world. However, as Hanau Santini argues, the main consequence of the EU's narrative was that it trapped itself into justifying coercion.[106] Diplomacy had failed because Iran simply could not be reasoned with—it was not "rational," German Foreign Minister Joschka Fischer said.[107] Such a narrative would embolden those seeking to use military means to change Iran's behavior and who understood the world in terms of actor types, for instance rogue states, as Bush had presented Iran as in 2002. Hence, in the US National Security Strategy of March 2006, when the US president presented the latest iteration of the US strategic narrative, it took the terms of the EU's own narrative by 2006, but was more explicit than the EU about the possible consequences or ending of the story: "The United States has joined with our EU partners and Russia to pressure Iran to meet its international obligations and provide objective guarantees that its nuclear program is only for peaceful purposes. This diplomatic effort must succeed *if confrontation is to be avoided.*"[108]

By early 2006 the EU had become sidelined. The Paris Agreement had failed and the EU had gone from narrative alignment with Iran and the IAEA to an unforeseen narrative overlap with the Bush administration. Through

2006–8, a third cycle saw an increase in pressure on all sides as Iran continued to fail to meet expectations about cooperating with the IAEA and evidence became disputed.

This cycle began with the March 2006 US National Security Strategy. That document represented the Iran nuclear problem as a byproduct of a more profound obstacle to peaceful order: Iran's regime itself. The "ultimate goal of U.S. policy" was to get Iran to "open up its political system, and afford freedom to its people."[109] Drawing on a geopolitical discourse rather than science or theology, the US argued it was now willing to take the lead on the issue. Iran might learn a lesson from how the US treated Saddam Hussein: "Saddam's strategy of bluff, denial and deception is a dangerous game that dictators play at their peril." His failure to prove Iraq was free of WMD set a precedent: "It was his refusal to remove the ambiguity that he created that forced the United States and its allies to act."[110] Could Iran prove it was not developing nuclear capacities that could be used for weapons?

"Our answer to those who are angry about Iran achieving the full nuclear fuel cycle," replied Ahmadinejad the next month, "is just one phrase. We say: 'Be angry at us and die of this anger.'"[111] Yet on May 8, 2006, Ahmadinejad took the unprecedented, dramatic step of sending a 3,901-word letter to President Bush and making that letter publicly available on the Internet, in English and Farsi. In the letter, Ahmadinejad responded directly to the US narrative about the nature of the international system and the question of whether Iran's defiance was the "test" or obstacle that had to be addressed for world society to move forward. The White House refused to respond to the content of the letter, but this can be interpreted as a miscalculation given that world opinion could read the letter and see Ahmadinejad's attempt to reach out. Ahmadinejad took a risk, for he could not anticipate how the letter would be interpreted around the world, or how Bush and his officials would respond. It also illustrates that what is significant is not necessarily the content of a narrative, but the manner of its projection and circulation.[112] Rejecting the letter would eventually trap the US. When Colin Powell told reporters, "We don't negotiate with evil," this strengthened the position of hawks in the US[113] and it was not until the Obama presidency that the US would be able to seek to engage diplomatically with Iran in a credible way.

Diplomacy was off the table. With no prospect of Iran accepting the P5+1 proposal or offer greater cooperation with the IAEA, UNSC resolution 1696 was adopted on July 31, 2006. If Iran had not fully cooperated with the IAEA by August 31, then the UNSC would decide upon sanctions that would be applied to Iran. In terms of our analysis, it is noteworthy that when the resolution was debated at the UN, the Iranian delegate, Javad Zarif, explicitly claimed that for some years US strategy had been to move the debate from the legal and technical orders of justification to a geopolitical order. "All along," Zarif said, "the threats by some to bring this issue before the Council and *take it out of its proper technical and negotiated structure* has loomed large over the negotiations."[114] He concluded by calling into question the intention of those trying to shift the discourse, yet he also then returned to the geopolitical register, arguing they would fail; the Iranian revolutionary state "had showed, time and again, their resilience in the face of pressure, threat, injustice and imposition."[115] In other words, having criticized the US for doing so, Zarif himself shifted to the geopolitical discourse using terms that would resonate with domestic publics in Iran.

The deadline for Iran to comply with UNSC Resolution 1696 passed on August 31, 2006, paving the way for sanctions. A few months later, on November 29, 2006, Ahmadinejad addressed a speech to the American people offering a narrative of US failure as a nation and actor in international affairs.[116] On December 23 the UN Security Council[117] passed Resolution 1737 imposing sanctions on materials related to missile technologies reaching Iran. These sanctions would be enhanced in March 2007 in UNSC Resolution 1747. Ahmadinejad responded by announcing that Iran had begun a new program of uranium enrichment at Natanz. He said, "With great honour, I declare that as of today our dear country has joined the nuclear club of nations."[118] Iran was positioned to do so partly because the IAEA had grown exasperated with US attempts to use intelligence to characterize Iran's intentions as disingenuous. In February 2007 the IAEA said of US intelligence, "Since 2002, pretty much all the intelligence that's come to us has proved to be wrong,"[119] and again in October the IAEA's Mohamed ElBaradei said he was worried about growing rhetoric from the US about Iran.[120] The likelihood of a military response from the US was also *seen to be* low when a survey of US foreign policy elites by *Foreign Policy* magazine showed little support for intervention.[121] The new media ecology made US intentions transparent to Iran. Hence, all parties became locked in rounds of threats of sanctions.

Finally, in 2009–10 both President Obama and the IAEA's ElBaradei called for a new start, with the EU sidelined and new actors emerging—Israel, Brazil, and Turkey all became part of any narrative about Iran's nuclear program. Iran and the US continued to present the issue through highly politicized narratives that ran parallel to one another, each using the nuclear issue to present different visions for the future of the international system and each presenting the other as flawed characters intent on obstructing a path to that future.

What narrative did the new US administration present to Iran? On the one hand, President Obama used his inaugural address to say, "To those who cling to power through corruption and deceit and the silencing of dissent, know that you are on the wrong side of history, but that *we will extend a hand if you are willing to unclench your fist.*"[122] He repeated the unclenched fist metaphor on Al Arabiya television on January 27, 2009. However, the US also used language to exert pressure. On April 22, 2009, US Secretary of State Hillary Clinton warned Iran of "crippling sanctions" if it did not enter negotiations, and spoke openly of its plans for a new regional security architecture, including US missiles based in Europe to guard against a nuclear Iran.[123] On Obama's more diplomatic approach to Iran, on August 6, 2009, US Secretary of State Hillary Clinton said, "We're not going to keep the window open forever."[124] Nevertheless, Obama at least acknowledged the longer history between the two countries. In his Cairo speech on June 4 he said:

> This issue has been a source of tension between the United States and the Islamic Republic of Iran. For many years, Iran has defined itself in part by its opposition to my country, and there is in fact a tumultuous history between us. In the middle of the Cold War, the United States played a role in the overthrow of a democratically elected Iranian government. Since the Islamic Revolution, Iran has played a role in acts of hostage-taking and violence against U.S. troops and civilians. This history is well known. Rather than remain trapped in the past, I've made it clear to Iran's leaders and people that my country is prepared to move forward. The question now is not what Iran is against, but rather what future it wants to build.
>
> I recognize it will be hard to overcome decades of mistrust, but we will proceed with courage, rectitude, and resolve. There will be many issues to discuss between our two countries, and we are willing to move forward without preconditions on the basis of mutual respect. But it is clear to all concerned that when it comes to nuclear weapons, we have reached a decisive point. This is not simply about America's interests. It's about preventing a nuclear arms race in the Middle East that could lead this region and the world down a hugely dangerous path.[125]

That same month the IAEA also offered a new start, a new narrative. "We have been going round in circles," declared IAEA Director General ElBaradei on June 17, 2009.[126] It had taken the IAEA twenty years to verify nuclear facilities in North Korea. The NPT was pointless because nuclear weapons states ignored it, continuing to expand their arsenals. "I would even dare say that we are not very useful," he admitted. However, Iran rejected a new IAEA fuel swap plan in which Iran's nuclear materials would be enriched overseas, saying this contradicted its right as a sovereign state under the NPT.

Hard-line responses followed from the UK[127] and US.[128] The EU instead created a new position, High Representative of the Union for Foreign Affairs and Security Policy, which was filled by the UK's Cathy Ashton. Her narrative on Iran was bureaucratic in content, stressing the legitimacy of the negotiation process, but again Iran was cast in the position of the character preventing cooperation and movement: "If Iran sets out on a more constructive course on the nuclear issue and on regional stability in general," she said, "it could play an important role in the Middle East and Gulf region, which would reflect its rightful place and proud history."[129] She spoke of Iran in terms of its economic potential but also its human rights problems.

The EU's position by 2010 reinforced a decontextualized view that Iran's reluctance to engage, rather than the terms of engagement, was responsible for the stalling of talks. Ashton asserted that, "We are ready, and have been since our last E3+3 meeting in October, to meet with Iranian officials to discuss international concerns about Iran's nuclear program."[130]

By early 2010, when we end this analysis, there was a narrative mirroring between the US and Iran, as each believed the other to be undermining the international system and progress on the nuclear issue because of deficiencies of character. The EU and IAEA could only offer a narrative promoting a return to the negotiating table and seek to limit any provocative language used by the US or Iran. The EU had led negotiations in 2002–4 and reached narrative alignment; by 2010 it was sidelined and there was little possibility of narrative alignment between the US and Iran.

In summary, the actors in this analysis have tried to make the others understand the international system and the nuclear issue through the terms of their own strategic narratives: their preferred vision of the international system, the obstacles it faces, the characterization of those involved, and the possible benign or malignant endings the future might hold. If other states' leaders and publics begin to act as if that narrative is desirable and build expectations based on that narrative unfolding, this offers the state that formed and projected that narrative a tremendous advantage in international relations.

This has entailed a lot of narrative work by these actors. Throughout these four cycles, certain objects and processes keep occurring and it is a continual challenge for actors to integrate these into their narratives. For example, the role of intelligence and certain spies and defectors, the science of nuclear processing and weaponizing, and the personality of individual leaders must all become narrativized, given character and meaning within the narratives the EU, US, and Iran tell. Some skill has been needed to identify the optimal times to take into account others' narratives, claims, and grievances, and when to switch from one discourse to another, thus undercutting the basis of other actors' narratives.

Throughout this period, the strategic narratives of the US, Iran, and IAEA were largely unchanged. The EU's strategic narrative shifted in 2005 when Iran would not implement the Paris Agreement of November 2004. As European leaders argued that reaching a deal with Iran was difficult because it was not "rational," so this undermined the credibility of diplomacy and opened a space for hawks in Europe, the US, and Iran. The 2006 US National Security Strategy began then to talk of "confrontation"; thereafter, dialogue broke down and a series of UN resolutions followed.

Actors did try to harness global media to shift the terms of debate, particularly when negotiations had reached an impasse for some years. Ahmadinejad and Obama have made the most dramatic efforts to make use of this ecology. Ahmadinejad's 2006 letter to President Bush, the first direct communication since 1979, was posted on the Internet for the world to read and for the world to see that Ahmadinejad was making the first move of conciliation. Obama's Cairo speech symbolized both "engagement" and "a new start." The IAEA even went public in 2008 to criticize US intelligence and hype about Iranian nuclear weaponization. However, it is arguable whether any of these acts made much difference to the likelihood of political agreement or strengthened those actors' positions.

This case study shows the limits of persuasion and communication: states can understand each other clearly and disagree. The US, Iran, EU, and IAEA know how the others are using communication, and even show reflexivity on occasion about this. Communication is just as much a way to wriggle free of agreement as to trap others into agreement or action.

CONCLUSION: THE MYTHS AND REALITIES OF CONTESTATION

This chapter has set out two dimensions of contestation we must consider to explain the role of strategic narratives in international relations. The first is a spectrum of persuasion. At one end are thin analyses that seek to explain how actors in a given system and situation seek to use narratives to trap, coerce, and undermine other actors in order to maneuver their behavior. At the other end are thick analyses that seek to explain how system, actor, or issue narratives are formed and become uncontested in the first place. In between are analyses of communicative action and reflexive actors, who look at how actors use narratives to shape each other's identities and interests and exploit each other's anxieties and narrative weaknesses to alter their behavior and their sense of self. Where to make the cut on this spectrum depends on the question being asked. And each approach offers a different measure of success and explains a different type of victory. Second, we introduced a set of aspects of narratives that are contested. This set involves qualities of the narrative itself, including its informational and emotional content, its epistemology or the form of truth it offers, the degree of ambiguity the narrative offers, and the narrative's relation to actual events and actions in the world. The practices of narrative formation, projection, and reception can also be contested. Consequently, understanding how narrative contestation operates can entail taking into account a range of processes, drawing on concepts from the study of media and communication as well as the study of international relations. We then illustrated how the spectrum of persuasion and aspects of narrative contestation play out by focusing on three case studies, the cases of Israel and its neighbors, the anti-whaling struggle, and contestation over the future of Iran's nuclear program.

This spectrum is evident in these three case studies. We find varying degrees and kinds of persuasion being achieved through actors' use of strategic narratives, and a range of types of effects on others' actions and even subjectivities. For Israel and its rivals, events unfolded as material to reinforce one's own narrative and challenge those of others, with the aim being to convince domestic and international publics and policy makers of the virtues of one's interests, identity, and goals. Achieving any long-term shift in others' understanding of one's country in this region is probably beyond the reach of any generation of leaders. It may need particularly far-sighted leaders to move Israel's conflicts from the issue/locale-specific narrative domain to that of system narratives; a resolution would be part of a new kind of international system or order altogether. For the anti-whaling activists, a long-term shift in attitudes and behavior was achieved on an impressive geographical scale and in a relatively short period. By crafting compelling narratives from prevailing Cold War and environmental discourses, and representing these visually through symbolic spectacles, activists were able to put whales and whaling within an entirely different set of meanings. Within a few decades, individual consumer-citizens and their elected representatives understood themselves to be living in a world in which killing whales was wrong and the international system was moving toward a state free of whaling. The discourses' generative power enabled a more behavioral exercise of power, resulting both in the constitution of new subjectivities and the organization of new behaviors around whaling production and consumption. Finally, getting others to buy in to a new narrative understanding was beyond any actors involved in diplomacy around Iran's nuclear program. For a brief period in 2003–4 the EU and Iran took into account each other's understandings. The EU publicly acknowledged Western involvement in Iran's recent history, its energy and security needs, and its right as an NPT signatory, while Iran acknowledged the EU's wishes to move toward a rule-governed, multilateral order. The two parties moved onto overlapping discursive ground. However, Iran's behavior and switch to a blood-over-the-sword narrative, reinforced by a parallel US narrative of distrust and antagonism, has since made any narrative alignment impossible. Consequently, the EU and IAEA have been unable to create a strategic narrative in which the US and Iran would buy into an agreement.

These case studies demonstrate how narrative contestation works in international relations; how the formation, projection, and reception of narratives in complex media ecologies can, under certain conditions, achieve discernible effects. We hope it is striking how difficult achieving strategic narrative success can be, however success is defined. And for that very reason, we hope readers will not take our argument as one more template for success in strategic communication or soft power. Yes, practitioners can learn to achieve short-term gains in the management of public opinion around specific issues and campaigns. But achieving long-term shifts in the meaning of international relations to others entails confronting how interests and identity form, and the limits of control any actor can have over these processes.

We wish to caution, then, against the construction of myths about narrative contestation. The sound bite "battle of the narratives" has an intuitive commonsense appeal that short-circuits further investigation into what the phrase could ever mean in practice. There is power in creating the template of successful contestation. In 1979 in Iran, the distant Ayatollah spread cassettes, moving from excluded and weak to included, strong, and in power. This case upset conventional wisdom and became a new textbook example.[131] From that point, strategic communication practitioners sought to learn from such events, look for such events, and (based on our conversations with leaders in this field) even try to create such events. More recently a new template for strategic communication took hold: Tahrir Square, the Arab Spring, and the myth of a Facebook revolution. It created expectation of further such results, and consequent support for the expansion of social media. We know there are templates of successful military action. Steele[132] argues these often have an aesthetic quality: a state's military moved with speed, grace, and precision. So, too, we see templates of beautiful persuasion and diplomatic maneuvering. These must be avoided.

Strategic narratives are an instrument of persuasion, tools of behavioral power and constitutive power. These two forms of power work in tandem. For all the skill that narrative practitioners can wield, any form of persuasion depends on the audience and the narrative work of other actors at the time. There are structural constraints within the nation and in international political and media systems. Leaders must assume that the likelihood of strategic narrative success will be low unless certain conditions are in place.

We have approached the questions of strategic narrative contestation and victory in our own way, and doubtless rationalist and communicative action scholars might defend their own analytic approaches to the same questions. However, we have articulated why our approach responds to specific processes. Brent Steele has called for a "productive dialogue between traditions" and it is in this spirit that we advance our approach to strategic narrative, which is one—important—phenomenon in communications and international relations.

In the next chapter we turn to another dimension of persuasion and contestation: the information infrastructure within which communication occurs. Control the infrastructure, win the narrative battle?

NOTES

1. Madeleine Albright, "MFN for China Would Advance America's Leadership in Asia," Senate Finance Committee, June 6, 1997, accessed May 21, 2013, http://www.usembassy-israel.org.il/publish/press/state/archive/1997/june/sd90612.htm.
2. Joseph S. Nye, Jr., "American and Chinese Power after the Financial Crisis," *The Washington Quarterly* 33 (2010): 149, 151.
3. At the time that this was being discussed, South Africa had not yet become part of the BRIC nations.
4. Robert B. Cooper, *The Breaking of Nations: Order and Chaos in the Twenty-First Century* (New York: Atlantic Books, 2004).
5. Jens Ringsmose and Berit K. Børgensen, "Shaping Public Attitudes toward the Deployment of Military Power: NATO, Afghanistan and the Use of Strategic Narratives," *European Security* 20 (2011).

6. Government of Canada, "Canada's Approach in Afghanistan," last modified August 24, 2011, accessed April 14, 2013, http://www.afghanistan.gc.ca/canada-afghanistan/approach-approche/index.aspx?lang=eng.
7. A similar question is asked in Diana Panke and Ulrich Petersohn, "Why International Norms Disappear Sometimes," *European Journal of International Relations* 18 (2012).
8. Michael Cox, "Power Shifts, Economic Change and the Decline of the West?" *International Relations* 26 (2012).
9. Brent J. Steele, *Defacing Power* (Ann Arbor: University of Michigan Press, 2012).
10. Ronald R. Krebs and Patrick Thaddeus Jackson, "Twisting Tongues and Twisting Arms: The Power of Political Rhetoric," *European Journal of International Relations* 13, no. 1 (2007).
11. Krebs and Jackson, "Twisting Tongues," 38, 41.
12. Robert M. Entman, *Projections of Power: Framing News, Public Opinion, and US Foreign Policy* (Chicago: University of Chicago Press, 2009); Patrick Thaddeus Jackson, "Defending the West: Occidentalism and the Formation of NATO," *Journal of Political Philosophy* 11, no. 3 (2003).
13. Marc Lynch, "Why Engage? China and the Logic of Communicative Engagement," *European Journal of International Relations* 8, no. 2 (2002): 214.
14. Jackson, "Defending the West."
15. David Campbell, *Writing Security* (Minneapolis: University of Minnesota Press, 1992).
16. Jackson, "Defending the West," 235.
17. Diana Coole, "Rethinking Agency: A Phenomenological Approach to Embodiment and Agentic Capacities," *Political Studies* 53, no. 1 (2005).
18. This dynamic is explored in Charlotte Epstein's work on norms and whaling. See for example: Charlotte Epstein, *The Power of Words in International Relations: Birth of an Anti-Whaling Discourse* (Cambridge, MA: MIT Press, 2008); Charlotte Epstein, "Moby Dick or Moby Doll? Discourse or How to Study 'the Social Construction of' All the Way Down." In *Constructing the International Economy*, edited by Rawi Abdelal, Mark Blyth, and Craig Parsons (Ithaca, NY: Cornell University Press, 2010).
19. Thomas Risse, "'Let's Argue!': Communicative Action in World Politics," *International Organization* 54, no. 1 (2000): 19.
20. Krebs and Jackson, "Twisting Tongues," 55; Risse, "'Let's Argue!'" 14–15.
21. Brian S. Brooks, George Kennedy, Daryl R. Moen, and Don Ranly, *News Reporting and Writing* (Boston: Bedford, 2005).
22. Marc J. Hetherington and Michael Nelson, "Anatomy of a Rally Effect: George W. Bush and the War on Terrorism," *Political Science and Politics* 36, no. 1 (2003).
23. Daniel C. Hallin, *The Uncensored War: The Media and Vietnam* (Berkeley: University of California Press, 1989).
24. Walter Benjamin, *Illuminations: Essays and Reflections* (New York: Schocken, 1969).
25. Barry Richards, *Emotional Governance: Politics, Media and Terror* (Basingstoke: Palgrave Macmillan, 2007).
26. William J.T. Mitchell, *Cloning Terror: The War of Images, 9/11 to the Present* (Chicago: University of Chicago Press, 2011), 98.
27. Mitchell, *Cloning Terror.*
28. Michael Freeden, *The Political Theory of Politics*, Full Research Report ESRC End of Award Report, RES-051-27–0098 (Swindon: ESRC, 2008).
29. Ringsmose and Børgensen, "Shaping Public Attitudes," 516.

30. Laura Roselle, *Media and the Politics of Failure: Great Powers, Communication Strategies, and Military Defeats,* 2nd ed. (New York: Palgrave Macmillan, 2011).
31. Roselle, *Media and the Politics of Failure.*
32. Jeffrey W. Legro, *Rethinking the World: Great Power Strategies and International Order* (Ithaca: Cornell University Press, 2005).
33. Vivien A. Schmidt, "Does Discourse Matter in the Politics of Welfare State Adjustment?" *Comparative Political Studies* 35, no. 2 (2002); Vivien A. Schmidt, and Claudio M. Radaelli, "Policy Change and Discourse in Europe: Conceptual and Methodological Issues," *West European Politics* 27, no. 2 (2004).
34. Tom Dyson, *Neoclassical Realism and Defence Reform in Post–Cold War Europe* (Basingstoke: Palgrave Macmillan, 2010).
35. Graeme A. M. Davies, "Coercive Diplomacy Meets Diversionary Incentives: The Impact of US and Iranian Domestic Politics during the Bush and Obama Presidencies," *Foreign Policy Analysis* 8, no. 3 (2012).
36. M. J. Williams, "(Un)Sustainable Peacebuilding: NATO's Suitability for Postconflict Reconstruction in Multiactor Environments," *Global Governance: A Review of Multilateralism and International Organizations* 17, no. 1 (2011).
37. Monroe Price, *Fierceness of Competition, Softness of Power: Freedom of Expression in a Time of Strategic Communicators* (forthcoming).
38. Janice Bially Mattern, *Ordering International Politics: Identity, Crisis, and Representational Force* (New York: Routledge, 2005), 14.
39. Richard K. Betts, "Is Strategy an Illusion?" *International Security* 25, no. 2 (2000).
40. David A. Lake, *Hierarchy in International Relations* (Ithaca, NY: Cornell University Press, 2009).
41. Jennifer Mitzen, "Governing Together: Global Governance as Collective Intention," in *Arguing Global Governance: Agency, Lifeworld and Shared Reasoning,* edited by Corneliu Bjola and Markus Kornprobst (London: Routledge, 2010); Jennifer Mitzen, "Ontological Security in World Politics: State Identity and the Security Dilemma," *European Journal of International Relations* 12, no. 3 (2006): 363.
42. Lara Nettelfield, *Courting Democracy in Bosnia and Herzegovina: The Hague Tribunal's Impact in a Postwar State* (New York: Cambridge University Press, 2010), 174–5, 192–209.
43. Martha Minow, "Stories in Law," in *Law's Stories: Narrative and Rhetoric in the Law,* edited by Peter Brooks and Paul Gewirtz (New Haven, CT: Yale University Press, 1996), 32–33.
44. Nettelfield, *Courting Democracy,* 178.
45. See also Lara Nettelfield, "Research and Repercussions of Death Tolls: The Case of the Bosnian Book of the Dead," in *Sex, Drugs, and Body Counts: The Politics of Numbers in Global Crime and Conflict,* edited by Peter Andreas and Kelly M. Greenhill (Ithaca, NY: Cornell University Press, 2010).
46. Nik Gowing, *"Skyful of Lies" and Black Swans: The New Tyranny of Shifting Information Power in Crises* (Oxford: Reuters Institute for the Study of Journalism, University of Oxford, 2009), 50; Andrew Hoskins and Ben O'Loughlin, *War and Media: The Emergence of Diffused War* (Cambridge: Polity, 2010); Ben D. Mor, "Public Diplomacy in Grand Strategy," *Foreign Policy Analysis* 2, no. 2 (2006): 165.
47. Ben D. Mor, "Using Force to Save Face: The Performative Side of War," *Peace & Change* 37, no. 1 (2012); see also Steele, *Defacing Power.*
48. Mor, "Public Diplomacy."

49. Emile Simpson, *War from the Ground Up: Twenty-First-Century Combat as Politics* (London: Hurst, 2012), 179.
50. Mor, "Public Diplomacy," 163.
51. Mor, "Public Diplomacy," 166.
52. Simpson, *War from the Ground Up*, 181.
53. Bially-Mattern, *Ordering International Politics*.
54. Mor, "Public Diplomacy," 167.
55. Ben D. Mor, "The Rhetoric of Public Diplomacy and Propaganda Wars: A View from Self-Presentation Theory," *European Journal of Political Research* 46, no. 5 (2007).
56. Ben D. Mor, "The Rhetoric of Public Diplomacy and Propaganda Wars," 675.
57. Mor, "Public Diplomacy," 173.
58. Mor, "Public Diplomacy," 173.
59. Mor, "Using Force to Save Face."
60. Cited in Ben D. Mor, "Accounts and Impression Management in Public Diplomacy: Israeli Justification of Force during the 2006 Lebanon War," *Global Change, Peace & Security* 21, no. 2 (2009): 234.
61. Mor, "Using Force to Save Face," 111.
62. Mor, "Using Force to Save Face," 112.
63. Mor, "Accounts and Impression Management."
64. Ben D. Mor, "Credibility Talk in Public Diplomacy," *Review of International Studies* 38, no. 2 (2012).
65. Mor, "Credibility Talk."
66. Cited in Mor, "Using Force to Save Face," 115.
67. Mor, "Accounts and Impression Management," 224.
68. Mor, "Credibility Talk," 394.
69. Mor, "Credibility Talk."
70. Mor, "Public Diplomacy," 173.
71. Mor, "Using Force to Save Face," 103.
72. Bernard Stiegler, *For a New Critique of Political Economy* (Cambridge: Polity, 2009).
73. BBC News, "Nine Killed as Afghans Rage at US," May 13, 2005, accessed May 21, 2013, http://news.bbc.co.uk/2/hi/south_asia/4544833.stm; Philip Seib, *The Al Jazeera Affect: How the New Global Media are Reshaping World Politics* (Washington, DC: Potomac Books, 2009), 52.
74. Ben O'Loughlin, "Images as Weapons of War: Representation, Mediation and Interpretation," *Review of International Studies* 37, no. 1 (2011).
75. Richard C. Eichenberg, "Victory Has Many Friends: U.S. Public Opinion and the Use of Military Force, 1981–2005," *International Security* 30, no. 1 (2005).
76. Susan Sontag, *Regarding the Pain of Others* (New York: Farrar, Straus and Giroux, 2003), 32–33, italics added.
77. Epstein, *The Power of Words*, vii.
78. Kevin M. DeLuca, *Image Politics: The New Rhetoric of Environmental Activism, Revisioning Rhetoric* (New York: Guilford Press, 1999).
79. Epstein, *The Power of Words*, 100.
80. Epstein, *The Power of Words*, 142.
81. Cited in Epstein, *The Power of Words*, 144.
82. Epstein, *The Power of Words*, 10.
83. Epstein, *The Power of Words*, 92–93.
84. For example: Emile Hokayem, "Foreign Policy: The Middle East Channel—The War of Narratives," *International Institute for Strategic Studies*, February 8, 2011, accessed May 21, 2013, http://www.iiss.org/whats-new/iiss-in-the-press/press-coverage-2011/february-2011/the-war-of-narratives/;

Ministry of Defence, "Strategic Communication: The Defence Contribution," Joint Doctrine Note 1/11, accessed May 23, 2013, http://www.mod.uk/NR/rdonlyres/7DAE5158-63AD-444D-9A3F-83F7D8F44F9A/0/20110310JDN111_STRAT_COMM.pdf; Wayne Porter and Mark Mykleby, *A National Strategic Narrative* (Washington, DC: Woodrow Wilson Center, 2011), accessed May 21, 2013, http://www.wilsoncenter.org/sites/default/files/A%20National%20Strategic%20Narrative.pdf.

85. Shahram Chubin, "The Iranian Nuclear Riddle after June 12," *The Washington Quarterly* 33, no. 1 (2010).

86. Wyn Q. Bowen and Jonathan Brewer, "Iran's Nuclear Challenge: Nine Years and Counting," *International Affairs* 87, no. 4 (2011): 925.

87. Fareed Zakaria, *The Post-American World* (London: Penguin, 2009), 235.

88. Mohamed ElBaradei, "Director General's Intervention on Non-Proliferation Issues at IAEA Board of Governors," International Atomic Energy Agency, June 17, 2009, accessed April 4, 2013, http://www.iaea.org/newscenter/statements/2009/ebsp2009n007.html.

89. George W. Bush, State of the Union Address, January 29, 2002 (Charlottesville: University of Virginia, Miller Center, 2013), transcript of published text of speech, accessed May 20, 2013, http://millercenter.org/president/speeches/detail/4540.

90. Felix S. Berenskoetter, "Mapping the Mind Gap: A Comparison of US and European Security Strategies," *Security Dialogue* 36, no. 1 (2005); Sven Biscop, *The European Security Strategy: A Global Agenda for Positive Power* (Abingdon: Ashgate, 2005); Roland Dannreuther and John Peterson, *Security Strategy and Transatlantic Relations* (London: Routledge, 2006).

91. IAEA, "Implementation of the NPT Safeguards Agreement in the Islamic Republic of Iran," GOV/2003/63, August 26, 2003, accessed April 4, 2013, http://www.iaea.org/Publications/Documents/Board/2003/gov2003-63.pdf.

92. Iran Ministry for Foreign Affairs, "Statement by the Iranian Government and visiting EU Foreign Ministers," *NuclearFiles.org*, October 21, 2003 (Santa Barbara, CA: Nuclear Age Peace Foundation, 1998–2013), accessed May 21, 2013, http://www.nuclearfiles.org/menu/key-issues/nuclear-weapons/issues/proliferation/iran/statement-visiting-eu-ministers.htm.

93. Iran Ministry for Foreign Affairs, "Statement," 3b, italics added.

94. White House, *The National Security Strategy of the United States of America*, Washington, DC: White House, September 2002, accessed May 21, 2013, http://www.state.gov/documents/organization/63562.pdf.

95. Office of the Director of National Intelligence, *Iran: Nuclear Intentions and Capabilities, National Intelligence Estimate*, November 2007, accessed April 4, 2013, http://graphics8.nytimes.com/packages/pdf/international/20071203_release.pdf, no page; for further explanation see Andrew Parasiliti, "Iran: Diplomacy and Deterrence," *Survival* 51, no. 5 (2009): 8.

96. IAEA, "Implementation of the NPT Safeguards Agreement in the Islamic Republic of Iran," GOV/2004/11, February 24, 2004, accessed May 21, 2013, http://www.iaea.org/Publications/Documents/Board/2004/gov2004-11.pdf, 12.

97. IAEA, "Communication on 5 March 2004 from the Permanent Mission of the Islamic Republic of Iran Concerning the Report of the Director General contained in GOV/2004/11," INFCIRC/628, March 5, 2004, accessed May 21, 2013, http://www.iaea.org/Publications/Documents/Infcircs/2004/infcirc628.pdf, 6.

98. Cited in Robert E. Hunter, "Engage, Don't Isolate, Iran," Rand Corporation, June 27, 2004, accessed April 4, 2013, http://www.rand.org/commentary/2004/06/27/SDT.html.

99. Ruth Hanau Santini, "European Union Discourses and Practices on the Iranian Nuclear Programme," *European Security* 19, no. 3 (2010): 477.

100. Jack Straw, "Interview with Foreign Secretary Jack Straw on UK Diplomatic Relations with Iran," UK Foreign and Commonwealth Office, July 4, 2004, accessed April 5, 2013, http://www.iranwatch.org/government/UK/uk-mfa-strawinterview-070404.htm.

101. IAEA, "Iran-EU Agreement on Nuclear Programme," November14, 2004, accessed April 5, 2013, http://www.iaea.org/newscenter/focus/iaeairan/eu_iran14112004.shtml.

102. *The Age*, "Iran Resumes Uranium Processing," August 9, 2005, accessed December 3, 2012, http://www.theage.com.au/news/world/iran-resumes-uranium-processing/2005/08/09/1123353289095.html.

103. IAEA, "Implementation of the NPT Safeguards Agreement in the Islamic Republic of Iran," GOV/2005/77, September24, 2005, accessed December 3, 2012, http://www.iaea.org/Publications/Documents/Board/2005/gov2005-77.pdf, 3.

104. Mahmood Ahmadinejad, "Address by H.E. Dr. Mahmood Ahmadinejad President of the Islamic Republic of Iran before the Sixtieth Session of the United Nations General Assembly," New York, September 17, 2005, accessed May 21, 2013, http://www.un.org/webcast/ga/60/statements/iran050917eng.pdf.

105. IAEA, "Communication Dated 13 January 2006 Received from the Permanent Missions of France, Germany and the United Kingdom to the Agency," INFCIRC/662, January13, 2006, accessed April 4, 2013, http://www.iaea.org/Publications/Documents/Infcircs/2006/infcirc662.pdf, 1.

106. Hanau Santini, "European Union Discourses"; see also Frank Schimmelfennig, "The Community Trap: Liberal Norms, Rhetorical Action, and the Eastern Enlargement of the European Union," *International Organization* 55, no. 1 (2001).

107. Joschka Fischer, "The Case for Bargaining with Iran," *Washington Post*, May 29, 2006, accessed May 21, 2013, http://www.washingtonpost.com/wp-dyn/content/article/2006/05/28/AR2006052800978.html.

108. White House, *The National Security Strategy of the United States of America*, March 2006, accessed April 4, 2013, http://www.comw.org/qdr/fulltext/nss2006.pdf, 20, italics added.

109. White House, *NSS 2006*, 20.

110. White House, *NSS 2006*, 24.

111. Cited in *Los Angeles Times*, "Iran Rejects U.N. Request to Halt Its Nuclear Activity," April14, 2006, accessed April 4, 2013, http://articles.latimes.com/2006/apr/14/world/fg-iran14.

112. Hoskins and O'Loughlin, *War and Media*.

113. Davies, "Coercive Diplomacy."

114. UN Security Council, "Security Council Demands Iran Suspend Uranium Enrichment by 31 August, or Face Possible Economic Sanctions," SC/8792, 5500th Meeting (AM), July 31, 2006, accessed May 21, 2013, http://www.un.org/News/Press/docs/2006/sc8792.doc.htm, italics added.

115. UN Security Council, "Security Council Demands."

116. Mahmood Ahmadinejad, "Message to the American People," November 29, 2006, accessed April 4, 2013, http://www.ahmadinejad.ir/en/Message_to_the_American_People_.

117. UN Security Council, *Resolution 1737*, S/RES/1737, December 23, 2006, accessed April 4, 2013, http://www.cfr.org/iran/un-security-council-resolution-1737-iran/p12334.

118. BBC News, "Iran 'Enters New Nuclear Phase,'" April 9, 2007, accessed April 4, 2013, http://news.bbc.co.uk/1/hi/world/middle_east/6538957.stm.

119. Bob Drogin and Kim Murphy, "U.N. Calls U.S. Data On Iran's Nuclear Aims Unreliable," *Los Angeles Times*, February 25, 2007, accessed May 21, 2013, http://articles.latimes.com/2007/feb/25/world/fg-usiran25.
120. NBC News, "Anti-Iran Rhetoric Worries U.N. Nuke Watchdog," October 28, 2007, accessed July 15, 2013, http://www.nbcnews.com/id/21516968/42739722#.UTTq9Y6PdgM.
121. Davies, "Coercive Diplomacy."
122. Barack Obama, Inaugural Address, Washington, DC, January 20, 2009, accessed April 4, 2013, www.whitehouse.gov/blog/inaugural-address, italics added.
123. Parasiliti, "Iran."
124. Cited in *Belfast Telegraph*, "World News in Brief: Clinton: No Iran Illusions," August 10, 2009, accessed May 21, 2013, http://www.belfasttelegraph.co.uk/news/world-news/world-news-in-brief-clinton-no-iran-illusions-28490233.html.
125. Barack Obama, "Remarks by the President on a New Beginning," Cairo University, Cairo, Egypt, June 4, 2009, accessed May 21, 2013, http://www.whitehouse.gov/the-press-office/remarks-president-cairo-university-6–04–09.
126. ElBaradei, "Director General's Intervention."
127. Julian Borger, Patrick Wintour, and Michael Oliver, "Iran Nuclear Plant: Miliband Refuses to Rule Out Military Action," *The Guardian*, September 26, 2009, accessed May 21, 2013, http://www.guardian.co.uk/world/2009/sep/26/miliband-iran-nuclear-plant.
128. *Haaretz*, "Obama: We'll Mull 'Sanctions that Bite' If Iran Nuclear Talks Fail," September 25, 2009, accessed April 4, 2013, http://www.haaretz.com/news/obama-we-ll-mull-sanctions-that-bite-if-iran-nuclear-talks-fail-1.7174.
129. Catherine Ashton, "Statement on Iran," European Parliament, January 19, 2010, accessed May 21, 2013, http://www.eu-un.europa.eu/articles/en/article_9421_en.htm.
130. Cited in *Trend*, "Iran May Be Willing to Talk on Nuclear Issue, Says EU's Ashton," May 22, 2010, accessed May 21, 2013, http://en.trend.az/regions/iran/1692278.html.
131. Monroe E. Price, *Fierceness of Competition, Softness of Power: Freedom of Expression in a Time of Strategic Communicators* (forthcoming), 131–2.
132. Steele, *Defacing Power*, 43.

5   Information Infrastructure

INTRODUCTION

To understand what difference a strategic narrative makes in international relations, we need to trace its trajectory and explore how it is received and interpreted by its audiences. We need to know how audiences evaluate that narrative alongside other narratives they might routinely hear or believe in, and how they behaved before encountering the strategic narrative and afterwards. We must account for the way in which a narrative is adapted, challenged, repackaged, twisted, and recontextualized as it travels through media ecologies. If policy makers want to know how to win the battle of the narratives, then mapping the circuits of communication, interpretation, and meaning making in media ecologies is a first step.

As if that is not hard enough, we must explain how actors in international relations try to manage and shape those media ecologies to ensure that their narrative gets heard and supported to the maximum degree while others get sidelined. They must exploit the media ecologies of the day, distributing their narrative within national and transnational public spheres, winning the arguments and the framing battles. But they must also compete to shape the infrastructure of these ecologies itself, since that infrastructure privileges certain voices and certain ways of communicating over others. As we suggested in Chapter 1, "Introduction," the United States has pursued an agenda of Internet freedom in the past decade that seeks to accomplish both of these goals. That agenda is made up of both a narrative *in media ecologies* about freedom and technology, and an effort to *shape media ecologies* so more voices can support the freedom narrative. Other actors in international relations are engaged in the same game, trying to ensure that media systems, the distribution of media technologies, and national and international media regulation all privilege their preferred model of communication. Hence, whose narrative "wins" is also a matter of institution-building, technology transfer, and political economy.

To explain the success of strategic narratives requires us to investigate how political actors approach both of these tasks and then analyze the interaction between how narratives circulate in media ecologies and how those narratives shape media ecologies. This chapter explores some of the difficulties that are emerging as states seek to put that interaction into practice. Both the US and UK are trying to both exploit and produce a new kind of media ecology and new hierarchy of international political communication in which "the people" are given an important role as vehicles of strategic narratives. Our analysis focuses on Obama's 2009 Cairo Speech and the BBC World Service's use of its Arabic language service. These cases show the strategic creation of communication spaces. Obama's team and the BBC both tried to cultivate horizontal networks of communication within which certain types of conversation would unfold between citizens in different countries. This is an explicit broadening of the range of actors participating in international relations. However, these were inescapably and transparently top-down efforts by powerful institutions to create bottom-up conversations between equals. Tensions were evident in each case between the intrinsic value of intercultural dialogue on the one hand, and the instrumental, interest-oriented goals of public diplomacy—goals that overseas publics are well aware of. Nevertheless, these are instructive instances of how strategic narrative requires attention to the reception and spaces of reception, not only to a narrative's content, formation, and projection.

We live in a world of actors experiencing different worlds.[1] Relations between actors do not take place in a vacuum, but rather in spaces of encounter. Leaders meet at summits or in bilateral meetings, young policy elites meet on cultural exchange programs or at universities, and publics increasingly meet through online spaces. Actors meet with known characteristics, attributions of power, and some overlapping experiences. Berenskoetter writes, "World politics is not simply about drawing, respecting or contesting demarcations of sovereignty—although this is important—but about negotiating and investing in a shared experience/envisioned space. The last century has produced significant experiences for many communities whose spaces and horizons now overlap, and the many 'inters' formed this way can be both sites of creativity and contestation."[2] It is here that cooperation and conflict can occur. In this chapter we focus on communicative spaces. Here, we can identify effects of narratives in the language used by online participants, in what issues and ideas they are willing to engage, and their attributions of credibility and legitimacy toward leaders and their policies.

We build on the arguments of previous chapters in a number of ways. First, control of infrastructures involves a range of actors with different economic, political, and cultural interests and motives. While states try to steer the development of infrastructure, the role of companies, media organizations, activists, and audiences cannot be overlooked. Second, infrastructure is a vital underpinning of international order. Actors' understandings of the international system, hierarchy, authority, sovereignty, and historical trajectories are generated through communication about these matters. That communication is made possible and shaped in important ways by the information infrastructure of the time. If communication and mediation are becoming more central to the ontology of international relations, then any account of that ontology must address the role of infrastructure. Third, narrative contestation occurs in the communication spaces these infrastructures enable. Those working in strategic communication and public diplomacy work to design communication spaces through which overseas audiences might be engaged, while also trying to penetrate and enter discussion in existing media spaces such as regional broadcast channels and Internet forums. We began the book by noting that there is an ineffable sense that how international relations is done, by whom, and what it involves, are all changing because of the way media ecologies are developing. This chapter rounds out that claim by penetrating, to the micro level, engagements states are seeking to construct as part of international relations, cultivating audiences and ensuring they engage with those states' narratives in order to generate long-term support for an envisioned international order.

INFORMATION INFRASTRUCTURE

Infrastructure refers to the basic physical and organizational structures and facilities needed for the operation of a society or enterprise, such as buildings, roads, power supplies, and communications systems. It can also refer to nonphysical entities such as standards, protocols, rules, and memories that allow a society or enterprise to function.[3] An information infrastructure refers to those structures and protocols through which the information storage and flows of a society or enterprise are achieved. Today, much attention is being given to *digital* information infrastructures and the connectivity they allow.[4] Economies and societies depend upon massive data servers, cloud services, software systems, and the power systems that keep them all running. Traditional infrastructure such as transport systems, buildings, and power stations themselves depend on digital infrastructures. Consequently, political leaders now seek to secure critical information infrastructure.[5] However, information infrastructures have always been vital to the functioning of societies and enterprises. Information infrastructures allow political leaders to exercise power at a distance to govern, monitor, and administer territory and populations, and to cultivate loyalty and consent through the distribution of ideological materials.[6] For instance, Michael Mann's survey of the organization of ancient and medieval societies shows how the Mesopotamian and Roman empires depended on the maintenance of a translocal culture among elites dispersed through their territories.[7] This translocal culture was able to sustain norms and codes because they were written on tablets and other artifacts. Challenges to these empires came from religious movements that harnessed either the elites' media or new media to spread their ideas more effectively than the ruling elites. Each information infrastructure allowed the embedding of a religion or culture that became the context for the next civilization—its religious and political narratives had to resonate with the values instantiated by the previous information infrastructure. The lesson of those early translocal systems for today's international system is clear. We must take into account the material organization of communication to explain how different ideas and narratives spread and become consensual.

The information infrastructure of a given age is the foundation for the communication processes of international relations—for the diffusion of norms, the cascading of frames, the generation of legitimacy, and to prevailing understandings of authority and legitimacy. Information infrastructure is the condition within which leaders can form and project strategic narratives, and the condition that shapes how audiences receive and interpret them. Information infrastructure is intrinsic to the ontology of international order. States, sovereignty, power, and rights are all conditioned by and constituted through systems of communication. Human experience of time, space, and connectivity—our orientation to the world—depends on the technologies we use in everyday life.[8] Without writing, there is no formal organization of human society. Gleick writes, "Before writing, communication is evanescent and local; sounds carry only a few yards and fade to oblivion."[9] Since McLuhan's association of media to the emergence of the sense of a global village, scholars have investigated how media and information infrastructure shapes experience of globality and locality, proximity and distance, continuity and rupture.[10] At the same time, accounts of modernity and the state emphasize how their development depended on the media technologies of the day not only for governance and administration but to create a qualitative sense of community, nationhood, and identity.[11] It stands to reason, then, that information infrastructure must be central to any account of international society and identity, of international norms, beliefs, and habits, or of how leaders and citizens experience international relations.

Policy makers understand this better than scholars.[12] Given the foundational role of information infrastructures for international relations, it is no surprise that information infrastructures themselves are politicized phenomena. Great powers, businesses, scientists, and activist groups all compete to shape the nature, development, and regulation of information infrastructure. Information infrastructure is not a merely technical background to "real" power politics. It determines the character of military, commercial, and political forces, as well as being determined by them.[13] It is in the context of this dualism that we can understand the US Internet freedom foreign policy of the Bush and Obama administrations. McCarthy's analysis of US foreign policy statements indicates that the meaning of the Internet has been creatively framed by key actors in the US to be associated with individual rights, freedom of expression, and enhanced democracy.[14] Within that sense-making framework, the spread of Internet access around the world would entail the spread of rights, freedom, and democracy; this is only reinforced when regimes such as China or Saudi Arabia limit Internet access. These assumptions have supported policies to increase information flows such as distributing antiblocking software, supporting NGOs that diffuse technology, and—infamously—asking Twitter to postpone its maintenance during the 2009 Iranian protests. "The desired transformation is a *physical* one," McCarthy writes, "an attempt to literally build the international system in line with the American vision for global politics" (italics in original).[15] This project is problematic in numerous ways; for instance, it overlooks US inability to limit its own technology firms supplying surveillance and other tools to authoritarian regimes, it conflates access to information with ability to use information, it ignores how nationalist and hate groups in numerous countries use Internet freedom to attack minorities, and it overlooks how US-backed intellectual property schemes limit information flows.[16] As Comor and Bean remind us, the medium is the message; and if the medium is Facebook, then the message is of individuals expressing their authentic selves in ever-expanding circles of trust.[17] That is a particular discourse about how individual and community should be integrated. Its spread can be narrativized as the movement toward individual freedom and network power, overcoming the obstacles of intransigent regimes. The diffusion of such social media spaces creates a condition of international order that embodies and extends the values US foreign policy supports.

There is a clear logic to states undertaking strategic action to shape information infrastructure. When foreign policy makers conceive of international communication, they must have a dual strategy. First, they must *shape conversations and interactions* and try to direct these toward topics, frames, and the overall narrative of international change that country is promoting. This dimension of strategic narrative work is a task routinely allocated to practitioners of public diplomacy. Diplomacy refers to communication between state representatives. *Public* diplomacy refers to "official communication with foreign publics" and nonstate groups in other countries,[18] and the increasing proliferation of state-led public diplomacy strategies in more and more countries leads to "a world in which all governments are assiduously cultivating each other's domestic constituencies on all issues at all levels."[19] Public diplomacy is therefore not restricted to communications by officials or state representatives. Corporations, nongovernmental organizations (NGOs), and cultural and educational institutions are all capable of public diplomacy, and public diplomacy strategies may operate through the cooperation of several such types of institution. Nor are foreign publics the only audience for such communications; unavoidably, domestic publics can learn about their state's public diplomacy strategies, so plural audiences must be simultaneously addressed and accounted for.

Achieving that first, the public diplomacy part of strategic narrative work is much easier for foreign policy makers if they can achieve the second part of the dual strategy. They must also *shape the environment within which such conversations and interactions occur.* They must ensure supportive voices have an opportunity to be heard, and—if we are being cynical here—that oppositional voices are sidelined, or at the very least countered. In a speech given in London in 2012, Anne-Marie Slaughter, Director of Policy Planning under the Obama Administration 2009–11, articulated exactly such a dual strategy.[20] Slaughter was explicit about how US foreign policy aims to shape the conditions of international order, not just the interactions in it. She began by saying that structures were being put in place whose effects would not be visible for some years. The structures the US was building were informed by the assumption that the biggest development in international relations is not the rise of the BRICs but the rise of society—"the people"—both within individual countries and across countries. The US had to build structures that harness societies as agents in the international system. Slaughter returned to Putnam's two-level game, the proposition that it is in the interaction of international and domestic politics that governments can play constituencies off against one another to find solutions to diplomatic and policy dilemmas.[21] Slaughter took up this framework: the US administration must see a country as comprised both of its government and its society, work with both, and enable US society to engage other countries' governments and societies. The latter involves the US acting not as "do-er" but as "convenor," using social media and organizing face-to-face platforms for citizens, civil society groups, and companies to form intra- and international networks. In other words, it depends upon guaranteeing these aspects of the global information infrastructure.

In the long run, this foreign policy aims to ensure that when a crisis develops overseas in a few decades' time, local and international publics find themselves supportive of US actions or at least willing to listen to what US leaders propose. Slaughter quoted former Secretary of State George P. Shultz. He suggested diplomacy is like gardening:

> You get the weeds out when they are small. You also build confidence and understanding. Then, when a crisis arises, you have a solid base from which to work.[22]

In this chapter we look at two cases of states harnessing the cutting edge of the information infrastructure to project strategic narratives to try to build the solid base Schultz speaks of. The first case examined is US President Obama's June 2009 speech to the Muslim world. Obama's strategic narrative operated on two levels: as storytelling, talking about how the world can be; and as story *making*, intervening in history by going to Cairo and attempting to create a new start. This required Obama to preview his own speech, constructing and teasing out potential responses to what he was yet to say, and for the White House to create multilingual platforms and channels to construct the global space of discussion about the speech. By examining these efforts, we can study the formation, projection, and subsequent interaction around a speech in an era in which political actors actively harness the nonlinearity and multidirectionality of political communication. We find that for all the effort the Obama communication team put into creating spaces of conversation, they failed to penetrate critical existing spaces, namely the national media of key Muslim-majority countries like Iraq.

In the second case study we analyze ongoing attempts by the BBC World Service to evaluate the impact of its programming on audiences by using online methodologies. This analysis draws on a series of articles and reports published by the media ethnographer Marie Gillespie, who had access to the production, social media analytics, and audience research teams at the BBC World Service.[23] It is an important example because the BBC World Service seeks to reconcile competing goals. It is primarily a news organization staffed by professional journalists. It also has a public diplomacy function, as its funding is dependent upon UK government foreign policy priorities. Its journalists have relative freedom for experimental programming to find ways to engage overseas audiences, while its audience research is relatively sophisticated, such that the BBC World Service is one of the few cases in world politics where there is significant data on the impact of strategic narratives on overseas opinion.

These analyses show that if international relations scholars take into account how communication works, a far richer picture opens up about their central concerns: the construction of the meaning of states and the state system, the diffusion of norms, and how interests are shaped and mediated by context and communication.

Information Infrastructure, Media Ecologies, and Capitalism

The role of commerce is unavoidable if we are to take a holistic view of information infrastructure. We must put strategic narrative work in the context of contemporary changes to capitalism and economic life. A useful starting point here is Nigel Thrift's thesis that "the underlying model of what constitutes 'economy' is changing to what might be termed a 'natural' model . . . concerned with producing environments."[24] If the first industrial revolution in the eighteenth century involved a break with the natural economy as livelihoods depended less on the land and more on the factory, the second industrial revolution, occurring today, involves returning to the land.[25] However, the land or terrain of economic activity has changed: it is proto-land, a sphere or zone of interpenetrating technological and social processes through which profit can be made, techno-social fields that produce waves of innovation. These might be cities or online spaces, or a combination of both. Thrift writes, "What is beginning to be produced by firms is a space based on a supercharged naturalism of ideas and affects that is in the business of reloading/recording on a constant basis, a space of continual composition that has grip through the different textures it produces in the world."[26] Whereas profit from land prior to the industrial revolution was based on enclosure and rent, now firms seek to create relatively unbounded spaces in which people produce new content, ideas, and virality together. This lets firms monitor how we are responding to their products, and chart shifting demands; ultimately, Thrift writes, "This new kind of massed and yet also individuated land will *feel us*" (italics added).[27]

The "space" of communication is not neutral; it offers affordances that guide us to communicate in certain ways and it is laced with monitoring software so our communications can be analyzed as proxy guidance for our thoughts and likely actions—as citizens, consumers, parents, or the numerous other roles we inhabit. International political communication occurs within these commercially driven spaces that build on capitalism's long tradition of reinventing invention, of trying to find new, optimal situations that will lead to creative thinking. In the 1980s the fashion was the learning organization with creative spaces in the institutions of production; then it was realized that instead of innovation only happening on the production end, consumers could be tapped for creative ideas. Firms softened the distinction between consumption and production, becoming what Victor Fung, William Fung, and Yoram Wind called "network orchestrators," actors managing circulations of information and desire that would build up to a moment of exchange.[28] By the 2000s and the emergence of social media, firms were tapping into what Thrift calls an *"expressive infrastructure."*[29] This allows for "cognitive capitalism." Thrift writes:

> Capitalism has to, needs to, intervene in the imagination. Thus, its main interest becomes what Moulier-Boutang calls "pollination," the systematic production and management of various kinds of publics and their opinions and affects through all kinds of imitative cascade that act as both supply and demand.[30]

By tracking our thoughts, firms can spot small differences in our behavior to exploit, they can work out how imitation works, and they can make tacit suggestions to nudge us to certain exchanges. Firms can monitor our talk about products, but our talk also becomes profitable—the model pursued by Facebook and Twitter. Firms must thicken our social space, making our interactions visible, to them and to us.

These marketing theories and practices are present in international political communication. We see varying degrees of this occurring in the Obama and BBC World Service case studies below. Their practices of public diplomacy work to thicken social spaces and foster connectivity. Beyond these two cases, the general task involves finding new ways to represent our interactions back to us individual users. This might include creating maps and diagrams of our social networks, which make us reflexive about how to optimize our interactions; thickening our relationships by creating transparency—websites through which we can see everyone else's interactions, likes, comments; and perhaps seeing where these people are, by persuading citizens-cum-users to use GPS, check in on Foursquare, and other digital tools to make our co-conversationalists' location visible.

Note that firms must allow for uncertainty about what people will do in these proto-lands or spaces. Indeed, this is where the source of profit is: by users creating new acts, surprising trends, and unforeseen demands.

Borrowing from Brian Massumi,[31] Thrift argues that the *power* of this "zone of continual emergence" is preemptive: "Preemptive power is environmental power. It alters the life environment's conditions of emergence . . . via incursive charges that alter the potential of a situation, pointing it in a new direction."[32] Such spaces prepare the ground, as Slaughter and Schultz put it:

> Since uncertainty is everywhere, the main solution is to produce a space that can work one small step in front of the moment in order to be able to charge the moment up with favorable ideas and affects, a space that can be thickened, gathered together, knotted in new ways, flowing through us, buoying us along, drawing us out and relating us back in new ways, changing our bearings.[33]

This is the dynamic of persuasion in today's information infrastructure. Firms, media organizations, and public diplomacy practitioners are seeking to harness this "mediatized emergence."[34] The term *emergence* is often used to describe the mechanism of social organization and change under conditions of complexity. Ontologically, society is more than the sum of its parts because relations, identities, and situations emerge that could not be foreseen by simply identifying the constituent units of that society. Yet the mediatization of social life massively expands the possibilities and parameters for the emergence of digital and digitized media data to transcend and transform what is known or thought to be known about events.[35] Mediatization is part of a long historical transformation in which institutions and practices assume a media form. Another way to understand this is in terms of media logics: certain mediums and the production and consumption practices that emerge around them privilege ways of acting. Television prioritizes a visually compelling and verbally fluent mode of action, which political leaders and organizations soon learnt to adapt to in the late twentieth century, such that politics was *done differently*.[36] Mediatization in political institutions becomes more intensive now that more of life is digitized—recorded, archived, retrieved, transformed—as media content. Under such conditions, digital media content can literally and suddenly emerge to force the reconsideration of some event or phenomenon. The emergence of the chaotic phone video of Saddam Hussein's execution, photos from Abu Ghraib, film of executions by Serb soldiers at Srebrenica; all resulted in the unsettling of established meanings around the American presence in Iraq or the criminality of Serb forces in the 1990s, respectively days, months, and years after the event.[37] Awareness that any event might have been recorded, and that this recording could emerge at any time, in any form, adds a permanent, "contingent openness" to social life.[38]

As we shall see below, this is what BBC Arabic could be seen to have done, to an extent, regarding the Egyptian uprising of 2011. So, if strategic narratives are a means for states to create shared meanings, and meanings are made through these spaces, then strategic narrative work entails working through and understanding these spaces and their dynamics of mediatized emergence and its real-time monitoring. This is especially the case for strategic narrative work aimed at overseas publics.

So far the focus in this chapter has been on state-public and public-public communication, but old media still matter to how strategic narratives are projected, received, and interpreted, as the examples in this chapter will show. After much anxiety among established or mainstream media in the early 2000s it is now clear that many old media organizations have adapted to the new media ecology and that mainstream journalism remains the main source of news to most citizens around the world.[39] Citizens may get news from niche online sources but usually this is interpreted with reference to and in the context of a lifetime of mainstream media consumption. Mainstream news editors and journalists remain important gatekeepers who can keep a strategic narrative out, or authoritatively reinterpret it for audiences. Journalists with established media have in some cases responded to the challenge of a proliferation of citizen journalists and more chaotic information flows by becoming more establishment-oriented in an effort to safeguard their identities as professional journalists; it is in this context that Handley and Rutigliano document ways in which US journalists are more likely to reinforce "the national narrative."[40] New information-news hybrids such as Wikileaks ultimately depended on the *Guardian, New York Times, Der Speigel, Le Monde*, and *El Pais* to splash the news of their embassy cables in December 2010.[41] Consequently, foreign policy and public diplomacy practitioners seeking to diffuse their strategic narrative need to understand how these renewed or hybrid media ecologies operate.

Returning to Thrift's suggestion of a second industrial revolution, not all economic life has shifted to the production of environments. There is still agriculture, manufacturing; we have not replaced one ideal type with another. Equally, not all international communication occurs through Web 2.0: what seemed like old and new media in the 1990s and 2000s have now combined into more settled ecologies. Thrift's "environmental" account aligns in productive ways with current conceptualizations of media ecologies, namely how interdependencies between the range of actors and technologies produce "climates," "waves," "modulations," and other dynamics that can be understood through analogies to processes occurring in nature.[42] The ways in which digital tools (even when harnessed by old or traditional institutions) make it possible to monitor, visualize, and even steer international communication offer rich promise to strategic narrative practitioners seeking to get a grip on climates and waves of opinion. How have they fared? The following two case studies are instructive.

OBAMA'S CAIRO SPEECH

On June 4, 2009, President Obama made a speech in Cairo, Egypt, to "the Muslim world."[43] He made great use of social media to enlarge the audience.

His words were disseminated through Facebook and MySpace, text messages and tweets, live streaming on the White House and State Department websites, and through live broadcast on Al Jazeera and other Arabic television channels. Translations in multiple languages were offered. Instead of simply getting a message out, the White House press secretary, Robert Gibbs, spoke of generating a "continuing dialogue"—in other words, sustained two-way communication in which Obama and his administration would listen as well as speak.[44] This marketing effort exemplifies the way a new media ecology has changed how political leaders can manage the expectation and responses to their speeches. The speech was extensively trailed, through predeparture interviews with NPR and the BBC, to hint at what audiences around the world might expect. The relentless self- and official commentary through tweets enabled interpretation to be subtlety steered as the speech was delivered. By creating spaces for feedback and electronic conversation, leaders could structure the responses in several ways. By moderating what gets published, Obama's team demonstrated the very fact of a global response, and that response fell into several categories (ecstatic, cautious, and perhaps—to suggest transparency and credibility—even a few critical comments). Obama's speech exemplifies the potential for projecting and managing strategic narratives in the new media ecology.

Turning first to the *formation* of the speech, the fact of the speech was as important as its content. The decision to give a speech in an Arabic country to the Muslim world was a gesture in itself. Obama was not just prepared to tell a story about US-Islamic relations, but also to insert himself into that story in order to move the story in a new direction. It was a deliberate attempt to perform a narrative into being. The novelty marked an attempt to interrupt a political temporality in which—Obama said—progress had become impossible, a political time shared by all of humanity but between followers of Islam, Christianity, and Judaism, the three Abrahamic religions, in particular. Obama described his speech as an attempt to break a "cycle of suspicion and discord"; to address "the complex questions that brought us to this point . . . in order to move forward." In narrative terms then, the story had ground to a halt, or rather reached an endless cycle of discord. An heroic actor was needed to seize the day, break the cycle, and allow a new unfolding, a new shared line to follow. Obama specified no telos or ending but appealed to a sense that the present situation was unacceptable. Part of the effect he tried to achieve was an agreement that this narrative was plausible; had we reached stalemate? Was it possible to move forward and break the cycle? If audiences did not accept these premises, the rest of the speech fell flat.

The speech was also a risk. If, in the months and years to follow, the Obama administration became associated with failed policies, for instance a disastrous or disappointing new Middle East peace initiative, then the gesture would come in retrospect to look hubristic at best, false at worst. This in turn would remove one tool from the diplomatic armory of future presidents, as any speech to the Muslim world would be looked upon with skepticism.[45] Years later, we might ask if in fact this is very much the case. In terms of the content of the speech assembled by Obama and his writers, Obama's narrative rested upon three epistemological bases of truth. First, Obama attempted to establish shared facts. That Al-Qaeda has killed predominantly Muslims is "not opinions to be debated; these are facts to be dealt with." That the Holocaust led to the death of millions of Jews in World War II was another fact to be dealt with, and to deny this would be "baseless, ignorant, and hateful." Second, Obama appealed to transcendent principles: "We do unto others as we would have them do unto us. This truth transcends nations and peoples. . . . We know that is God's vision." Third, he offered foreign policy "red lines," that is, foundational or essential markers of national interest that he attempted to position as beyond discussion, for example, "America's bonds with Israel are well known. This bond is unbreakable."[46]

Each of these bases for the truth of his narrative performed functions, for instance by establishing a settled historical record from which future-oriented talks could begin, or tying identity groups together as all under the Abrahamic figure of God, or appealing to domestic constituencies by invoking national interests. Do these plural bases for claims making generate contradictions or schisms—Bially-Mattern's "intolerable ambiguities"—that opponents could exploit and might lead even open-minded but skeptical audiences to question Obama's credibility? This was a classic case of a speech projected to multiple audiences and, in the narrative's formation and preparation, the Obama team must have anticipated a degree of dissent.

A second major theme in his speech was the form of the narrative. Obama said:

I do have an unyielding belief that all people yearn for certain things; the ability to speak your mind and have a say in how you are governed; confidence in the rule of law. . . . Now, *there is no straight line to realize* this promise. . . . But I also know human progress cannot be denied. (emphasis added)[47]

This conception of linear history (not straight, but overall moving on a line forward) parallels a definition of politics offered by Bruno Latour:

When one says that someone or something is "political," one signals above all this fundamental disappointment, as if it were no longer possible to move forwards in a straight line, reasonably, quickly, efficiently, but necessary to "take into account," "a whole lot of " "extra-rational factors" of which one fails to clearly understand all the ins and outs.[48]

Obama was managing expectations by pointing to the indirect and cumbersome processes through which peace processes and international diplomacy proceed. It anticipated the response that his attempt to create a new start was overly optimistic by acknowledging that he realized things would not move forward quickly in a straight line to peace. Yet still the message was one of liberal universalism and a telos that "cannot be denied"; he was both the person pointing to this *and* the person kick-starting that telos after it had hit an obstacle; he offered a philosophy of history and tried to become the philosopher-prince who realizes through praxis what he purports initially to only describe.

The *projection* of the speech was achieved through a proliferation of channels and spaces, over time and across languages. The White House (whitehouse.gov) offered not just a video available on its website and on Facebook, but also posted the video on the White House channel on YouTube within minutes of its conclusion, and a transcript of the speech— with this material translated into Arabic, Chinese, Dari, French, Hebrew, Hindi, Indonesian, Malay, Pashto, Persian, Punjabi, Russian, Turkish, and Urdu.

Alhurra Television station and Radio Sawa broadcast the speech live with simultaneous Arabic translation and a live stream of the speech was available on Alhurra.com. The White House and other arms of the US government also offered a suite of accompanying promotional materials. These included:

- A video about Muslims serving in the US government.
- A podcast recording of the speech and transcripts of the entire address in a variety of languages, posted at www.america.gov, for instance in Arabic at http://www.america.gov/ar/multimedia/podcast.html.
- A behind-the-scenes video about Obama's trip, 2–7 June 2009.
- A blog post about how Muslim women in the US who want to wear the headscarf are protected by the US Constitution (http://www.white house.gov/blog/Nashalas-Story).
- Photographs of the event were posted on the White House page on photo-sharing site Flickr at flickr.com/photos/whitehouse.
- The White House Twitter feed—@whitehouse—posted about twenty 140-character-or-less real-time updates during the speech to its approximately 250,000 followers around the world.
- The US embassy in Ottawa linked to a fact sheet about the United States outreach to Muslims on its Twitter feed.
- The US embassy in London posted a transcript of officials' prespeech spin on Twitter as well.
- The US embassy in Bangkok, in Thai, posted a preview of administration talking points.
- The State Department offered SMS text messages with highlights of the speech to mobile phone users in four languages: Arabic, English, Farsi, and Urdu. SMS recipients were invited to send back their comments on the speech. Selected messages were posted at america.gov/ sms-comments.html. (US citizens could not participate, as taxpayer money cannot be used for domestic propaganda.)

White House spokesman Robert Gibbs said:

> Our goal is to ensure that the greatest number of people with an interest to see this—not just through newspapers and television—but can see this through Web sites. . . . The Internet team here is working with a host of others to get this information to as many platforms as humanly possible so that people will get a chance all over the world to see what the president has to say.[49]

As we see, Gibb's rather broadcast-era, monological ambition was supplemented by a series of platforms that offered a small degree of interactivity. People from around the world were invited to send SMS text messages. Publics were granted a sliver of voice in international affairs here, and since people could see what others had texted in and could respond, then there was potential for public-to-public, horizontal communications, which we might label "citizen public diplomacy." Paul Sharp describes these multilevel diplomatic practices with a footballing analogy: as "'total diplomacy,' echoing the old Dutch idea of 'total football' in which all players attack and defend."[50] The White House encouraged such total diplomacy by providing channels and spaces through which multiple domestic and overseas publics could deliberate about the speech and the issues it raised. Simply projecting a speech into the international communication ether, or relying on closed-door diplomacy with the leaders of Muslim-majority states, would have suggested a failure to harness new public diplomacy techniques made possible by the Web 2.0 information infrastructure of 2009. However, as we describe below, the BBC World Service case study to follow demonstrates far greater innovation here.

Turning finally to the *reception* and interpretation of Obama's speech, it is striking that Obama himself and oppositional leaders in the region tried to preempt the speech and prepare the ground for its reception. Obama was not projecting a narrative in isolation. Earlier the same day, June 4, 2009, Ayatollah Ali Khamenei gave a speech marking the 20th anniversary of the death of Ayatollah Khomenei, founder of the current Iranian republic. Khamenei argued that action was needed by the US, not "beautiful and sweet words."[51] "If the new president of America wants a change of face," he said, "America should change this behavior. Words and talk will not result in change."[52] Nevertheless, Obama focused on words as a starting point. In his first prespeech interview, to France's Canal Plus, Obama introduced the purpose of going to Cairo as to present a framework:

> I am delivering on a promise I made during the campaign to provide a framework, a speech of how I think we can remake relations between the United States and countries in the Muslim world.[53]

To Canal Plus, Obama spoke openly about the process of communication itself rather than about any particular message or end point to which he'd like "the Muslim world" to be persuaded:

Well, you know, this is a start of what I think will be a long-term process. We'll have a speech, we'll have a roundtable discussion. It will give an opportunity I think for people around the world to engage in this discussion. It will be telecast in a wide variety of languages on our White House Web site, whitehouse.gov. And my hope is, is that as a consequence you start seeing discussions not just at the presidential level, but at every level of life. And I hope I can spark some dialogue and debate within the Muslim world, because I think there's a real struggle right now between those who believe that Islam is irreconcilable to modern life and those who believe that actually Islam has always been able to move side by side with progress.[54]

The three major themes Obama attempted to establish as anchoring interpretations of his speech were (1) the speech as the beginning of an interaction, (2) that he acknowledged the problem of foreign policy creating discrepancies between words and deeds, and (3) that he was approaching the Muslim world with openness and respect. Media coverage in the days before his speech indicated some success with this framing. The *New York Times* columnists Thomas Friedman and James Traub each followed Obama's three themes exactly, and Obama was able to express them clearly on the BBC and Canal Plus.[55] However, even in the US other media outlets chose to report the speech with a focus on different themes. The *Los Angeles Times* was more interested in the formation of the speech—Obama's speechwriters—and the statement Obama was making simply by making that speech in that country. Understandably, Egyptian media such as *Al-Ahram Weekly* focused on Cairo as a venue, though also reported using the theme of possible discrepancies between US foreign policy and Obama's rhetoric, which he himself was highlighting. Predictably, perhaps, when news media the next day did report the speech, this was through a local prism. The *New York Times* column View from Tel Aviv and Al-Jazeera English both reported the speech in terms of the Israel-Palestinian conflict; the latter also put Obama's speech within the context of the war on terror and US policies against violent extremism in the region.

While Obama's speech was broadcast live on Al-Jazeera across the region, there were important country-specific variations in the old media landscape. It was not broadcast on Iranian television or radio (though audiences could find it via satellite channels), so there are doubts he reached key audiences there.[56] The main story on Iraqi TV that day was the death of three people arrested by Iraqi counter-terrorism forces. Obama's Cairo speech was reported on main news channels but, apart from the US-sponsored station Al-Hurra and state-sponsored Al-Iraqiya, it was not shown in its entirety and it was framed by critical responses.[57] The US also found it difficult to persuade ordinary people online. Khatib, Dutton, and Thelwall studied the engagement efforts of the US State Department's Digital Outreach Team from May until December 2009.[58] Before and after the Obama Cairo speech, this team of ten civil servants intervened and participated in numerous overseas Web forums used by Arabic-speaking users. Their interactions offer a useful lens on reaction in the Middle East and North Africa. The Digital Outreach Team seemed to generate negative comments—ridicule, hostility, as well as the recurring substantive critique that the US must deliver "action, not words." Users posted visual images that the Digital Outreach Team found difficult to counter. The Cairo speech became a symbol of disappointment users could refer to. In short, all the Digital Outreach Team could do was put a positive spin on policies towards the region set not at the State Department but by the White House.

The reaction to Obama's Cairo speech raises questions about what kind of impact can be expected, and therefore what the role and aims of public diplomacy are; indeed, even what the role of communication is more broadly in international relations. First, the speech raises the question of *what counts as value?* Is strategic narrative work a process of communication ethics where dialogue is valuable for its own sake, or is this a process in which value lies in measurable attitudinal change or observable behavioral change? In terms of the spectrum of persuasion set out in the previous chapter, thin rationalists would argue the latter, but scholars of communicative action would argue that dialogue for its own sake generates trust that can provide a platform, ultimately, for measurable attitudinal or behavioral change.[59] Second, the speech brings into question *the transparency of instrumental public diplomacy.* It would appear that public relations-led strategic narrative work is extremely limited, even delusional, because overseas audiences and their leaders anticipate and are reflexive about the intentions behind such speeches. Facing this dilemma, some argue that the US should instead embrace genuine dialogue, which involves listening and being seen to take into account others' perspectives.[60] However, what it means to listen and take into account is a recurring problem in political communication. As the leader of a country with a great power identity, Obama could hardly admit that, having listened to audiences in Cairo, he was willing to change his foreign policy toward the region.

We might ask then, third, *does great power identity prevent genuine dialogue?* Are there limits to the kind of "dialogue" the US can enter into while it still self-identifies as the leading power? The public diplomacy scholar Paul Sharp writes, "American diplomacy under Obama remains framed by the increasingly questionable assumption that its renewed openness to talking, its continued military superiority and its claim to embody universal values will continue to confer upon it the mantle of global leadership."[61] Great power identity creates an anxiety to be seen to fulfill the expectations of a great power.[62] To enter a dialogue as an equal partner would entail either renouncing or redefining the role and meaning of great power.

Fourth and finally, we might ask: *Will civil society be co-opted?* In domestic politics online participation has drawn in fringe political actors (party activists, well-known bloggers) but pushed out ordinary citizens, creating a "fat," elitist democracy.[63] Have activist bloggers and citizen journalists operating in IR been co-opted into power structures? Are relatively free spaces of the Web being colonized by public diplomacy teams with real-time opinion monitoring tools and network analysis technique to identify influential users? This would undermine the broader US strategic narrative of Internet freedom.

In summary, the projection of Obama's Cairo speech was organized to take advantage of the information infrastructure of 2009. An examination of how it was received makes clear a number of unresolved tensions concerning how strategic narratives can be expected to function. On the one hand the speech brought forth a rhetoric of dialogue and engagement, the promise of Web 2.0 horizontal interaction, and the genuine aspiration among a proportion of global public that Obama's public diplomacy might signal a new approach in US foreign policy. On the other hand the relations and platforms of engagement were set by the US, which could not mask the power asymmetries between the US and its audiences, and the US did not successfully penetrate mainstream Arabic media television.

Instrumentally, there was no observable benefit. What remains to be seen is whether, in the long term, this attempt to put the narrative into practice does contribute to what Slaughter and Schultz described as cultivating the ground, such that in ten or twenty years, attitudes have shifted so that audiences in the Middle East and North Africa are more receptive to US strategic narratives.

BBC World Service: Creating and Monitoring Impact

The reputation of the BBC World Service around the world reflects that of Britain generally.[64] It is an institution tied to colonial history and hence is an object both of suspicion but also long-term connection for many former British colonies. It aspires to global reach and thus exemplifies UK governments' rhetoric of "punching above our weight" in international affairs. Through its journalism it tries to uphold values of impartiality and objectivity, which produces an attractive, soft-power dimension such that the BBC is well regarded by overseas public opinion.[65] As an institution, however, it cannot escape appearing partial—it is funded by the British state, and audiences can infer that the state only funds it to the extent that the service is serving Britain's interests. Indeed, historically the BBC World Service has been funded by a direct grant from the Foreign and Commonwealth Office (FCO), Britain's State Department. While a Royal Charter prevented the FCO interfering in the editorial content of World Service programming, the FCO could decide which foreign language services were strengthened or cut. During the 2000s, Arabic and other strategically important language services tended to retain funding. It is impossible to avoid the suspicion that these decisions were unrelated to the audiences the UK government chose as targets for its strategic narrative. In 2010 the government announced the

World Service would be funded through the annual license fee people in Britain must pay in order to receive BBC content legally. The World Service became just another part of the BBC Global News, its tie to the FCO less obvious. This means it had to demonstrate its value in new ways. However, with such a legacy of strategic narrative projection and in-house expertise about producing content for overseas audiences and measuring its impact, the BBCWS remains a fascinating cauldron for strategic narrative development and experimentation.

The researchers Marie Gillespie and Hugh Mackay spent 2010–12 inside the BBCWS exploring how the organization understands impact and value. Impact is expected to be on audiences, not necessarily on political systems, social change, or business and commerce. However, the goals in the BBC's global strategy are quite ambitious. It aims "to meet particular audience needs or enhance the influence of values the UK treasures," for instance, "a free media independent of government."[66] It also aims to create global "public value"—"civic, social and cultural benefits"—including global citizenship.[67] While impact is considered in terms of effects, influence, and engagement, in practice this could refer to affecting, influencing, and engaging individuals, communities, or even whole political systems. Some such effects may not be visible in the short term but may mesh with other forces, for instance the overseas policy interventions of the UK's Foreign and Commonwealth Office and Department for International Development (DfID), to create longer-term effects. One of the most striking criteria the BBCWS must work toward is to promote a "global conversation."[68] The BBC Trust defines the global conversation as:

> an informed and intelligent dialogue which transcends international borders and cultural divides; by giving communities around the world opportunities to create, publish, and share their own views and stories; and, thereby, enabling people to make sense of increasingly complex regional and global events and developments.[69]

For the BBC this creates a problem of knowing and knowledge as well as a problem of definition—what is a global conversation, how global is global enough, and what counts as a conversation? It must demonstrate it is producing these effects, to retain its funding. How? Ninety years of audience research within the organization created a set of theories and models akin to a science, but a new paradigm emerged in the late 2000s and early 2010s: digital media allow for new ways of monitoring, measuring, and evaluating the impact of BBCWS programming and online content. These include quantitative metrics such as reach, time spent with BBCWS content, amount of Twitter followers and retweets, and positivity of sentiment. These can be evaluated in real time and networks of engagement plotted. The environmental space Nigel Thrift writes about (see above) can be turned into diagrams—the circulation of ideas, actions, and affects becomes visible or thickened. However, such metrics do not illuminate "the meaning or significance of interactions, and their qualitative dimensions."[70] It doesn't capture the *quality* of engagement, and what follows from it. For instance, it does not help the BBCWS understand how people then talk about what they have heard on BBCWS with friends, family, or colleagues, not does it help the BBCWS identify how it makes audiences think differently. It does not identify how narratives in BBC programming mesh with narratives held by audiences. The research of Gillespie and Mackay suggests that to get at relations of cause and effect regarding impact, qualitative research is needed.

In line with Thrift's conception of the contemporary economy, *impact* also means allowing creativity in both production and consumption. Regarding production, by the mid-1990s the BBCWS held to rather didactic theories of cultural change whereby programming is expected to educate audiences. For instance, a radio soap opera for Afghanis rewrote a story line from the postwar British radio show *The Archers* in which a young man's impending wedding depended on him successfully rearing pigs. The story line was designed to instruct rural British audiences in the austere years after World War II how to keep pigs themselves. By the 1990s, rural Afghanis were listening to the tale of a young man trying to raise sheep. The young hero regularly lost sheep to landmines, but eventually raised and sold enough to pay a dowry to his bride's father.[71] This was the same narrative, transposed to a different time, space, and context. In the 2000s the BBCWS turned to less didactic story lines. They tried instead what Gillespie calls "creative coalescence" between London-based journalists and those in the target country who coproduce programming. This entails London's editors surrendering any hope of exactness and mastery and giving space for playfulness. At the consumption end, this entails creating platforms through which users can engage with others from other societies and cultures. Thus, both production and consumption become contact zones not only for the transmission of ideas and the FCO's strategic narratives, but more ritualistically for the forging of relationships and production of cultural literacy.[72]

Such practices again "ready the ground," as Schultz and Slaughter said, creating certain subjectivities, norms, and expectations. In the spectrum of persuasion, the BBC was putting into practice a poststructural approach. The BBC could present itself as going with the grain of the new media ecology, for instance the notion that the Internet allows the diffusion of authority in religion and politics as horizontal, peer-to-peer communication enables individuals to look to people whom they perceive as being like them for information rather than distant, traditional authority figures.[73] The BBC could say it was creating the spaces for organic, emergent dynamics to flourish, while at the same time exposing audiences to its norms and values.

However, the BBCWS tried to go further with creativity and engagement. In line with Thrift's account of how firms sought to generate innovation by meshing together production and consumption, the BBCWS turned to a format that let audiences share the practice of producing the show.

A ZONE OF ENGAGEMENT: "GREENWICH 710"

BBC Arabic was created in 2007. Its director, Hosam Sokkari, suggested the station's aim was to rewire habitual responses in English-language and Arabic-language media cultures in which rhetorics of suspicion and blame are routinely triggered. As he put it, the station's role was for "piercing the blood-brain barrier that exists between the Anglo and Arab media spheres and facilitating an increased flow of high quality, impartial debate from the UK to the Middle East and vice versa."[74] Such a task is made difficult because linguistic media spaces do not map easily onto geographical spaces. More than 50 percent of users of BBC foreign language services are diasporic, not living in the country and region of birth.[75] From the perspective of foreign policy makers trying to craft and send strategic narratives, the audiences are not where they should be. However, these distributions create different kinds of conversations. Diaspora dwellers in, say, London, Melbourne, or Chicago can act as mediators, other times as cheerleaders, but certainly open up nonhabitual patterns of communication across borders and between cultures. BBC Arabic is well placed to facilitate this.

As an experiment to create engagement and cross-cultural impact, BBC Arabic launched a program on March 4, 2010, called "Greenwich 710" in which audience members had the opportunity to participate in its content and production. "Greenwich 710" was a weekly 50-minute political talk show broadcast on satellite TV across the Middle East and Arab-speaking world on Thursday evenings at 7:10 GMT (Greenwich Mean Time) (19:10 was not chosen). Specifically, it was produced by three groups: BBC Arabic producers, volunteer "produsers," namely users entering into regular production activity in spaces granted by the BBC producers, and finally general audiences participating via platforms such as the "Greenwich 710" website and Facebook page. Produsers were encouraged to see themselves as "citizens" of the show—"citizens of the republic of Greenwich 710."[76] Again, the BBC's practices were akin to the application of a poststructural, thick approach to persuasion, since it was creating and constituting subject positions that audience members were encouraged to take on and speak from. When asked to describe how this complex production process played out, Hosam Sokkari drew an hourglass figure. Produsers and fans would make a large number of suggestions for potential guests and questions for the show. These filtered into the narrow middle, at which point BBC Arabic producers imposed some editorial experience and sought to ensure that the BBC's journalistic ethos would not be compromised by any choices; the show would then flow out again to the produsers and wider fan base. The editorial contingent was strengthened as Sokkari recruited what he called a Board of Wise Men—prominent Egyptian social media activists who met in a closed Facebook group to discuss the show's content and agenda and how it could be promoted across Arabic social media spaces—how its conversation could extend beyond the official website.

Did "Greenwich 710" create a global conversation—or at least a regional one? How successfully did it harness the new media ecology to help engage people? "Greenwich 710" was cut after six weeks of broadcast. The number of users being reached was in the thousands rather than the millions BBCWS radio reaches. The show's content upset the Egyptian government—prominent dissidents were given a platform and the political process in Egypt was satirized.[77] "Greenwich 710" also failed to meet the expectations of being either global or a conversation: users were overwhelmingly Egyptian and interactions were sometimes hostile and gendered. Political tensions between Arabic countries played out in the online "Greenwich 710" community. Nevertheless, in that short period some interesting developments occurred. There was a clear didactic process whereby produsers and fans on the Facebook page were exposed to and participated in debates about journalistic impartiality and reliability. The show had to meet BBC standards, so participants learnt what that meant in practice, and had the chance to debate the norms and values these standards embodied. The show also legitimized in public what many in the region felt in private. Since produsers and fans could shape the questions asked, this meant political figures faced the kind of questions being asked in virtual forums but rarely expressed on air.

There is a curious and perhaps significant back story to "Greenwich 710." The Board of Wise Men became pivotal figures in the uprisings that followed. Gillespie notes that the digital, networked form and ideological content of "Greenwich 710" "prefigured and connected with the Egyptian protests a year later." She writes:

> *Greenwich 7/10* foreshadowed in interesting ways the events leading up to Mubarak's resignation, and the way that digital devices and data were implicated in these events . . . the downfall of Mubarak. . . . After being axed—G7/10 had lain dormant for a while but the digital network was being re-animated. For example, Hossam and other G7/10 members began to raise the issue of torture practiced by the Egyptian army during and even before the revolution.[78]

In what way does the BBCWS experiment in public diplomacy point to a changed global order? Recall that in Chapter 3 we argued that the way in which order becomes meaningful and narrativized is changing because the new media ecology increases the volume of contributors and contributions to the range of narratives being projected. In the same way, the US emphasis on harnessing "the people" and the BBCWS concept of a "global conversation" appear to follow the same logic and to be encouraging this direction. These multiplatform phenomena create new patterns, new processes, and new kinds of encounters and transactions through which strategic narratives and their discursive raw materials can be projected and exchanged between ordinary people.[79] However, both the US and UK initiatives are on their own terms, not the terms of their audiences. There is thus a trade-off between empowering and monitoring users, and a need to recognize that the aim of producing new subjectivities is the exercise of behavioral power through the practices of generative power. There are also tensions involving authority, control, creativity, and style. The BBC would like spontaneous cross-cultural dialogue but has cumbersome moderation procedures of selection and sometimes translation of audience comments such that its forums are less spaces of conversation and more a public screen where people simply view isolated statements.[80]

Transparency and increased media literacy may generate as much cynicism as engagement. A more media-literate cross-section of overseas audiences might appear to create a pool of latency, a reservoir of potential support in the future. However, audiences might feel they see engagement programs for what they are—instrumental tools to persuade audiences. Hence, the US Digital Outreach Team found Arab responses to Obama's Cairo speech to be calls for action, not words: engagement does not imply changed policy. The projection of strategic narratives is a difficult, risky enterprise since those narratives are received and interpreted by audiences in the context of their experiences of that country and its foreign policies, historically, today, and in the foreseeable future. And while state departments and national broadcasters have immediate goals of audience reach and engagement, creating long-term buy-in to a strategic narrative so that those audiences *"live the experience* of the . . . identity" projected by a particular state's narrative, thinking and acting as if this identity is definitely obtained will be a hard and fraught process.[81] However, this exercise in what Janice Bially-Mattern calls "language-power," and to which we would add *infrastructure creation*, is equally hard to avoid, since it is how international order becomes possible.[82]

CONCLUSION

International relations are entangled in changing forms of economic life because firms are the primary creators of spaces of public communication. It must be recognized that international relations take place within and alongside changing forms of economic life. Contemporary capitalism is characterized by practices that encourage and exploit continual fluidity, creativity, and uncertainty. It is no surprise to see those tasked with strategic narrative work, such as state departments and national broadcasters, adopting these practices, and this trend is only likely to continue. Paradoxically, policy makers must embrace the seeming flux and emergence of these spaces because that is the only route to a measure of control. In recent years it already seems that political leaders have realized that communication in IR involves multiple uncertainties. These include how to communicate to multiple audiences, how to balance the forces of chaos and control to retain credibility, how to employ long-term communicative action and even poststructural approaches to obtain instrumental, strategic goals.

One way to obtain some control of communication processes is to shape the infrastructure within which persuasion and identity formation occur, and to find formats that audiences find engaging. Public diplomacy organizations like BBCWS are experimenting with these forms. At the production end of strategic narratives, they employ diasporic intellectuals and local producers. At the consumption or reception end, they create spaces and content that might not appear political and that audiences may wish to engage with as much for fun and entertainment as for political information seeking. A format such as "Greenwich 710" combined these developments by involving audiences in the show's design and production, in order to disseminate norms of public civility and journalistic standards. The purpose of these public diplomacy practices is to prepare the ground, and it is notable that both theorists of online space like Nigel Thrift and political leaders and international relations experts like Anne-Marie Slaughter are employing nature metaphors to express the need to cultivate audiences.[83] The task is to create subjectivities, literacies, and relationships. "Greenwich 710" *did* cultivate a network that contributed to political change. It became a space where the prodemocracy, promedia freedom strategic narrative could flourish, and expanded the network where this narrative could flourish. We need reflexive and poststructural approaches to research how subjects' experiences of international relations change as they engage with these spaces, conversations, and initiatives. Showing that that engagement is what leads to them experiencing international affairs through the projected narrative is an important task.

It must be acknowledged that not all international relations is about cultivating long-term support overseas. That has been this chapter's focus, but there is also a need to create short-term support for particular treaties or interventions, and to target overseas elites as well as publics. State public diplomacy outfits require different communication strategies depending on the type of event, process, and target. Different relations and varying patterns of engagement can be cultivated or exploited if events are scheduled or unscheduled, domestic or international. Sometimes audiences may be participating intentionally, other times audiences may be unwittingly harnessed. Study is required in which case studies are selected to compare a range of these structural scenarios. We begin this task in the edited volume that follows this book.[84]

NOTES

1. Felix Berenskoetter, "Parameters of a National Biography," *European Journal of International Relations* (2012). Article first published online, 16 October, DOI: 10.1177/1354066112445290: 20.
2. Berenskoetter, "Parameters of a National Biography," 21.
3. Geoffrey C. Bowker and Susan Leigh Star, *Sorting Things Out: Classification and its Consequences* (Cambridge, MA: MIT Press, 1999).

4. Geoffrey C. Bowker et al., "Toward Information Infrastructure Studies: Ways of Knowing in a Networked Environment," in *International Handbook of Internet Research*, edited by Jeremy Husinger, Lisbeth Klastrup, and Matthew Allen (Heidelberg, Germany: Springer, 2010).

5. Barack Obama, "Remarks by the President on Securing Our Nation's Cyber Infrastructure" (The White House, Office of the Press Secretary, May 29, 2009), accessed August 29, 2012, http://www.whitehouse.gov/the-press-office/remarks-president-securing-our-nations-cyber-infrastructure; Neelie Kroes, "Working Together to Protect Cyber Security," in Telecom Ministerial Conference on Critical Information Infrastructure Protection (Balatonfüred, Hungary, April 15, 2011), accessed July 15, 2013, http://europa.eu/rapid/press-release_SPEECH-11-275_en.htm.

6. Michel Callon, "Some Elements of a Sociology of Translation: Domestication of the Scallops and the Fishermen of St Brieuc Bay," in *Power, Action and Belief: A New Sociology of Knowledge*, edited by John Law (London: Routledge and Kegan Paul, 1986); Stewart R. Clegg, *Frameworks of Power* (London: Sage, 1989), 88; Robert A. Dahl, "The Concept of Power," *Behavioral Science* 2, no. 3 (1957): 204; Bruno Latour, "Visualisation and Cognition: Thinking With Hands and Eyes," *Knowledge and Society* 6 (1987): 1–40; Nikolas Rose, "Governing 'Advanced' Liberal Democracies," in *Foucault and Political Reason: Liberalism, Neo-Liberalism, and Rationalities of Government*, edited by Andrew Barry, Thomas Osborne, and Nikolas Rose (London: UCL, 1996); Nikolas Rose and Peter Miller, "Political Power beyond the State: Problematics of Government," *British Journal of Sociology* 61 (1992): 271–303.

7. Michael Mann, *The Sources of Social Power*, Vol. 2A: *A History of Power from the Beginning to AD 1760* (Cambridge: Cambridge University Press, 1986).

8. Walter Ong, *Orality and Literacy: The Technologizing of the Word* (London: Routledge, 1988).

9. James Gleick, *The Information: A History, a Theory, a Flood* (London: Fourth Estate, 2011), 31.

10. Marsall McLuhan, *Understanding Media: The Extensions of Man* (London: Routledge & Kegan Paul, 1964); Steven Livingston, "The CNN Effect Reconsidered (Again): Problematizing ICT and Global Governance in the CNN Effect Research Agenda," *Media, War & Conflict* 4, no. 1 (2011): 20–36; James N. Rosenau, *Distant Proximities: Dynamics beyond Globalization* (Princeton, NJ: Princeton University Press, 2003); John Tomlinson, "Global Immediacy," in *Cultural Politics in a Global Age: Uncertainty, Solidarity and Innovation*, edited by David Held and Henrietta L. Moore (Oxford: Oneworld, 2008).

11. Benedict Anderson, *Imagined Communities* (rev. ed.) (London: Verso, 1991); Jürgen Habermas, *The Structural Transformation of the Public Sphere: An Inquiry into a Category of Bourgeois Society* (Cambridge, MA: MIT Press, 1989); Walter Lippmann, *The Phantom Public* (New Brunswick and London: Transaction, 2002); Michael Mann, *The Sources of Social Power*, Vol. 2: *The Rise of Classes and Nation-States, 1760–1914* (Cambridge: Cambridge University Press, 1993); Mark Thompson, "Delivering Public Value: The BBC and Public Sector Reform," Smith Institute Media Lecture, Westminster, London, October 11, 2006, accessed September 4, 2012, http://www.bbc.co.uk/pressoffice/speeches/stories/thompson_smith.shtml.

12. There are empirical studies of the difference information infrastructure makes to political phenomena, but for each area of study these are relatively few and far between. These include, on cyber security: David Barnard-Wills and Debi Ashenden, "Securing Virtual Space: Cyber War, Cyber Terror, and Risk,"

Space and Culture 15, no. 2 (2012): 110–23; Mary M. Manjikian, "From Global Village to Virtual Battlespace: The Colonizing of the Internet and the Extension of Realpolitik," *International Studies Quarterly* 54, no. 2 (2010): 381–401. On terrorism and radicalization: Akil N. Awan, Andrew Hoskins, and Ben O'Loughlin, *Radicalisation and Media: Connectivity and Terrorism in the New Media Ecology* (London: Routledge, 2011); Andrew Hoskins and Ben O'Loughlin, *War and Media: The Emergence of Diffused War* (Cambridge, Polity: 2010). On citizenship and democracy: Bruce Bimber, "The Study of Information Technology and Civic Engagement," *Political Communication* 17, no. 4 (2000): 329–33; Bruce Bimber, *Information and American Democracy: Technology in the Evolution of Political Power* (Cambridge: Cambridge University Press, 2003); Philip N. Howard, *The Digital Origins of Dictatorship and Democracy: Information Technology and Political Islam* (New York and Oxford: Oxford University Press, 2010). On imperialism: Linda Main, "The Global Information Infrastructure: Empowerment or Imperialism?" *Third World Quarterly* 22, no. 1 (2001): 83–97.

13. Tim Wu, *The Master Switch: The Rise and Fall of Information Empires* (London: Atlantic Books, 2010).
14. Daniel R. McCarthy, "Open Networks and the Open Door: American Foreign Policy and the Narration of the Internet," *Foreign Policy Analysis* 7, no. 1 (2011): 89–111.
15. McCarthy, "Open Networks and the Open Door," 104.
16. Evgeny Morozov, *The Net Delusion: How Not to Liberate the World* (New York: Penguin, 2011); McCarthy, "Open Networks and the Open Door"; Edward Comor and Hamilton Bean, "America's 'Engagement' Delusion: Critiquing a Public Diplomacy Consensus," *International Communication Gazette* 74, no. 3 (2012).
17. Comor and Bean, "America's 'Engagement' Delusion."
18. Jan Melissen, *The New Public Diplomacy* (Basingstoke: Palgrave, 2007), xvii.
19. Paul Sharp, *Diplomatic Theory of International Relations* (Cambridge: Cambridge University Press, 2009), 269.
20. Ben O'Loughlin, "How the US Is Slowly Cultivating the Conditions for a Renewed International Order," *Global Policy*, May 31, 2012, accessed August 29, 2012, http://www.globalpolicyjournal.com/blog/31/05/2012/how-us-slowly-cultivating-conditions-renewed-international-order-0.
21. Robert D. Putnam, "Diplomacy and Domestic Politics: The Logic of Two-Level Games," *International Organization* 42, no. 3 (1988).
22. George P. Schultz, "Diplomacy in the Information Age," paper presented at the Conference on Virtual Diplomacy, U.S. Institute of Peace, Washington, DC, April 1, 1997.
23. Gillespie led a three-year AHRC funded project, "Tuning In: Diasporic Contact Zones at BBCWS"; see http://www.open.ac.uk/socialsciences/diasporas/. Award Ref: AH/ES58693/1. The project was based at the ESRC-funded Centre for Research on Socio-Cultural Change at the Open University (see www.cresc.ac.uk). O'Loughlin worked alongside Gillespie in a follow-on study of the BBC World Service, social media, and the 2012 Olympics (see http://newpolcom.rhul.ac.uk/npcu-blog/2012/9/4/new-project-the-olympics-twitter-and-the-bbc.html).
24. Nigel Thrift, "The Insubstantial Pageant: Producing an Untoward Land," *Cultural Geographies* 19, no. 2 (2012): 161.
25. Thrift, "The Insubstantial Pageant," 141.
26. Thrift, "The Insubstantial Pageant," 156.
27. Thrift, "The Insubstantial Pageant," 155.

28. Victor K. Fung, William K. Fung, and Yoram R. Wind, *Competing in a Flat World: Building Enterprises in a Borderless World* (Upper Saddle River, NJ: Prentice Hall, 2007).
29. Thrift, "The Insubstantial Pageant," 146. Emphasis in original.
30. Thrift, "The Insubstantial Pageant," 146.
31. Brian Massumi, "National Enterprise Emergency Steps Toward an Ecology of Powers," *Theory, Culture & Society* 26, no. 6 (2009): 167.
32. Thrift, "The Insubstantial Pageant," 155.
33. Thrift, "The Insubstantial Pageant," 156–57.
34. Mina Al-Lami, Andrew Hoskins, and Ben O'Loughlin, "Mobilisation and Violence in the New Media Ecology: The Dua Khalil Aswad and Camilia Shehata Cases," *Critical Studies on Terrorism* 5, no. 2 (2012): 237–56.
35. The study of strategic narratives in these terms could contribute to an understanding of what Tomlinson calls "complex connectivity" as part of a wider theorization and empirical explication of mediatization that is emerging. On complex connectivity see John Tomlinson, *Globalization and Culture* (Chicago: University of Chicago Press, 1999). On mediatization see: Knut Lundby, ed., *The Mediatization of Communication* (Berlin: De Gruyter Mouton, forthcoming).
36. David L. Altheide and Robert P. Snow, *Media Logic* (London: Sage, 1979); for its application see Andrew Hoskins and Ben O'Loughlin, "Security Journalism and 'The Mainstream' in Britain since 7/7: Translating Terror but Inciting Violence?" *International Affairs* 86, no. 4 (2010): 103; Andrew Chadwick, *The Hybrid Media System: Power and Politics* (Oxford: Oxford University Press, 2013).
37. Hoskins and O'Loughlin, "Security Journalism."
38. John Urry, "The Complexity Turn," *Theory, Culture, and Society* 22, no. 5 (2005): 3.
39. Pippa Norris and Ronald Inglehart, *Cosmopolitan Communications* (Cambridge: Cambridge University Press, 2009).
40. Robert L. Handley and Lou Rutigliano, "Journalistic Field Wars: Defending and Attacking the National Narrative in a Diversifying Journalistic Field," *Media, Culture & Society* 34, no. 6 (2012).
41. Chadwick, *The Hybrid Media System*.
42. Hoskins and O'Loughlin, "Security Journalism"; Brian Massumi, "Fear (The Spectrum Said)," *Positions: East Asia Cultures Critique* 13, no. 1 (2005): 31–48; Massumi, "National Enterprise Emergency."
43. Barack Obama, "A New Beginning", Cairo University, Cairo, Egypt, June 4, 2009, accessed August 29, 2012, http://www.whitehouse.gov/the_press_office/ Remarks-by-the-President-at-Cairo-University-6–04–09.
44. Philip Elliot, "White House Relays Obama's Cairo Message to Web," ABC News, June 4, 2009, story no longer available online.
45. David Bromwich, "Advice to the Prince," *New York Review of Books* 56 (2009): 12, accessed August 29, 2012, http://www.nybooks.com/articles/ archives/2009/jul/16/advice-to-the-prince/.
46. Obama, "A New Beginning."
47. Obama, "A New Beginning."
48. Bruno Latour, "What If We Talked Politics a Little?" *Contemporary Political Theory* 2, no. 2 (2003): 143.
49. ABC News, "White House Relays Obama's Cairo Message to Web."
50. Sharp, *Diplomatic Theory of International Relations*, 270.
51. BBC News, "Iran Marks Ayatolla Khomeini Anniversary," June 4, 2009, accessed May 23, 2013, http://news.bbc.co.uk/2/hi/8082386.stm.
52. BBC News, "Iran Marks Ayatolla Khomeini Anniversary."

53. Cited in Laura Haim, "Interview of the President," Canal Plus, June 1, 2009, accessed May 23, 2013, http://www.whitehouse.gov/the-press-office/transcript-interview-president-laura-haim-canal-plus-6-1-09.

54. Ibid.

55. Thomas L. Friedman, "Obama on Obama," *New York Times*, June 3, 2009, accessed May 22, 2013, http://www.nytimes.com/2009/06/03/opinion/03friedman.html?_r=0; James Traub, "Obama Realism May Not Play Well in Cairo Streets," *New York Times*, May 30, 2009, accessed May 22, 2013, http://www.nytimes.com/2009/05/31/weekinreview/31traub.html.

56. "Obama Speech Gets Solid Reaction World-Wide," *Wall Street Journal*, June 4, 2009, accessed September 1, 2012, http://online.wsj.com/article/SB124412266343885095.html.

57. "Iraq TV: Obama in Cairo, Dog Eaten Corpses," *Iraq Slogger*, June 4, 2009, accessed September 4, 2012, http://iraqslogger.powweb.com/index.php/post/7742?PHPSESSID= 86b6121176d9268d5067ebce23e8a267.

58. Lina Khatib, William Dutton, and Michael Thelwall, "Public Diplomacy 2.0: An Exploratory Case Study of the US Digital Outreach Team," *Middle East Journal* 2 (2011).

59. Craig Hayden, *The Rhetoric of Soft Power: Public Diplomacy in Global Contexts* (Lanham, MD: Lexington Books, 2012); Marc Lynch, "Why Engage? China and the Logic of Communicative Engagement," *European Journal of International Relations* 8, no. 2 (2002): 187–230.

60. Comor and Bean, "America's 'Engagement' Delusion."

61. Paul Sharp, "Obama, Clinton and the Diplomacy of Change," *The Hague Journal of Diplomacy* 6, no. 3–4 (2011): 393.

62. Brent J. Steele, "The Limit(ation)s of International Society?" In *Maritime Piracy and the Construction of Global Governance*, edited by Michael Streutt, Jon D. Carlson, and Mark Nance (Abingdon, UK: Routledge, 2012).

63. Aeron Davis, "New Media and Fat Democracy: The Paradox of Online Participation," *New Media & Society* 12, no. 5 (2010): 745–61.

64. Ben O'Loughlin, "New Deal for BBC World Service Weakens Britain's Soft Power?" *The Duck of Minerva*, June 26, 2011, accessed May 23, 2013, http://duckofminerva.blogspot.co.uk/2011/06/new-deal-for-bbc-world-service-weakens.html.

65. Foreign and Commonwealth Office, *Public Diplomacy Review* (London, December 2005), accessed September 1, 2012, http://www.britishcouncil.org/home-carter-report.

66. BBC Trust, "The BBC's Global Strategy: An Overview from the Executive," February, 2011, accessed September 1, 2012, http://www.bbc.co.uk/bbctrust/assets/files/pdf/review_report_research/strategic_review/global_strategy.txt.

67. Thompson, "Delivering Public Value."

68. Marie Gillespie. "BBC Arabic, Social Media and Citizen Production: An Experiment in Digital Democracy before the Arab Spring," *Theory, Culture and Society* 30, no. 4 (2013, forthcoming), doi: 10.1177/0263276413482382; Hugh Mackay and Jingrong Tong, "Interactivity, the Global Conversation and World Service Research: Digital China," *Participations: Journal of Audience and Reception Studies* 8, no. 1 (2011): 48–74, accessed September 1, 2012, http://www.participations.org/Volume%208/Issue%201/PDF/mackay.pdf.

69. BBC Trust, "Operating Agreement: BBC World Service," June, 2007, accessed September 1, 2012, http://www.bbc.co.uk/bbctrust/assets/files/pdf/regulatory_framework/other_activities/world_service_op_agreement.txt.

70. "Understanding Impact," Report for the BBC World Service, 2012, para 9.8, accessed November 4, 2012, http://www8.open.ac.uk/researchprojects/diasporas/news/public-policy-fellowship-at-the-bbc-world-service.

71. Andrew Skuse, Marie Gillespie, and Gerry Power, eds., *Drama for Development: Cultural Translation and Social Change* (London: Sage, 2011).
72. Skuse, Gillespie, and Power, *Drama for Development.*
73. Bryan S. Turner, "Religious Authority and the New Media," *Theory, Culture & Society* 24, no. 2 (2007): 117–34.
74. Gillespie, "BBC Arabic, Social Media and Citizen Production," 6.
75. Matilda Andersson, Marie Gillespie, and Hugh Mackay, "Mapping Digital Diasporas @ BBC World Service: Users and Uses of the Persian and Arabic Websites," *Middle East Journal of Culture and Communication* 3, no. 2 (2010): 256–78.
76. Gillespie, "BBC Arabic, Social Media and Citizen Production," 11.
77. Gillespie, "BBC Arabic, Social Media and Citizen Production."
78. Gillespie, "BBC Arabic, Social Media and Citizen Production."
79. Gillespie, "BBC Arabic, Social Media and Citizen Production."
80. Marie Gillespie, David Herbert, and Matilda Andersson, "The Mumbai Attacks and Diasporic Nationalism: BBC World Service Online Forums as Conflict, Contact and Comfort Zones," *South Asian Diaspora* 2, no. 1 (2010): 109–29.
81. Janice Bially Mattern, *Ordering International Politics: Identity, Crisis, and Representational Force* (Abingdon, UK: Routledge, 2005), 14.
82. Bially Mattern, *Ordering International Politics.*
83. Schultz, "Diplomacy in the Information Age."
84. Alister Miskimmon, Ben O'Loughlin, and Laura Roselle, eds., *Forging the World: Strategic Narratives and International Relations* (Ann Arbor: University of Michigan Press, forthcoming).

6 Conclusions
Thinking Ahead

Strategic narratives are a means for political actors to construct a shared meaning of the past, present, and future of international relations in order to shape the opinions and behavior of actors at home and overseas. Throughout this book we have examined examples of actors trying to craft and project narratives in order to give sense to international affairs in a way that gives them a strategic benefit. From Kennan and Nitze creating a Cold War narrative that legitimized policies that generated an international system, to attempts by states, international organizations, terrorist groups, and activists to give meaning to economic crises, environmental change, and wars and conflicts, strategic narratives make a difference to political change. The difficulty is knowing how and when they matter. We have provided an approach that helps explain the limitations and conditions that determine how and when strategic narratives matter.

We must take seriously what we say about the world and how we see ourselves, if we are to explain the major processes in international relations. Narratives are integral to how actors involved in those processes experience, understand, and communicate. Human beings think in narratives, and tell stories to make sense of the world around them. Narratives stitch events together into a past, a present, and possible futures. Narratives set out actors and their characters, create expectations about the roles they might play, give meaning to the context and setting, and organize events into a plot while sidelining or silencing other ways of seeing events. Narratives are central to the identity and behavior of actors in the international system, the structure of the system itself, and how ideas, issues, and policies are contested.

It is because narratives give sense to international relations that actors seek to use them strategically. A lot of effort and resources go into strategic communication, impression management, diplomatic signaling, and public diplomacy campaigns. Behind these efforts lurk assumptions, concepts, and models of communication that often prove hard to put into practice. Our study of strategic narrative makes clear a set of considerations that policy makers and communications professionals must account for when designing a strategy to create some effect in international relations. This includes joining up the formation, projection, and reception of strategic narratives and the interactions and feedback loops that ensue. It includes deciding where the strategic aims lie on the spectrum of persuasion: is the aim simply to rhetorically trap opponents into signing up to a treaty, or are there more long-term ambitions to alter how those opponents understand themselves and their role in the international system? It also includes understanding how a narrative will be contested in various media ecologies. Both the content and the process of narrative formation, projection, and reception can be contested. We hope that these many dimensions of narrative contestation make clear how difficult it is to craft and use a strategic narrative to achieve change in international relations. Nevertheless, political leaders have no option but to try.

In addition, we show how a new media ecology both affects the use of strategic narratives and is affected by them. New technologies and an expanded number of communicators change the dynamics of system, identity, and issue narratives. Today leaders are less able to control the flow of media content because of the proliferation of media sources and rapid dissemination of information via the Internet, cell phones, and other new media. In particular, there is more of an opportunity for non-elite media and nongovernmental sources to affect media coverage and the broader narrative on international relations. This is important because we know that news media within a state tend to focus on their own state's involvement.[1] We also know that non-elite media, including blogs and social media spaces, can provide alternative narratives, as can nongovernmental individual sources. We should look at the construction of narratives as multifaceted, nonlinear, and broad in scope. This is the insight of Castells' work on communication, power, and the terrain of international relations.

In Chapter 2 we addressed actors depicted in strategic narratives and actors' uses of strategic narratives. For example, system narratives set out who are the important actors in the world, what characteristics they have, and what role they play. Thus, great powers, normal powers, rising powers, and rogue states are expected to behave in a particular way, and their actions are shaped, in part, by those expectations. Great powers must live up to their role not simply in their actions but through offering a compelling narrative of world order. This suggests the idea of a "say-do gap" can be problematic.[2] Saying is doing. A narrative that suggests, for example, that one stands shoulder to shoulder is to make a commitment. It is a concrete act that compels an actor toward certain behavior or face the label of hypocrite.

But strategic narratives are not just central in constructing or constraining international behavior. Political actors attempt to use strategic narratives. We understand national interest as Jutta Weldes does, as constructed "out of shared meanings through which the world, particularly the international system and the place of the state in it, is understood," in other words, through narratives.[3] These narratives are, in part, strategically constructed as political actors champion their own preferred narratives. In addition, actors choose to use particular narratives because they support or legitimize preferred policies, and these narratives may then structure future decisions and/or preferences.

Chapter 3 focused on how narratives shape our understanding of international order. The Libya crisis of 2011 illustrates how states sought to narrate what was happening and tried to define their response. The role of France and the UK in spearheading diplomatic efforts to enforce a no-fly zone rested on their efforts to project a strategic narrative of the crisis that would generate international support within the United Nations. Central to this strategic narrative were conceptions of international order—the nature of sovereignty, the responsibility of powerful states to ensure the safety of citizens under R2P, and the role of international multilateral institutions in maintaining order. By appealing to the United States' sense of global leadership and its prior involvement in crisis management operations in the European region, France and the UK were able to generate enough support for UN1973. The Franco-British strategic narrative's stress on the severity of the threat posed to Libyan civilians also helped generate international support for UN1973 and secured the abstention of China, Germany, and Russia, despite their reservations. As Orford has argued, the heroic narrative of the West to undertake crisis management has dominated discussions on military interventions since the 1990s.[4] This narrative of responsibility for the fate of Libyan civilians in Benghazi proved very compelling in the diplomacy of the crisis. The narrative that underpinned the British and French diplomacy proved effective in securing the enforcement of the no-fly zone and the involvement of President Obama in supporting the decision. This case illustrates how the components of international relations such as law, cooperation, and sovereignty became narrativized by France and the UK to achieve their immediate interests in a way that also served to support a broader understanding of how the international order should operate.

The Libya example neatly illustrates the main argument of Chapter 4. We asked what happens when narratives clash and what counts as success or even victory. Scholars from different theoretical perspectives have addressed a variety of forms of contestation. Contestation can involve short-term framing of issues and trapping of one state by another around a particular issue, such as the way France and the UK framed the Libya crisis in order to generate a behavioral response from the US. However, contestation can also involve long-term discursive shifts purposefully driven by actors seeking to define or redefine the core terms through which international relations are understood and experienced. Chapter 4 offered two analytical frameworks through which these dynamics can be disentangled. First, persuasion can be treated in thin or thick terms, depending on the type of interactions and power relations the analyst seeks to explain. In an ideal world, analysts would be able to follow how thick and thin dynamics shape each other, and a few studies have been able to achieve this. Second, we asked what it was about a narrative that is contested. We proposed that both the content of the narrative and the processes of its formation, projection, and reception are open to contestation by opponents. We illustrated some of the aspects of each framework through three examples of narrative contestation in the last half century: the narrative contests that emerge during Israel's conflicts with its neighbors, the narrative work involved when the majority of states and citizens shifted from pro-whaling to anti-whaling in the 1960s and 1970s, and contestation of Iran's nuclear program. The whaling case appears one of long-term narrative success for activists as states and publics around the world began to interpret whales through a different narrative, resulting in major policy change. However, Iran's ability to undermine the formation of a shared, settled narrative about its nuclear program was also a success insofar as talking continues and its program has not been halted. What these cases suggest is that there can be no template or model of narrative success.

Chapter 5 explored ways states are seeking to harness the new media ecology to cultivate audiences overseas who might become receptive to strategic narratives. Some claim we are witnessing a new great game. The spread of participatory media and communication power brings "the people" into international relations as an actor to be courted, whose views should be engaged with, and whose agency should be managed. We argued that governments are playing a twin-track strategy. First, they must win arguments and gain narrative traction with audiences by working within the media ecologies of the day, making sure their narrative is relayed by credible figures within national and transnational public spheres. Second, states must also compete to shape the infrastructure of these ecologies itself, since that infrastructure privileges some voices and some ways of communicating over others. Thus, shaping the infrastructure conditions whether supporters or opponents are able to express themselves in the narrative battle. The US has promoted an agenda of Internet freedom that works on both tracks. Internet freedom is a narrative circulating *in* media ecologies about freedom. However, it is also a narrative that legitimizes and rationalizes efforts to *shape* media ecologies so more voices can support the freedom narrative. Other countries are engaged in the same twin-track game, including the EU and China. Both levels or tracks present problems and can be understood through different theories of communication and persuasion. These media spaces are a crucial site of communication power and where strategic narrative contestation is being waged, but the way relations unfold presents difficult conceptual, methodological, and normative problems. What we mean by "the people" or "the audience" is itself contestable, how influence works in these spaces is hard to empirically measure or demonstrate, and skeptics rightly ask whether states' rhetoric of engagement and listening is likely to have any substantive effect on their foreign policy making.

OUR CONTRIBUTION

Our theory of strategic narrative contributes to explaining many processes in international relations.[5] Strategic narratives construct and shape expectations of the nature and workings of the *international system*. These include actors' understandings of the structure of the system, and its polarity. Actors also identify with categorizations of states and seek to socialize others to accept these identities; expectations about the behavior of kinds of states, such as great powers and rogue states, are generated through narratives; the desirability and possibility of collaboration, cooperation, integration; predictions about rising and falling powers, threats, enemies, and allies; and the identification of interests all involve narrative constructions. Strategic narrative is central to *foreign policy*, including the formation of policy agendas, understandings of policy options and preferences, the formation of coalitions, and the legitimation of policy.

A focus on strategic narratives can also contribute to addressing many key questions in a range of literatures:

IR systems theories and power transition: Strategic narrative analysis speaks to IR systems theories and analyses of power transition by assessing how actors come to understand power transitions. Hard-power capabilities and even the actors that make up the system may change, but a new order must be narratively constructed. In fact we are living in a world surrounded by contestation over a new world order. Seen through the lens of strategic narratives, one can study how new orders are constructed and why this is a challenge. It is important to note once again that we still understand hard-power capabilities to be important. Still, the most powerful states cannot always use their hard-power capabilities, and even when they do, the use of those capabilities is constrained by the narratives that define interests and threats.

Influence: Persuasion, socialization, norm diffusion, soft power, normative power: Strategic narrative analysis addresses the role of influence in international relations and foreign policy, giving scholars insight on why ideas or norms spread, what contributes to socialization, and what underlies soft power or normative power. Effective narratives contribute to all of these processes, as we outlined in Chapter 4 on contestation. There are various characteristics associated with narratives that contribute to the relative success of narratives in norm diffusion, socialization, and soft power, from content to communication process and technique to enhance credibility of the communicator. Strategic narrative analysis focuses attention on agents both as communicator and as audience-cum-users, adding significantly to the constructivist agenda in international relations theory. Recognition that the new media ecology shapes these processes is also important, as a traditional conception of audience as receptor changes in some circumstances to users who interact with information and with each other, making networks more important and the communication process more horizontal and nonlinear than in the past. This has the potential to significantly change the nature of power and influence in the international system, to the extent that in Chapter 3 we asked whether the ontology of IR must be reexamined.

Language in IR: Studies of discourse, framing and narrative: The importance of narrative highlights the centrality of language in international relations. This ties in directly to studies of discourse and framing. For example, there are a number of ways to define and use the term *framing* and there are a number of conceptual overlaps with the notion of strategic narratives. Entman, for example, defines framing as "selecting and highlighting some facets of events or issues, and making connections among them so as to promote a particular interpretation, evaluation, and/or solution."[6] Wolfsfeld defines an interpretive frame as "central organizing idea[s] for making sense of relevant events and suggesting what is at issue."[7] Entman's making of connections and Wolfsfeld's organizing ideas come close to the development of a narrative. However, narrative as a concept pinpoints a very specific form of experience based around a sense of time and movement. A narrative entails an initial order or status quo, a problem that disrupts that order, and a resolution that reestablishes order, often bringing about a slightly altered situation in which characters have demonstrated their qualities. Narrative is a particular structure made up of actors and events, plot and time, and setting and space. Aspects of narrative may be framed, but framing does not imply this broader structure of experience. Meanwhile, narratives and frames draw upon enduring discourses, by which we mean bodies of knowledge and the practices that sustain them. In Chapter 4 we saw how actors crafted elements of legal, scientific, or religious discourse into narratives about Iran's nuclear program. It is not that narrative lies in a hierarchal relationship to frames and discourse. Each analysis of one helps illuminate how the other two work. These three forms of representation continually interact and must be analyzed together to identify how actors understand the meaning of immediate events and long-term change in international relations.

Public diplomacy and international political communication: It is imperative for foreign policy makers to try to persuade their international rivals of the validity of their narrative of the international system. However, the era of communication power opens up opportunities for practitioners of public diplomacy to reach beyond elite circles and reach overseas publics. Those publics become targets whose support is valued for two reasons. Those foreign publics may pressure their political elites into policy change. They may also be part of a culture that is more receptive to economic, cultural, and geopolitical relations with your state and narrative in the longer-term future. Consequently, the formation, projection, and reception of strategic narrative pulls in classic questions in international political communication concerning how agendas are set, which audiences are exposed to or contributing to whose content, and who owns the national and international media organizations that mediate the flow of strategic narratives. In the new media ecology, however, the operation of agenda-setting, patterns of exposure, and the nature of ownership have all altered. The gatekeepers of news agenda are now networked, with audiences gatekeeping their own news agendas through their clicking and sharing of news stories online. Patterns of exposure are both less predictable, due to unforeseeable dynamics of virality and emergence, and routinized, since national old media still remain vital to most audiences worldwide. Ownership too is disrupted, as the dominance of Western private-sector media organizations that characterized the late twentieth century undergoes a power transition that overlaps with that in international relations generally. Media based in the BRICS and other rising powers are growing stronger. Meanwhile, there is a greater range of types of actors in the media space thanks to the emergence of open source publishing, private media that allow mass self-publication (think Facebook), and the endurance of public sector media in different parts of the world. As a result, public diplomacy practitioners who aim to generate a receptive audience for their strategic narrative need to understand how these hybrid media ecologies operate if they are to fully realize the possibilities of communication power.

Strategic communication in war and conflict: Finally, strategic narrative analysis offers a way to understand the full context of war and conflict. It is clearly not enough to analyze only hard-power capabilities when studying war. In all types of conflict, there must be an explanation for the appalling price of war. Narratives are important as they set out the story of why a state is involved in a conflict, who is with the state and against the state, and how the conflict will be resolved.[8] Narratives serve as the bridge between images of other states and foreign policy behavior.[9] There must be narratives about the nature of the international system, the identity of the force for which one fights, and the specific issues in dispute. Yet, preexisting narratives—about great power status, for example—can shape and constrain narratives about war and conflict. This is seen clearly in the cases of US involvement in Vietnam and USSR involvement in Afghanistan, where great power identity constrained policies and narrative explanations and made candor unattractive.[10] It is also seen during protracted conflict, when one serious challenge involves maintaining alliances. Narratives about abandonment and entrapment within alliances constrain behavior, for example.

Our approach is the unifying strand that connects these disparate approaches and trajectories of research in international relations and communication. Engagement with strategic narrative analysis would add explanatory capability in all of the areas listed above.

FUTURE AGENDAS

The study of strategic narrative can help explain current phenomena in IR and would be valuable to future studies in a number of areas. Below are some examples.

1. Identifying whether Strategic Narratives Make More of a Difference at Turning Points and Critical Junctures

Future research is required to establish whether strategic narratives play different roles, or are used differently, in moments of change or stasis. Was narrative work more important as the Cold War ended, or did narrative work make that change possible or legitimize it afterwards? In the introduction (Chapter 1) we argued that political leaders can be reflexive about the nature and malleability of core features of international relations. The natures of borders, states, law, and rights do change, and leaders wish to understand the conditions within which narrative work can help them alter the meanings of these core features and thus how they are practiced. Whether conditions of rupture or continuity present more windows of opportunity is important to those seeking to act strategically.

Equally, do different conditions make it easier or more difficult to change narratives? Political actors may construct meaning as multiple narratives come into conflict in one case and overlap in another. For example, in the Soviet Union, political leaders eschewed narratives associated with the tsar as legitimate ruler, transforming the narrative to one focused on the new Soviet man and communist ideals. Under Putin, however, Hill and Gaddy argue that there is an interesting continuity in narrative. Statues of Lenin are left up or resurrected in places even as depictions of the tsars again adorn the Kremlin, emphasizing a common history for one great Russia.[11] Putin has been able to achieve narrative continuity, or even a narrative return.

Explaining narrative continuity and change requires analysis that operates across the full spectrum of persuasion, from behavioral, tactical maneuvering as events unfold to the strategic harnessing of constitutive power to work upon identities and the ecologies through which targets of narratives come to understand and experience international relations. Analysis must also account for the constraints on action. Leaders, nations, and narratives are often resistant to change, but they can change. These processes are not static, even if it is unrealistic to expect any actor to achieve unilateral change and win broad consent for a new issue or system narrative.

2. Explaining How National Cultures Are Expressed in the World

Peter Katzenstein's work highlights the importance of culture and civilization in international politics.[12] Our work on strategic narrative addresses how ideas of culture or civilization may be both (re)constructed and constrained through communication of narratives. For example, in our analysis of the Iran nuclear program in Chapter 4 it was clear that narrative contestation was not only a matter of tactically shifting the terrain or discourse under discussion. Each actor was bound by cultural constraints about what their leaders could say. Why is it that US presidents cannot say that proliferation might be a good thing, might bring stability, but a leading US international relations scholar such as Kenneth Waltz can?[13] Why is there no denunciation of India's nuclear weapons from EU or US leaders but immediate and preemptive securitization in Iran's case?

3. Identifying the Impact and Effect of Narratives

Addressing questions of impact and effect is a major endeavor, and one to which we turn in a forthcoming edited volume.[14] A range of scholars will address the impact and effect of strategic narratives in a number of specific cases including:

- within the US ad Russian Federation in the post–Cold War world;
- within the European Union as economic challenges mount;
- within China about foreign policy;
- within international organizations in the area of international development;
- at the intersection of social networks, public diplomacy, and the international community;
- in the contestation of narratives about terrorism;
- in narratives about global uncertainty.

Specifically, these case studies will bring in issues such as networks, technology, and institutions, and will address the methodological issues associated with the study of strategic narratives.

There is a need for empirical studies of how actors operationalize strategic narrative in international relations. State departments and media organizations have invested a great deal of thinking in the past decade about how to identify who has received a narrative and what effects the narrative has on attitudes and behavior. This is an extremely complex area, however. Establishing the difference made by the presence, reception, and interpretation of a narrative and its mediation vis-à-vis other narratives and other factors requires a number of methods as well as theories and concepts from different disciplines. It is striking that Castells,[15] for instance, turned to neuroscience to understand how individuals receive and interpret narratives about the 2003 Iraq war, for example. We deal with this methodological challenge at greater length in our subsequent volume, but some important points can be advanced here.

The first point is both the most obvious and yet the least practiced. The processes of formation, projection, and reception must be traced. What are the connections between the initial, intentional strategic narrative design, the way in which the narrative is projected, by whom, through what intermediaries, languages, and formats, and the meanings attributed to the narrative by intended and unintended recipients of the narrative? We must also guard against viewing this as a linear process. How does a state anticipate reactions and build those into the narrative formation and projection such that audience responses are folded back into the process without them even knowing?

Second, it would appear that the proliferation of digital communications in the international system offers unprecedented opportunities to analyze the formation, projection, and reception of strategic narratives. However, narratives are also projected and circulated through face-to-face conversation, through paper materials, and via other nondigital formats. Those who have studied narratives of conflict in rich and poor states attest to the importance of routine discussion about news and politics among friends, family, coworkers and even strangers to the interpretation of elite narratives.[16] At the time of writing, there is a great deal of excellent analysis emerging on digital communications and global waves of protest.[17] However, just as elite behind-the-scenes interaction is vital but hard to access, so it requires a mix of methodologies to connect online narrative work with the ways in which meanings circulate through offline social interaction.

Third, the question of reception has *not* been blown apart by the arrival of digital media and apparent pluralization of authors and diffusion of content. Rather, it has become more challenging. Gatekeeping still exists and steers where narratives go. Mass media editors have traditionally held a gatekeeping role, deciding what stories would make the scarce pages or minutes of the news. Their position appeared fatally undermined by the infinite capacity of the Internet, the fragmentation of news audiences, and the ability of audiences to gatekeep their own news through personalized filters—what Negroponte termed "the daily me."[18] Instead, the past decade has witnessed new forms of gatekeeping that are networked,[19] institutional,[20] and often multilingual, hinting at more subtle changes in the form and loci of power in international communication.[21] In 2010 CNN announced that 75 percent of its news hits came from links from social networking sites (e.g. Facebook, Twitter).[22] Instead of mainstream media gatekeeping and sustaining predictable news agendas, citizens have independently begun to perform this function in their daily news and social media routines. Gates still exist and states seeking to project strategic narratives must understand and work with them, even as the nature of gates and gatekeeping adapt in form and personnel. For narrative content that lies beyond these networked gatekeeping processes, much Internet content can be tracked through social media monitoring methods. Big data, increased computer processing power, and linguistic analysis software make it possible to track narratives through the messy grammars and multiple languages of everyday digitized global communication.

Strategic narrative offers a promising framework to chart the emergence of a potential multipolar world during a period of power transition. Understanding changes in the distribution of power and influence drove our initial thoughts on how narrative analysis could play a central role in explaining some of the major themes in international relations. Strategic narrative is a way to understand current developments. Each of the chapters in this book has sought to highlight how narrative is central to communication in an increasingly competitive media ecology. Presidents, prime ministers, and heads of state all seek to exert influence through the projection of strategic narratives, aimed at generating domestic support for foreign policy and at maximizing the scope for persuasion of their parties. Material power is not enough to shape the conditions of international affairs—although it helps. The major developments that have shaped the world since the end of the Cold War have concerned the claims of existing and emerging powerful actors to shape the political, economic, and social foundations of the globe. Influencing the ideas that shape policies is a growing preoccupation of governments, NGOs, business, and ordinary citizens. An organization such as the European Union has emerged as a major economic player in the world. With this has come influence over the rules and norms of the global economy. This has led Peter van Ham to highlight the social power that the EU has.[23]

Ikenberry has been the leading figure in explaining power transition through a liberal lens.[24] Ikenberry argues that the existing liberal order will not fundamentally change, which is to the future benefit of existing powers. We believe that strategic narrative can help analyze whether the liberal model will remain the dominant international force by analyzing the strategic narratives of emerging powers such as Brazil, India, and China. Shashi Tharoor argues in his book *Pax Indica* that existing conventions may over time face challenges as new powerful voices emerge, such as India.[25] Barry Buzan's argument that we are destined to inherit a more decentered world can only add to the range of competing perspectives.[26] The global financial crisis of 2008 and the United States' challenging military interventions in Afghanistan and Iraq have pressured President Obama to construct a new strategic narrative to retain US global influence.[27] As Obama has said, "In an age when ideas and images can travel the globe in an instant, our response to terrorism can't depend on military or law enforcement alone. We need all elements of national power to win a battle of wills, a battle of ideas."[28] With new powerful voices emerging and the nature of communication and power changing how international relations is done, the study of strategic narratives offers a way to understand the contestation surrounding power transition and potential avenues to overcome potential conflicts.

NOTES

1. Cristina Archetti, "Unamerican Views: Why US-Developed Models of Press-State Relations Don't Apply to the Rest of the World," *Westminster Papers in Communication and Culture* 5, no. 3 (2008): 4–26.
2. Emile Simpson, *War from the Ground Up: Twenty-First-Century Combat as Politics* (London: Hurst, 2012), 181.
3. Jutta Weldes, "Constructing National Interests," *European Journal of International Relations* 2, no. 3 (1996).
4. Anne Orford, *Reading Humanitarian Intervention* (Cambridge: Cambridge University Press, 2003).

5. Alister Miskimmon, Ben O'Loughlin, and Laura Roselle, "Forging the World: Strategic Narratives and International Relations." Centre for European Politics / New Political Communications Unit Working Paper, 2012. Accessed May 23, 2013, http://newpolcom.rhul.ac.uk/storage/Forging%20the%20World%20Working%20Paper%202012.pdf.

6. Robert M. Entman, *Projections of Power: Framing News, Public Opinion, and US Foreign Policy* (University of Chicago Press, 2009), 5.

7. Gadi Wolfsfeld, *Media and Political Conflict: News from the Middle East* (Cambridge University Press, 1997), 35.

8. Andreas Antoniades, Alister Miskimmon, and Ben O'Loughlin, "Great Power Politics and Strategic Narratives." March 2010. Working Paper No. 7, The Centre for Global Political Economy, University of Sussex. Accessed May 22, 2013, https://www.sussex.ac.uk/webteam/gateway/file .php?name=cgpe-wp07-antoniades-miskimmon-oloughlin.pdf&site=359.

9. Amy Skonieczny, "Trade Talk: Narratives of US Identity in the Making of Economic Policy," paper prepared for the Annual Meeting of the American Political Science Association, Toronto, Canada, September 3–6, 2009.

10. Laura Roselle, *Media and the Politics of Failure: Great Powers, Communication Strategies, and Military Defeats*, 2nd ed. (New York: Palgrave Macmillan, 2011), 123.

11. Fiona Hill and Clifford G. Gaddy, *Mr. Putin: Operative in the Kremlin* (Washington, DC: The Brookings Institution, 2013), 67, 73.

12. Peter Katzenstein, *Anglo-America and Its Discontents: Civilizational Identities beyond West and East* (New York: Routledge, 2012); *Sinicization and the Rise of China: Civilizational Processes beyond East and West* (New York: Routledge, 2012); *Civilizations in World Politics: Plural and Pluralist Perspectives* (New York: Routledge, 2009).

13. Kenneth N. Waltz, "Why Iran Should Get the Bomb: Nuclear Balancing Would Mean Stability," *Foreign Affairs* 91 (2012).

14. Alister Miskimmon et al., eds., *Forging the World: Strategic Narratives in International Relations.*

15. Manuel Castells, *Communication Power* (Oxford: Oxford University Press, 2009).

16. Andrew Skuse, Marie Gillespie, and Gerry Power, eds., *Drama for Development: Cultural Translation and Social Change* (London: Sage, 2011); Marie Gillespie, "Security, Media, Legitimacy: Multi-Ethnic Media Publics and the Iraq War 2003," *International Relations* 20, no. 4 (2006); Monroe Price, *Fierceness of Competition, Softness of Power: Freedom of Expression in a Time of Strategic Communicators,* (forthcoming).

17. Lance W. Bennett and Alexandra Segerberg, "The Logic of Connective Action: Digital Media and the Personalization of Contentious Politics," *Information, Communication & Society* 15, no. 5 (2012); Sharon Meraz and Zizi Papacharissi, "Networked Gatekeeping and Networked Framing on# Egypt," *The International Journal of Press/Politics* 18, no. 2 (2013).

18. Nicholas Negroponte, *Being Digital* (New York: Knopf, 1995).

19. Karine Barzilai-Nahon, "Toward a Theory of Network Gatekeeping: A Framework for Exploring Information Control," *Journal of the American Society for Information Science and Technology* 59, no. 9 (2008); Sharon Meraz and Zizi Papacharissi, "Networked Gatekeeping and Networked Framing on Egypt," *The International Journal of Press/Politics* 18, no. 2 (2013).

20. Lance W. Bennett, Kirsten Foot, and Michael Xenos, "Narratives and Network Organization: A Comparison of Fair Trade Systems in Two Nations," *Journal of Communication* 61, no. 2 (2011).

21. Andrew Hoskins and Ben O'Loughlin, "Remediating Jihad for Western News Audiences: The Renewal of Gatekeeping?" *Journalism* 12, no. 2 (2011).
22. Doug Gross, "Survey: More Americans Get News from Internet than Newspapers or Radio," CNN Tech, March 1, 2010. Accessed May 23, 2013, http://articles.cnn.com/2010–03–01/tech/social.network.news_1_social-networking-sites-social-media-social-experience?_s=PM:TECH.
23. Peter van Ham, *Social Power* (London: Routledge, 2010).
24. G. John Ikenberry, *Liberal Leviathan: The Origins, Crisis, and Transformation of the American World Order* (Princeton: Princeton University Press, 2011).
25. Shashi Tharoor, *Pax Indica* (London: Allen Lane, 2012).
26. Barry Buzan, "The Inaugural Kenneth N. Waltz Lecture 'A World without Superpowers: Decentred Globalism,'" *International Relations* 25, no. 1 (2011).
27. Nancy Birdsall and Francis Fukuyama, "The Post-Washington Consensus: Development after the Crisis," *Foreign Affairs* 90, no. 2 (2011).
28. Barack Obama, "Remarks by the President at the National Defense University," Fort McNair, Washington D. C. May 23, 2013, accessed May 23, 2013, http://www.whitehouse.gov/the-press-office/2013/05/23/remarks-president-national-defense-university.

Bibliography

The Age. "Iran Resumes Uranium Processing," August 9, 2005, accessed December 3, 2012, http://www.theage.com.au/news/world/iran-resumes-uranium-processing/2005/08/09/1123353289095.html.

Agnew, John. *Globalization and Sovereignty.* Lanham, MD: Rowman and Littlefield, 2009.

———. "The Territorial Trap: The Geographical Assumptions of International Relations Theory." *Review of International Political Economy* 1, no. 1(1994): 53–80.

Ahmadinejad, Mahmood. "Address by H.E. Dr. Mahmood Ahmadinejad President of the Islamic Republic of Iran before the Sixtieth Session of the United Nations General Assembly." New York, September 17, 2005. Accessed May 21, 2013, http://www.un.org/webcast/ga/60/statements/iran050917eng.pdf.

———. "Message to the American People." November 29, 2006. Accessed April 4, 2013, http://www.ahmadinejad.ir/en/Message_to_the_American_People_.

Albright, Madeleine. "MFN for China Would Advance America's Leadership in Asia." Senate Finance Committee, June 6, 1997. Accessed May 21, 2013, http://www.usembassy-israel.org.il/publish/press/state/archive/1997/june/sd90612.htm.

Albrow, Martin, Helmut K. Anheier, Marlies Glasius, Mary Kaldor, and Monroe E. Price, eds. *Global Civil Society 2007/8: Communicative Power and Democracy.* London: Sage, 2007.

Al-Lami, Mina, Andrew Hoskins, and Ben O'Loughlin. "Mobilisation and Violence in the New Media Ecology: The Dua Khalil Aswad and Camilia Shehata Cases." *Critical Studies on Terrorism* 5, no. 2 (2012): 237–56.

Altheide, David L., and Robert P. Snow. *Media Logic.* London: Sage, 1979.

Anderson, Benedict. *Imagined Communities* (rev. ed.). London: Verso, 1991.

Andersson, Matilda, Marie Gillespie, and Hugh Mackay. "Mapping Digital Diasporas@ BBC World Service: Users and Uses of the Persian and Arabic Websites." *Middle East Journal of Culture and Communication* 3, no. 2 (2010): 256–78.

"Anti-Iran Rhetoric Worries U.N. Nuke Watchdog." *NBC News*, October 28, 2007. Available at: http://www.nbcnews.com/id/21516968/42739722#.UTTq9Y6PdgM.

Antoniades, Andreas, Alister Miskimmon, and Ben O'Loughlin. "Great Power Politics and Strategic Narratives." Working paper no. 7, The Centre for Global Political Economy, University of Sussex, March 2010. Accessed May 22, 2013, https://www.sussex.ac.uk/webteam/gateway/file.php?name=cgpe-wp07-antoniades-miskimmon-oloughlin.pdf&site=359.

Archetti, Cristina. "People, Processes & Practices: Agency, Communication and the Construction of International Relations." Paper prepared for the International Studies Association meeting, San Francisco, CA, April 3–6, 2013.

———. "Unamerican Views: Why US-Developed Models of Press-State Relations Don't Apply to the Rest of the World." *Westminster Papers in Communication and Culture* 5, no. 3 (2008): 4–26.

————. *Understanding Terrorism in the Age of Global Media: A Communication Approach.* Basingstoke: Palgrave Macmillan, 2013.

Ashton, Catherine. "Statement on Iran," European Parliament, January 19, 2010. Accessed May 21, 2013, http://www.eu-un.europa.eu/articles/en/article_9421_en.htm.

Atlas, James. "What Is Fukuyama Saying?" *New York Times Magazine,* October 22, 1989. Accessed March 13, 2013, http://www.nytimes.com/1989/10/22/magazine/what-is-fukuyama-saying-and-to-whom-is-he-saying-it.html?pagewanted=print&src=pm.

Awan, Akil, Andrew Hoskins, and Ben O'Loughlin. *Radicalisation and Media: Connectivity and Terrorism in the New Media Ecology.* London: Routledge, 2011.

Bach, Jonathan P. G. *Between Sovereignty and Integration: German Foreign Policy and National Identity after 1989.* Vol. 23. Münster: LIT Verlag, 1999.

Barnard-Wills, David, and Debi Ashenden. "Securing Virtual Space: Cyber War, Cyber Terror, and Risk." *Space and Culture* 15, no. 2 (2012): 110–23.

Barnett, Michael. "Culture, Strategy and Foreign Policy Change: Israel's Road to Oslo." *European Journal of International Relations* 5, no. 1 (1999): 5–36.

————. *The International Humanitarian Order.* New York: Taylor & Francis, 2010.

Bacevich, Andrew J. *American Empire: The Realities and Consequences of US Diplomacy.* Cambridge, MA: Harvard University Press, 2002.

Barzilai-Nahon, Karine. "Toward a Theory of Network Gatekeeping: A Framework for Exploring Information Control." *Journal of the American Society for Information Science and Technology* 59, no. 9 (2008): 1493–1512.

BBC. "The BBC's Global Strategy: An Overview from the Executive." February, 2011. Accessed September 1, 2012, http://www.bbc.co.uk/bbctrust/assets/files/pdf/review_report_research/strategic_review/global_strategy.txt.

————. "Operating Agreement: BBC World Service." June, 2007. Accessed September 1, 2012, http://www.bbc.co.uk/bbctrust/assets/files/pdf/regulatory_framework/other_activities/world_service_op_agreement.txt.

BBC News. "Iran 'Enters New Nuclear Phase.'" April 9, 2007. Accessed April 4, 2013, http://news.bbc.co.uk/1/hi/world/middle_east/6538957.stm.

————. "Iran Marks Ayatolla Khomeini Anniversary." June 4, 2009. http://news.bbc.co.uk/2/hi/8082386.stm,

Beck, Ulrich. *German Europe.* London: Polity, 2013.

Benjamin, Walter. *Illuminations: Essays and Reflections.* New York: Schocken, 1969.

Bennett, W. Lance, and Alexandra Segerberg. "The Logic of Connective Action: Digital Media and the Personalization of Contentious Politics." *Information, Communication & Society* 15, no. 5 (2012): 739–68.

Bennett, W. Lance, and Jarol B. Manheim. "The One-Step Flow of Communication." *The Annals of the American Academy of Political and Social Science* 608, no. 1 (2006): 213–32.

Bennett, W. Lance, Kirsten Foot, and Michael Xenos. "Narratives and Network Organization: A Comparison of Fair Trade Systems in Two Nations." *Journal of Communication* 61, no. 2 (2011): 219–45.

Bentley, Michelle. "War and/of Words: Constructing WMD in US Foreign Policy." *Security Studies* 22, no. 1 (2013): 68–97.

Berenskoetter, Felix S. "Mapping the Mind Gap: A Comparison of US and European Security Strategies." *Security Dialogue* 36, no. 1 (2005): 71–92.

————. "Parameters of a National Biography." *European Journal of International Relations.* Online First Version, October 16, 2012.

Berenskoetter, Felix, and Bastian Giegerich. "From NATO to ESDP: A Social Constructivist Analysis of German Strategic Adjustment after the End of the Cold War." *Security Studies* 19, no. 3 (2010): 407–52.

Bernardi, Daniel Leonard, Pauline Hope Cheong, Chris Lundry, and Scott W. Ruston. *Narrative Landmines: Rumors, Islamist Extremism, and the Struggle for Strategic Influence.* New Brunswick, NJ: Rutgers University Press, 2012.

Betts, Richard K. "Is Strategy an Illusion?" *International Security* 25, no. 2 (2000): 5–50.

Bially Mattern, Janice. *Ordering International Politics: Identity, Crisis, and Representational Force.* New York: Routledge, 2005.

Billig, Michael. *Arguing and Thinking: A Rhetorical Approach to Social Psychology.* Cambridge: Cambridge University Press, 1987.

———. *Banal Nationalism.* London: Sage, 1995.

Bimber, Bruce. *Information and American Democracy: Technology in the Evolution of Political Power.* Cambridge: Cambridge University Press, 2003.

———. "The Study of Information Technology and Civic Engagement." *Political Communication* 17, no. 4 (2000): 329–33.

Birdsall, Nancy, and Francis Fukuyama. "The Post-Washington Consensus: Development after the Crisis." *Foreign Affairs* 90, no. 2 (2011): 45–53.

"The Birth of an Obama Doctrine." *Economist* (Lexington), March 28, 2011. Accessed September 1, 2011, http://www.economist.com/blogs/lexington/2011/03/libya_4.

Biscop, Sven. *The European Security Strategy: A Global Agenda for Positive Power.* Abingdon: Ashgate, 2005.

———, ed. "The Value of Power, the Power of Values: A Call for an EU Grand Strategy." *Egmont Paper 33.* Egmont Royal Institute for International Relations, October, 2009.

Blanchard, Christopher M. "Libya: Unrest and U.S. Policy." CRS Report for Congress 7–5700. Accessed August 21, 2011, http://www.fpc.state.gov/documents/organization/159788.pdf.

Blitz, James. "Public Opposes Wider Libya Campaign." *Financial Times,* June 20, 2011, including Harris Opinion Poll for the *Financial Times,* June 20, 2011. Accessed August 21, 2011, http://www.ft.com/cms/s/0/19f0dc8a-9b5c-11e0-bbc6-00144feabdc0.html#axzz1qPRjAE6X.

Borger, Julian, Patrick Wintour, and Michael Oliver. "Iran Nuclear Plant: Miliband Refuses to Rule Out Military Action." *The Guardian,* September 26, 2009. Accessed May 21, 2013, http://www.guardian.co.uk/world/2009/sep/26/miliband-iran-nuclear-plant.

Bostdorff, Denise M. "Harry S. Truman, 'Special Message to the Congress on Greece and Turkey: The Truman Doctrine' (12 March 1947)." *Voices of Democracy* 4 (2009): 1–22.

Bowen, Wyn Q., and Jonathan Brewer. "Iran's Nuclear Challenge: Nine Years and Counting." *International Affairs* 87, no. 4 (2011): 923–43.

Bowker, Geoffrey C., Karen Baker, Florence Millerand, and David Ribes. "Toward Information Infrastructure Studies: Ways of Knowing in a Networked Environment." In *International Handbook of Internet Research,* edited by Jeremy Husinger, Lisbeth Klastrup, and Matthew Allen. Heidelberg, Germany: Springer, 2010.

Bowker, Geoffrey C., and Susan Leigh Star. *Sorting Things Out: Classification and its Consequences.* Cambridge, MA: MIT Press, 1999.

Brand, Laurie A. "National Narratives and Migration: Discursive Strategies of Inclusion and Exclusion in Jordan and Lebanon." *International Migration Review* 44, no. 1 (2010): 78–110.

Bromwich, David. "Advice to the Prince." *New York Review of Books* 56 (2009): 12. Accessed August 29, 2012, http://www.nybooks.com/articles/archives/2009/jul/16/advice-to-the-prince/.

Brooks, Brian S., George Kennedy, Daryl R. Moen, and Don Ranly. *News Reporting and Writing.* Boston: Bedford, 2005.

Brooks, Stephen G., and William C. Wohlforth. *World Out of Balance: International Relations and the Challenge of American Primacy.* Princeton, NJ: Princeton University Press, 2008.

Brown, Robin. "Getting to War: Communication and Mobilization in the 2002–03 Iraq Crisis." In *Media and Conflict in the Twenty-First Century,* edited by Philip Seib. New York: Palgrave, 2005. 57–82.

Bucher, Jessica, Lena Engel, Stephanie Harfensteller, and Hylke Dijkstra. "Domestic Politics, News Media and Humanitarian Intervention: Why France and Germany Diverged over Libya." *European Security.* Published Online, 2013. Accessed May 21, 2013, http://www.tandfonline.com/doi/full/10.1080/09662839.2013.766597#.UePH2haLBgI.

Bull, Hedley. *The Anarchical Society* (4th ed.). Basingstoke: Palgrave. 2012.

Bulmer, Simon, and William E. Paterson. "Germany and the European Union: From 'Tamed Power' to Normalized Power?" *International Affairs* 86, no. 5 (2010): 1051–73.

Bush, George W. State of the Union Address, January 29, 2002. Accessed May 20, 2013, http://millercenter.org/president/speeches/detail/4540.

———. *The National Security Strategy of the United States of America (NSS 2002).* Washington, DC: Executive Office of the President, 2002.

———. *The National Security Strategy of the United States of America (NSS 2006).* Washington, DC: Executive Office of the President, 2006.

Buzan, Barry. "Civilisational Realpolitik as the New World Order?" *Survival* 39, no. 1 (1997): 180–83.

———. "The Inaugural Kenneth N. Waltz Annual Lecture: A World Order Without Superpowers: Decentred Globalism." *International Relations* 25, no. 1 (2011): 3–25.

Buzan, Barry, Ole Waever, and Jaap De Wilde. *Security: A New Framework for Analysis.* London: Lynne Rienner, 1998.

Callahan, William A. *China: The Pessoptimist Nation.* Oxford: Oxford University Press, 2010.

———. "Forum: The Rise of China: How to Understand China: The Dangers and Opportunities of Being a Rising Power." *Review of International Studies* 31 (2005): 701–14.

Calleo, David P. "The Tyranny of False Vision: America's Unipolar Fantasy." *Survival* 50, no. 5 (2008): 61–78.

Callon, Michel. "Some Elements of a Sociology of Translation: Domestication of the Scallops and the Fishermen of St Brieuc Bay." In *Power, Action and Belief: A New Sociology of Knowledge,* edited by John Law. London: Routledge and Kegan Paul, 1986.

Campbell, David. *Writing Security.* Minneapolis, MN: University of Minnesota Press, 1992.

"Canada's Approach in Afghanistan." *Canada's Engagement in Afghanistan,* August 24, 2011. Government of Canada/Gouvernement du Canada. Accessed May 21, 2013, http://www.afghanistan.gc.ca/canada-afghanistan/approach-approche/index.aspx?lang= eng.

Carter, Patrick (Lord Carter of Coles). *Public Diplomacy Review.* London: Foreign and Commonwealth Office, December 2005. Accessed September 1, 2012, http://www.britishcouncil.org/home-carter-report.

Casey, Steven. "Selling NSC-68: The Truman Administration, Public Opinion, and the Politics of Mobilization, 1950–51." *Diplomatic History* 29, no. 4 (2005): 655–90.

Castells, Manuel. *The Internet Galaxy: Reflections on the Internet, Business, and Society.* New York: Oxford University Press, 2003.

———. "Communication, Power and Counter-Power in the Network Society." *International Journal of Communication* 1, no. 1 (2007): 238–266.

———. *Communication Power.* Oxford: Oxford University Press, 2009.

———. *The Information Age: Economy, Society, and Culture.* Vol. 1, *The Rise of the Network Society.* Oxford: Wiley-Blackwell, 2011.

———. *The Information Age: Economy, Society, and Culture.* Vol. 2, *The Power of Identity.* Oxford: Wiley-Blackwell, 2011.

———. *Networks of Outrage and Hope.* Cambridge: Polity, 2012.

Chadwick, Andrew. *The Hybrid Media System: Power and Politics.* Oxford: Oxford University Press, 2013.

Checkel, Jeffrey T. *Ideas and International Political Change: Soviet/Russian Behavior and the End of the Cold War.* New Haven: Yale University Press, 1997.

———. "Social Constructivisms in Global and European Politics: A Review Essay." *Review of International Studies* 30, no. 2 (2004): 229–44.

Chollet, Derek, and James M. Goldgeier. *America between the Wars: From 11/9 to 9/11: The Misunderstood Years between the Fall of the Berlin Wall and the Start of the War on Terror.* New York: Public Affairs, 2008.

Chubin, Shahram. "The Iranian Nuclear Riddle after June 12." *The Washington Quarterly* 33, no. 1 (2010): 163–72.

Churkin, Vitaly. "Statement by Mr. Vitaly Churkin, Permanent Representative of the Russian Federation to the United Nations, at the Official UN Security Council Meeting during the Vote on the Resolution on Libya, New York, March 17, 2011." Accessed August 21, 2011, http://www.rusembassy.ca/node/546.

Chyi, Hsiang Iris, and Maxwell McCombs. "Media Salience and the Process of Framing: Coverage of the Columbine School Shootings." *Journalism & Mass Communication Quarterly* 81, no. 1 (2004): 22–35.

Ciută, Felix. "Narratives of Security: Strategy and Identity in the European Context." In *Discursive Constructions of Identity in European Politics*, edited by Richard Mole. Basingstoke: Palgrave MacMillan, 2007.

Clark, Ian. *Legitimacy in International Society.* Oxford: Oxford University Press, 2005.

Clegg, Stewart R. *Frameworks of Power.* London: Sage, 1989.

Clunan, Anne L. *The Social Construction of Russia's Resurgence.* Baltimore: Johns Hopkins University Press, 2009.

Comor, Edward, and Hamilton Bean. "America's 'Engagement' Delusion: Critiquing a Public Diplomacy Consensus." *International Communication Gazette* 74, no. 3 (2012): 203–20.

Conrad, Sebastian, and Dominic Sachsenmaier. *Competing Visions of World Order: Global Moments and Movements, 1880s–1930s.* Basingstoke: Palgrave Macmillan, 2007.

Coole, Diana. "Rethinking Agency: A Phenomenological Approach to Embodiment and Agentic Capacities." *Political Studies* 53, no. 1 (2005): 124–42.

Cooper, Robert. *The Post-Modern State and the World Order.* London: Demos, 2000.

———. *The Breaking of Nations: Order and Chaos in the Twenty-First Century.* London: Atlantic Books, 2004.

Corman, Steven R., Angela Trethewey, and H. L. Goodall, Jr. *Weapons of Mass Persuasion: Strategic Communication to Combat Violent Extremism.* Vol. 15. New York: Peter Lang, 2008.

Cover, Robert M. "The Supreme Court, 1982 Term—Foreword: Nomos and Narrative." *Harvard Law Review* 97 (1983): 1–4.

Cox, Michael. "Power Shifts, Economic Change and the Decline of the West?" *International Relations* 26, no. 4 (2012): 369–88.

Cox, Robert W. "Social Forces, States and World Orders: Beyond International Relations Theory." *Millennium: Journal of International Studies* 10, no. 2 (1981): 126.

Croft, Stuart. *Securitizing Islam: Identity and the Search for Security.* Cambridge: Cambridge University Press, 2012.

Cruz, Consuelo. "Identity and Persuasion: How Nations Remember Their Past and Make Their Futures." *World Politics* 52, no. 3 (2000): 275–312.

Daalder, Ivo H., and James G. Stavridis. "NATO's Victory in Libya." *Foreign Affairs* 91, no. 2, (2012): 2–7.

Dahl, Robert A. "The Concept of Power." *Behavioral Science* 2, no. 3 (1957): 201–15.

D'Andrade, Roy. "Schemas and Motivations." In *Human Motives and Cultural Models*, edited by Roy G. D'Andrade and Claudia Strauss. Cambridge: Cambridge University Press, 1992.

Dannreuther, Roland, and John Peterson. *Security Strategy and Transatlantic Relations*. London: Routledge, 2006.

Davis, Aeron. "New Media and Fat Democracy: The Paradox of Online Participation." *New Media & Society* 12, no. 5 (2010): 745–61.

Davies, Graeme A. M. "Coercive Diplomacy Meets Diversionary Incentives: The Impact of US and Iranian Domestic Politics during the Bush and Obama Presidencies." *Foreign Policy Analysis* 8, no. 3 (2012): 313–31.

DeLuca, Kevin M. *Image Politics: The New Rhetoric of Environmental Activism, Revisioning Rhetoric*. New York: Guilford Press, 1999.

Derrida, Jacques. *Of Grammatology*. Baltimore: Johns Hopkins University Press, 1974.

Deibert, Ronald J. *Parchment, Printing, and Hypermedia: Communication in World Order Transformation*. New York: Columbia University Press, 1997.

Domke, David, David Perlmutter, and Meg Spratt. "The Primes of Our Times? An Examination of the 'Power' of Visual Images." *Journalism* 3, no. 2 (2002): 131–59.

Douglas, Frank Scott. "Waging the Inchoate War: Defining, Fighting, and Second-Guessing the 'Long War.'" *The Journal of Strategic Studies* 30, no. 3 (2007): 391–420.

Drogin, Bob, and Kim Murphy. "U.N. Calls U.S. Data on Iran's Nuclear Aims Unreliable." *Los Angeles Times*, February 25, 2007. Accessed May 21, 2013, http://articles.latimes.com/2007/feb/25/world/fg-usiran25.

Dryzek, John S. *Deliberative Global Politics: Discourse and Democracy in a Divided World*. London: Polity, 2006.

Dyson, Tom. *Neoclassical Realism and Defence Reform in Post–Cold War Europe*. Basingstoke: Palgrave Macmillan, 2010.

Eder, Klaus. "A Theory of Collective Identity: Making Sense of the Debate on a 'European Identity.'" *European Journal of Social Theory* 12, no. 4 (November 2009): 427–47.

Eichenberg, Richard C. "Victory Has Many Friends: U.S. Public Opinion and the Use of Military Force, 1981–2005." *International Security* 30, no.1 (2005): 7–45.

ElBaradei, Mohamed. "Director General's Intervention on Non-Proliferation Issues at IAEA Board of Governors." *Statements of Director General*. International Atomic Energy Agency, June 17, 2009. Accessed April 4, 2013, http://www.iaea.org/newscenter/statements/2009/ebsp2009n007.html.

Elliot, Philip. "White House Relays Obama's Cairo Message to Web." *ABC News*, June 4, 2009. http://abcnews.go.com/Technology/wireStory?id=7755103.

Entman, Robert M. *Projections of Power: Framing News, Public Opinion, and US Foreign Policy*. Chicago: University of Chicago Press, 2009.

———. Review of *Framing Public Life: Perspectives on Media and Our Understanding of the Social World*, edited by Stephen D. Reese, Oscar H. Gandy, Jr., and August E. Grant (Mahwah, NJ: Lawrence Erlbaum, 2001). *Political Communication* 23, no. 1 (2006): 121–2.

Epstein, Charlotte. "Constructivism or the Eternal Return of Universals: Why Returning to Language is Vital for Prolonging the Owl's Flight." *European Journal of International Relations*, 19, no. 3 (forthcoming).

———. "Moby Dick or Moby Doll? Discourse or How to Study 'the Social Construction of' All the Way Down." In *Constructing the International Economy*, edited by Rawi Abdelal, Mark Blyth, and Craig Parsons. Ithaca, NY: Cornell University Press, 2010.

——. *The Power of Words in International Relations: Birth of an Anti-Whaling Discourse.* Cambridge, MA: MIT Press, 2008.

——. "Stop Telling Us How to Behave: Socialization or Infantilization?" *International Studies Perspectives* 13, no. 2 (2012): 135–45.

Erlanger, Steven. "Sarkozy puts France at Vanguard of West's War Effort." *New York Times*, March 21, 2011: 12.

Fearon, James D. "Signaling Versus the Balance of Power and Interests." *Journal of Conflict Resolution* 38 (1994): 68–90.

Feaver, Peter. "Holding Out for the National Security Strategy." *Foreign Policy*, January 20, 2010. Accessed May 22, 2013, http://shadow.foreignpolicy.com/posts/2010/01/20/holding_out_for_the_national_security_strategy.

Feller, Ben. "Obama Doctrine on Military Intervention Tested in Libya." *Huffington Post*, March 9, 2011. Accessed September 1, 2011, http://www.huffingtonpost.com/2011/03/09/obama-libya-military-intervention_n_833345.html.

Fierke, Karin M. *Changing Games, Changing Strategies: Critical Investigations in Security.* Manchester: Manchester University Press, 1998.

——. *Diplomatic Interventions: Conflict and Change in a Globalizing World.* Basingstoke: Palgrave Macmillan, 2005.

Finnemore, Martha. "Legitimacy, Hypocrisy, and the Social Structure of Unipolarity: Why Being a Unipole Isn't All It's Cracked Up to Be." *World Politics* 61, no. 1 (2009): 58–85.

——. "Legitimacy, Hypocrisy, and the Social Structure of Unipolarity: Why Being a Unipole Isn't All It's Cracked Up to Be." In *International Relations Theory and the Consequences of Unipolarity*, edited by G. John Ikenberry, Michael Mastanduno, and William C. Wohlforth. Cambridge: Cambridge University Press, 2011. 67–98.

Fischer, Frank. *Reframing Public Policy: Discursive Politics and Deliberative Practices.* Oxford: Oxford University Press, 2003.

Fischer, Joschka. "The Case for Bargaining with Iran." *Washington Post*, May 29, 2006. Accessed May 21, 2013, http://www.washingtonpost.com/wp-dyn/content/article/2006/05/28/AR2006052800978.html.

Fishman, Brian. "Using the Mistakes of al Qaeda's Franchises to Undermine Its Strategies." *Annals of the American Academy of Political and Social Science* 618 (2008): 48–54.

Foucault, Michel. *The Archaeology of Knowledge.* Translated by A.M. Sheridan Smith. London: Tavistock, 1972.

——. *The History of Sexuality: An Introduction.* Translated by Robert Hurley. London: Penguin Books, 1984.

——. *Power/Knowledge: Selected Interviews and Other Writings, 1972–1977.* London: Vintage Books, 1980.

"France and Germany Clash over No Fly Zone." *EurActiv*, March 15, 2011. Accessed September 1, 2011, http://www.euractiv.com/en/global-europe/france-germany-clash-libya-fly-zone-news-503090.

Freeden, Michael. *The Political Theory of Politics.* Full Research Report: ESRC End of Award Report, RES-051–27–0098. Swindon: ESRC, 2008.

Freedman, Lawrence. *The Evolution of Nuclear Strategy.* London: MacMillan Press, 1981.

——. "Networks, Culture and Narratives." *Adelphi Papers Series* 45, no. 379 (2006): 11–26. Available at: http://dx.doi.org/10.1080/05679320600661640.

——. "Order and Disorder in the New World." *Foreign Affairs* 71, no. 1 (1991): 20–37.

Friedman, Thomas L. "Obama on Obama." *New York Times*, June 3, 2009. http://www.nytimes.com/2009/06/03/opinion/03friedman.html?_r=0.

"French German Libya Rift Deepens." *European Voice*, March 25, 2011. Accessed August 21, 2011, http://www.europeanvoice.com/article/2011/march/french-german-libya-rift-deepens/70661.aspx.

Fukuyama, Francis. "The End of History?" *The National Interest* 16 (1989): 3–18.

———. *The Origins of Political Order: From Prehuman Times to the French Revolution*. London: Profile Books, 2012.

Fung, Victor, William K. Fung, and Yoram R. Wind. *Competing in a Flat World: Building Enterprises in a Borderless World*. Upper Saddle River, NJ: Prentice Hall, 2007.

Gaddis, John Lewis. "Was the Truman Doctrine a Real Turning Point?" *Foreign Affairs* 52, no. 2 (January 1974): 386–402.

Gallie, Walter B. *Philosophy and the Historical Understanding*. New York: Schocken Books, 1964.

Garton-Ash, Timothy. "1989!" *New York Review of Books* 56, no. 17 (November 5, 2009). Accessed May 22, 2001, http://www.nybooks.com/articles/archives/2009/nov/05/1989/.

Gebauer, Matthias. "Are German Soldiers Secretly Helping Fight Gadhafi?" *Spiegel Online*, August 19, 2011. Accessed September 1, 2011, http://www.spiegel.de/international/world/0,1518,781197,00.html.

Geertz, Clifford. *The Interpretation of Cultures: Selected Essays*. Vol. 5019. London: Basic Books, 1973.

George, Alexander. "Domestic Constraints on Regime Change in US Foreign Policy: The Need for Policy Legitimacy." In *American Foreign Policy: Theoretical Essays*, edited by G. J. Ikenberry. Glenview: Scott, Foresman, 1989. 583–608.

———. *Bridging the Gap: Theory and Practice in Foreign Policy*. Washington, DC: United States Institute of Peace Press, 1993.

"German Defends Cautious Approach to Libya, Denies Isolation." *Deutsche Welle*, March 21, 2011. Accessed September 1, 2011, http://www.dw-world.de/dw/article/0,,14926360,00.html.

Gilboa, Eytan. "Global Television News and Foreign Policy: Debating the CNN Effect." *International Studies Perspectives* 6, no. 3 (2005): 325–41.

Gillespie, Marie, David Herbert, and Matilda Andersson. "The Mumbai Attacks and Diasporic Nationalism: BBC World Service Online Forums as Conflict, Contact and Comfort Zones." *South Asian Diaspora* 2, no. 1 (2010): 109–29.

Gillespie, Marie. "BBC Arabic, Social Media and Citizen Production: An Experiment in Digital Democracy before the Arab Spring." *Theory, Culture and Society* 30, no. 4 (2013): 1–39. doi: 10.1177/0263276413482382.

Gilpin, Robert. *War and Change in World Politics*. Princeton, NJ: Princeton University Press, 1981.

Gleick, James. *The Information: A History, a Theory, a Flood*. London: Fourth Estate, 2011.

Goldmann, Kjell. *The Logic of Internationalism: Coercion and Accommodation*. London: Routledge, 1994.

Gomis, Benoit. "Franco-British Defence and Security Treaties: Entente While It Lasts?" Royal Institute for International Affairs/Chatham House, Programme Paper: ISP PP 2001/01, 2011.

Gorst, Isabelle, and Neil Buckley. "Medvedev and Putin Clash over Libya." *Financial Times*, March 21, 2011. Accessed May 22, 2013, http://www.ft.com/cms/s/0/2e62b08e-53d2–11e0-a01c-00144feab49a.html.

Gould, Stephen Jay. *Full House: The Spread of Excellence from Plato to Darwin*. Cambridge, MA: Harvard University Press, 2011.

Gourevitch, Peter. "The Second Image Reversed: The International Sources of Domestic Politics." *International Organization* 32, no. 4 (1978): 881–912.

Gow, James, and Milena Michalski. *War, Image and Legitimacy: Viewing Contemporary Conflict*. Vol. 47. London: Routledge, 2007.

Gowing, Nik. *"Skyful of Lies" and Black Swans: The New Tyranny of Shifting Information Power in Crises.* Oxford: Reuters Institute for the Study of Journalism, University of Oxford, 2009.

Grant, Mark. L. "Evidence to House of Commons Defence Select Committee HC905." October 12, 2011, London. Accessed March 1, 2012, http://www.publications.parliament.uk/pa/cm201012/cmselect/cmdfence/950/11101201.htm.

———. "Explanation of Vote Delivered by Sir Mark Lyall Grant, Ambassador and Permanent Representative of the UK Mission to the United Nations, on Security Council Resolution on Libya." March 17, 2011, New York. Accessed September 1, 2011, http://ukun.fco.gov.uk/en/news/?view=News&id=568282782.

Gross, Doug. "Survey: More Americans Get News from Internet than Newspapers or Radio." *CNN Tech*, March 1, 2010. Accessed May 23, 2013, http://articles.cnn.com/2010–03–01/tech/social.network.news_1_social-networking-sites-social-media-social-experience?_s=PM:TECH.

Habermas, Jürgen. *The Structural Transformation of the Public Sphere: An Inquiry into a Category of Bourgeois Society.* Cambridge, MA: The MIT Press, 1989.

Hague, William. Foreign Secretary Comments on UN Vote on Libya No Fly Zone. March 18, 2011, London. Accessed August 21, 2011, http://ukun.fco.gov.uk/en/news/?view=News&id=568543282.

———. Statement to the House of Commons, March 24, 2011, London. Accessed August 21, 2011, http://www.fco.gov.uk/en/news/latest-news/?view=PressS&id=571853282.

———. Statement to the House of Commons on North Africa and the Middle East. House of Commons Official Report. Parliamentary Debates (*Hansard*), Vol. 525, no. 139 (March 24, 2011): 1113—1130.

Hajer, Martin A. *The Politics of Environmental Discourse: Ecological Modernization and the Policy Process.* Oxford: Oxford University Press, 1995.

Hallin, Daniel C. *The Uncensored War: The Media and Vietnam.* Berkeley: University of California Press, 1989.

Halverson, Jeffry R., H. Lloyd Goodall, and Steven R. Corman. *Master Narratives of Islamist Extremism.* Basingstoke: Palgrave Macmillan, 2011.

Hanau Santini, Ruth. "European Union Discourses and Practices on the Iranian Nuclear Programme." *European Security* 19, no. 3 (2010): 467–89.

Handel, Michael. *Weak States in the International System.* London: Frank Cass, 1990.

Handley, Robert L., and Lou Rutigliano. "Journalistic Field Wars: Defending and Attacking the National Narrative in a Diversifying Journalistic Field." *Media, Culture & Society* 34, no. 6 (2012): 744–60.

Hansen, Lene. *Security as Practice.* London: Routledge, 2006.

———. "Theorizing the Image for Security Studies: Visual Securitization and the Muhammad Cartoon Crisis." *European Journal of International Relations* 17, no. 1 (2011): 51–74.

Hanson, Elizabeth. *The Information Revolution and World Politics.* Lanham: Rowman and Littlefield, 2008.

Hayden, Craig. *The Rhetoric of Soft Power: Public Diplomacy in Global Contexts.* Lanham, MD: Lexington Books, 2012.

He, Kai. "Undermining Adversaries: Unipolarity, Threat Perception, and Negative Balancing Strategies after the Cold War." *Security Studies* 21, no. 2 (2012): 154–91.

Hendrickson, Ryan C. "Libya and American War Powers: Barak Obama as Commander in Chief." Paper presented to the Annual Convention of the International Studies Association, San Diego, April 2–5, 2012.

Herman, Robert G. "Identity, Norms, and National Security: The Soviet Foreign Policy Revolution and the End of the Cold War." In *The Culture of National Security: Norms and Identity in World Politics,* edited by Peter Katzenstein. New York: Columbia University Press, 1996. 272–316.

Hetherington, Marc J., and Michael Nelson. "Anatomy of a Rally Effect: George W. Bush and the War on Terrorism." *Political Science and Politics* 36, no. 1 (2003): 37–42.

Hill, Fiona, and Clifford G. Gaddy. *Mr. Putin: Operative in the Kremlin.* Washington, DC: Brookings Institution Press, 2013.

Hogan, Michael J. *A Cross of Iron.* Cambridge: Cambridge University Press, 1998.

Hokayem, Emile. "Foreign Policy: The Middle East Channel—The War of Narratives." International Institute for Strategic Studies, February 8, 2011. Accessed March 2, 2013, http://www.iiss.org/whats-new/iiss-in-the-press/press-coverage-2011/february-2011/the-war-of-narratives/.

Holsti, Kaleavi J. "National Role Conceptions in the Study of Foreign Policy." *International Studies Quarterly* 14, no. 3 (1970): 233–309.

Hopf, Ted. *Social Construction of International Politics: Identities & Foreign Policies, Moscow, 1955 and 1999.* Ithaca, NY: Cornell University Press, 2002.

Hoskins, Andrew. *Televising War: From Vietnam to Iraq.* London: Continuum, 2004.

———. "Temporality, Proximity, and Security: Terror in a Media-drenched Age." *International Relations* 20 (2007): 453–66.

Hoskins, Andrew, and Ben O'Loughlin. *Television and Terror: Conflicting Times and the Crisis of News Discourse.* Basingstoke: Palgrave Macmillan, 2007.

———. *War and Media.* Cambridge: Polity, 2010.

———. "Security Journalism and 'The Mainstream' in Britain since 7/7: Translating Terror but Inciting Violence?" *International Affairs* 86, no. 4 (2010): 903–24.

———. "Remediating Jihad for Western News Audiences: The Renewal of Gatekeeping?" *Journalism* 12, no. 2 (2011): 199–216.

Howard, Philip N. *The Digital Origins of Dictatorship and Democracy: Information Technology and Political Islam.* New York: Oxford University Press, 2010.

Howorth, Jolyon, and Anand Menon. "Still Not Pushing Back: Why the European Union Is Not Balancing the United States." *Journal of Conflict Resolution* 53, no. 5 (2009): 727–44.

Hunter, Robert E. "Engage, Don't Isolate, Iran." Rand Corporation, June 27, 2004. Accessed April 4, 2004, http://www.rand.org/commentary/2004/06/27/SDT.html.

Hurrell, Andrew. *On Global Order: Power, Values and the Constitution of International Society.* Oxford: Oxford University Press, 2007.

Hutcheson, John, David Domke, Andre Billeaudeaux, and Philip Garland. "US National Identity, Political Elites, and a Patriotic Press Following September 11." *Political Communication* 21, no. 1 (2004): 27–50.

Huth, Paul, and Bruce Russett. "What Makes Deterrence Work: Cases from 1900 to 1980." *World Politics* 36 (1984): 496–526.

Hyde-Price, Adrian, and Charlie Jeffery. "Germany in the European Union: Constructing Normality." *Journal of Common Market Studies* 39, no. 4 (Nov. 2001): 689–717.

IAEA (International Atomic Energy Agency). "Communication Dated 13 January 2006 Received from the Permanent Missions of France, Germany and the United Kingdom to the Agency." INFCIRC/662, January 13, 2006. Accessed April 4, 2013, http://www.iaea.org/Publications/Documents/Infcircs/2006/infcirc 662.pdf.

———. "Communication on 5 March 2004 from the Permanent Mission of the Islamic Republic of Iran Concerning the Report of the Director General Contained in GOV/2004/11." INFCIRC/628, March 5, 2004. Accessed May 21, 2013, http://www.iaea.org/Publications/Documents/Infcircs/2004/infcirc628.pdf.

———. "Implementation of the NPT Safeguards Agreement in the Islamic Republic of Iran." GOV/2003/63, August 26, 2003. Accessed April 4, 2013, http://www .iaea.org/Publications/Documents/Board/2003/gov2003–63.pdf.

————. "Implementation of the NPT Safeguards Agreement in the Islamic Republic of Iran." GOV/2004/11, February 24, 2004. Accessed May 21, 2013, http://www.iaea.org/Publications/Documents/Board/2004/gov2004-11.pdf.

————. "Implementation of the NPT Safeguards Agreement in the Islamic Republic of Iran." GOV/2005/77, September 24, 2005. Accessed December 3, 2012, http://www.iaea.org/Publications/Documents/Board/2005/gov2005-77.pdf.

————. "Iran-EU Agreement on Nuclear Programme." November14, 2004. Accessed April 5, 2013, http://www.iaea.org/newscenter/focus/iaeairan/eu_iran14112004.shtml.

IFOP (Institut Français d'Opinion Publique). "Survey of French Views of Libya Crisis from March 2011—June 2011." Accessed March 1, 2013, http://www.ifop.com/media/poll/1558-2-study_file.pdf.

Ignatieff, Michael. "The Diplomatic Life: The Dream of Albanians." *The New Yorker*, January 11, 1999: 34–39.

Ikenberry, G. John. *After Victory: Institutions, Strategic Restraint, and the Rebuilding of Order after Major Wars*. Princeton, NJ: Princeton University Press, 2001.

————, ed. *America Unrivalled: The Future of the Balance of Power*. Ithaca, NY: Cornell University Press, 2002.

————. "Liberal Internationalism 3.0: America and the Dilemmas of Liberal World Order." *Perspectives on Politics* 7, no. 1 (2009): 71–87.

————. *Liberal Leviathan: The Origins, Crisis, and Transformation of the American World Order*. Princeton, NJ: Princeton University Press, 2011.

————. 2008. "The Rise of China and the Future of the West: Can the Liberal System Survive." *Foreign Affairs* 87, no. 1 (January/February 2008): 23–37.

————. "A Weaker World." *Prospect*, November (2010): 30–33.

Ikenberry, G. John, Michael Mastanduno, and William C. Wohlforth, ed. *International Relations Theory and the Consequences of Unipolarity*. Cambridge: Cambridge University Press, 2011.

Infratest diMap. Poll on Libya for ARD, March 8–9, 2011. Accessed August 21, 2011, http://www.infratest-dimap.de/uploads/media/dt1103_bericht.pdf.

Ipsos MORI. "Military Action in Libya: Topline Results." April 12, 2011. Accessed August 21 2011, http://www.ipsos-mori.com/Assets/Docs/Polls/Reuters-Libya-topline-Apr11.PDF.

Iran Ministry for Foreign Affairs. "Statement by the Iranian Government and visiting EU Foreign Ministers." *NuclearFiles.org*, October 21, 2003. Accessed May 21, 2013, http://www.nuclearfiles.org/menu/key-issues/nuclear-weapons/issues/proliferation/iran/statement-visiting-eu-ministers.htm.

Irish, John, and Tim Hepher. "France Fails to Get G-8 Accord on Libya No Fly Zone." *Reuters*, March 15, 2011. Accessed September 1, 2011, http://www.reuters.com/article/2011/03/15/us-g8-libya-idUSTRE72E0BX20110315.

Irwin-Zarecka, Iwona. *Frames of Remembrance: The Dynamics of Collective Memory*. Somerset, NJ: Transaction, 1994.

Isaacson, Walter, and Evan Thomas. *The Wise Men: Six Friends and the World They Made*. New York: Simon & Schuster, 2012.

Jackson, Patrick Thaddeus. "Defending the West: Occidentalism and the Formation of NATO." *Journal of Political Philosophy* 11, no. 3 (2003): 223–52.

Jamieson, Kathleen Hall. *Dirty Politics: Deception, Distraction, and Democracy*. Oxford: Oxford University Press, 1992.

Jentleson, Bruce W., and Steven Weber. "America's Hard Sell." *Foreign Policy* 1 (2008): 169.

Jones, Ben. "Franco-British Defence Co-operation: A New Engine for European Defence?" *Occasional Paper No.88*, European Union Institute for Security Studies, February 2011. Accessed April 14, 2011, http://www.iss.europa.eu/uploads/

media/op88—Franco-British_military_cooperation—a_new_engine_for_Euro
pean_defence.pdf.

Jones, Bruce D. "Libya and the Responsibilities of Power." *Survival* 53, no. 3 (2011): 51–60.

Juppé, Alain. "Libya—Speech by Alain Juppé, Minister of Foreign Affairs and European Affairs, to the United Nations Security Council, March 17, 2011." France in the United Kingdom, French Embassy in London. *Ambafranc-uk.org*. Accessed May 22, 2013, http://www.ambafrance-uk.org/Alain-Juppe-backs-UN-resolution.

Kagan, Robert. *Paradise and Power: America and Europe in the New World Order.* London: Atlantic Books, 2003.

Kaldor, Mary. *New & Old Wars: Organized Violence in a Global Era.* Stanford, CA: Stanford University Press, 2007.

Kaldor, Mary, Mary Martin, and Sabine Selchow. "Human Security: A New Strategic Narrative for the EU." *International Affairs* 83, no.2 (2007): 273–88.

Kang, David C. *China Rising: Peace, Power, and Order in East Asia.* New York: Columbia University Press, 2007.

Katzenstein, Peter J., ed. *The Culture of National Security: Norms and Identity in World Politics.* New York: Columbia University Press, 1996.

———. *Tamed Power: Germany in Europe.* Ithaca, NY: Cornell University Press, 1997.

Keck, Margaret E., and Kathryn Sikkink. *Activists beyond Borders: Advocacy Networks in International Politics.* Ithaca, NY: Cornell University Press, 1998.

Kelley, Colleen E. *The Rhetoric of First Lady Hillary Rodham Clinton: Crisis Management Discourse.* London: Praeger, 2001.

Khatib, Lina, William Dutton, and Michael Thelwall. "Public Diplomacy 2.0: An Exploratory Case Study of the US Digital Outreach Team." *The Middle East Journal* 2 (2011). http://ssrn.com/abstract=1734850.

Kinnvall, Catarina. "Globalization and Religious Nationalism: Self, Identity, and the Search for Ontological Security." *Political Psychology* 25, no. 5 (2004): 741–67.

———. "European Trauma Governance and the Psychological Moment." *Alternatives: Global, Local, Political* 37, no. 3 (2012): 266–81.

Knorr-Cetina, Karin. "Complex Global Microstructures: The New Terrorist Societies." *Theory, Culture & Society* 22, no. 5 (2005): 213–34.

Krauthammer, Charles. "Decline Is a Choice. The New Liberalism and the End of American Ascendancy." *The Weekly Standard* 15, no. 5 (2009). Accessed May 22, 2013, http://www.weeklystandard.com/Content/Public/Articles/000/000/017/056lfnpr.asp.

Krebs, Ronald R., and Patrick Thaddeus Jackson. "Twisting Tongues and Twisting Arms: The Power of Political Rhetoric." *European Journal of International Relations* 13, no. 1 (2007): 35–66.

"Krieg in Libyen: Über 60 Prozent der Deutschen befürworten den Angriff." *Bild am Sonntag*, March 20, 2011. Accessed August 21, 2011, http://www.bild.de/politik/2011/libyen-krise/aber-mehrheit-lehnt-beteiligung-ab-16933388.bild.html.

Kroes, Neelie. "Working Together to Protect Cyber Security." In *Telecom Ministerial Conference on Critical Information Infrastructure Protection.* Balatonfüred, Hungary, April 15, 2011. http://europa.eu/rapid/pressReleasesAction.do?reference=SPEECH/11/275&format= HTML&aged=0&language=EN&guiLanguage=en.

Krotz, Ulrich, and Joachim Schild. *Shaping Europe: France, Germany, and Embedded Bilateralism from the Elysee Treaty to Twenty-First Century Politics.* Oxford: Oxford University Press, 2012.

Kubálková, Vendulka. *Foreign Policy in a Constructed World.* Vol. 4. Armonk, NY: M. E. Sharpe, 2001.

Kupchan, Charles A. "After Pax Americana: Benign Power, Regional Integration, and the Sources of a Stable Multipolarity." *International Security* 23, no. 2 (1998): 40–79.

———. *The End of the American Era: US Foreign Policy and the Geopolitics of the Twenty-First Century.* New York: Knopf, 2002.

Lake, David A. *Hierarchy in International Relations.* Ithaca, NY: Cornell University Press, 2009.

Lapid, Yosef, and Friedrich V. Kratochwil, eds. *The Return of Culture and Identity in IR Theory.* Boulder, CO: Lynne Rienner, 1996.

Latour, Bruno. "Visualisation and Cognition: Thinking With Hands and Eyes." *Knowledge and Society* 6 (1987): 1–40.

———. "What If We Talked Politics a Little?" *Contemporary Political Theory* 2, no. 2 (2003): 143–64.

Lawson, George. "The Eternal Divide? History and International Relations." *European Journal of International Relations* 18, no. 2 (2012): 203–26.

Layne, Christopher. "The Global Power Shift from West to East." *The National Interest* 119 (2012): 22.

———. "A Matter of Historical Debate." *Foreign Affairs* 85, no. 6 (2006): 181–82.

———. "The Unipolar Illusion: Why New Great Powers Will Rise." *International Security* 17, no. 4 (1993): 5–51.

———. "The Unipolar Illusion Revisited: The Coming End of the United States' Unipolar Moment." *International Security* 31, no. 2 (2006): 7–41.

Leavy, Patricia. *Iconic Events: Media, Politics, and Power in Retelling History.* Lanham, MD: Lexington Books, 2007.

Lebow, Richard Ned, and Benjamin Valentino. "Lost in Transition: A Critical Analysis of Power Transition Theory." *International Relations* 23, no. 3 (2009): 389–410.

Leffler, Melvyn P., and Jeffrey W. Legro, eds. *To Lead the World: American Strategy after the Bush Doctrine.* Oxford: Oxford University Press, 2008.

Legro, Jeffrey W. "What China Will Want: The Future Intentions of a Rising Power." *Perspectives on Politics* 5, no. 3 (2007): 515–34.

———. *Rethinking the World: Great Power Strategies and International Order.* Ithaca, NY: Cornell University Press, 2005.

Leonard, Mark, ed. *China 3.0,* London: European Council on Foreign Relations, 2012.

———. *What Does China Think?* New York: Public Affairs, 2008.

Levy, Jack. *War in the Modern Great Power System.* Lexington: University Press of Kentucky, 1983.

Li, Baodong. "Explanation of Vote by Ambassador Li Baodong after Adoption of Security Council Resolution on Libya, March 17, 2011." *China-UN.org.* Accessed August 21, 2011, http://www.china-un.org/eng/gdxw/t807544.htm.

Lippmann, Walter. *The Phantom Public.* New Brunswick: Transaction, 2002.

———. *Public Opinion* (1921). Accessed May 1, 2013, http://xroads.virginia.edu/~Hyper2/CDFinal/Lippman/cover.html.

Lipset, Seymour Martin. *American Exceptionalism: A Double-Edged Sword.* New York: Norton, 1997.

Livingston, Steven. "The CNN Effect Reconsidered (Again): Problematizing ICT and Global Governance in the CNN Effect Research Agenda." *Media, War & Conflict* 4, no. 1 (2011): 20–36.

———. "Transparency and the News Media." In *Power and Conflict in the Age of Transparency,* edited by Bernard I. Finel and Kristin M. Lord. New York: Palgrave, 2003. 115–35.

Litwak, Robert. *Rogue States and U.S. Foreign Policy: Containment after the Cold War.* Baltimore: Johns Hopkins University Press, 2000.

Los Angeles Times. "Iran Rejects U.N. Request to Halt its Nuclear Activity." April 14, 2006. Accessed April 4, 2013, http://articles.latimes.com/2006/apr/14/ world/ fg-iran14.

Lundby, Knut, ed. *The Mediatization of Communication.* Berlin: De Gruyter Mouton, forthcoming.

Lynch, Marc. *State Interests and Public Spheres: The International Politics of Jordan's Identity.* New York: Columbia University Press, 1999.

———. "Why Engage? China and the Logic of Communicative Engagement." *European Journal of International Relations* 8, no. 2 (2002): 187–230.

Mackay, Hugh. "Understanding Impact." Report for the BBC World Service, 2012. Accessed November 4, 2012, http://www8.open.ac.uk/researchprojects/diasporas/ news/public-policy-fellowship-at-the-bbc-world-service.

Mackay, Hugh, and Jingrong Tong. "Interactivity, the Global Conversation and World Service Research: Digital China." *Participations: Journal of Audience and Reception Studies* 8, no. 1 (2011): 48–74. Accessed September 1, 2012, http:// www.participations.org/Volume%208/Issue%201/PDF/mackay.pdf.

MacMillan, Margaret. *Paris 1919: Six Months that Changed the World.* London: Random House, 2007.

Main, Linda. "The Global Information Infrastructure: Empowerment or Imperialism?" *Third World Quarterly* 22, no. 1 (2001): 83–97.

Manjikian, Mary M. "From Global Village to Virtual Battlespace: The Colonizing of the Internet and the Extension of Realpolitik." *International Studies Quarterly* 54, no. 2 (2010): 381–401.

Mann, Michael. *The Sources of Social Power.* Vol. 2A, *A History of Power from the Beginning to AD 1760.* Cambridge: Cambridge University Press, 1986.

———. *The Sources of Social Power.* Vol. 2, *The Rise of Classes and Nation-States, 1760–1914.* Cambridge: Cambridge University Press, 1993.

Manners, Ian. "The European Union as a Normative Power: A Response to Thomas Diez." *Millennium-Journal of International Studies* 35, no. 1 (2006): 167–80.

———. "Normative Power Europe: A Contradiction in Terms?" *JCMS: Journal of Common Market Studies* 40, no. 2 (2002): 235–58.

Massumi, Brian. "Fear (The Spectrum Said)." *Positions: East Asia Cultures Critique* 13, no. 1 (2005): 31–48.

———. "National Enterprise Emergency: Steps toward an Ecology of Powers." *Theory, Culture & Society* 26, no. 6 (2009): 153–85.

Mastanduno, Michael. "Preserving the Unipolar Moment: Realist Theories and US Grand Strategy after the Cold War." *International Security* 21, no. 4 (1997): 49–88.

March, James G., and Johan P. Olsen. *The Logic of Appropriateness.* ARENA Working Papers 04/09, Centre for European Studies, University of Oslo, 2004. Accessed May 22, 2013, http://www.sv.uio.no/arena/english/research/publications/ arena-publications/workingpapers/working-papers2004/wp04_9.pdf.

Maull, Hanns W. "Germany and Japan: The New Civilian Powers." *Foreign Affairs* 69, no. 5 (Winter, 1990): 91–106.

McCarthy, Daniel R. "Open Networks and the Open Door: American Foreign Policy and the Narration of the Internet." *Foreign Policy Analysis* 7, no. 1 (2011): 89–111.

McEvoy-Levy, Siobhan. *American Exceptionalism and US Foreign Policy.* Basingstoke: Palgrave, 2001.

McGregor, Richard, and Daniel Dombey. "Foreign Policy: A Reticent America." *Financial Times*, March 23, 2011. Accessed September 1, 2011, http://www.ft.com/ cms/s/0/3ddd2d0c-557e-11e0-a2b1–00144feab49a.html#axzz2QtWEz7j3.

McLuhan, Marshall. *Understanding Media: The Extensions of Man.* Cambridge, MA: MIT Press, 1994.

Mearsheimer, John J. *The Tragedy of Great Power Politics.* New York: Norton, 2001.
Melissen, Jan. *The New Public Diplomacy.* Basingstoke: Palgrave Macmillan, 2005.
Meraz, Sharon, and Zizi Papacharissi. "Networked Gatekeeping and Networked Framing on Egypt." *The International Journal of Press/Politics* 18, no. 2 (2013): 138–66.
"Merkel Cabinet Agrees AWACS for Afghanistan." *Spiegel Online,* March 23, 2011. Accessed August 21, 2011, http://www.spiegel.de/international/world/0,1518, 752709,00.html.
Miller, Derek B. *Media Pressure on Foreign Policy: The Evolving Theoretical Framework.* Basingstoke: Palgrave Macmillan, 2007.
Ministry of Defence. "Strategic Communication: The Defence Contribution." Joint Doctrine Note 1/11, 2011. Accessed May 22, 2013, https://www.gov.uk/govern ment/uploads/system/uploads/attachment_data/file/33710/20120126jdn112_ Strategic_CommsU.pdf.
Minow, Martha. "Stories in Law." In *Law's Stories: Narrative and Rhetoric in the Law,* edited by Peters Brooks and Paul Gewirtz. New Haven, CT: Yale University Press, 1996. 24–36.
Miskimmon, Alister. "Falling into Line? Kosovo and the Course of German Foreign Policy." *International Affairs* 85, no. 3 (2009): 561–73.
———. "German Foreign Policy and the Libya Crisis." *German Politics* 21, no. 4 (2012): 392–410.
Miskimmon, Alister, Ben O'Loughlin, and Laura Roselle. "Forging the World: Strategic Narratives and International Relations." Centre for European Politics/New Political Communications Unit Working Paper, 2012. Accessed May 23, 2013, http://newpolcom.rhul.ac.uk/storage/Forging%20the%20World%20Working %20Paper%202012.pdf.
———, ed. *Strategic Narrative in International Relations.* Ann Arbor: Michigan University Press, 2014.
Mitchell, William John Thomas. *Cloning Terror: The War of Images, 9/11 to the Present.* Chicago: University of Chicago Press, 2011.
———. "There Are No Visual Media." *Journal of Visual Culture* 4, no. 2 (2005): 257–66.
Mitzen, Jennifer. "Governing Together: Global Governance as Collective Intention." In *Arguing Global Governance: Agency, Lifeworld and Shared Reasoning,* edited by Corneliu Bjola and Markus Kornprobst. London: Routledge, 2010. 52–66.
———. "Ontological Security in World Politics: State Identity and the Security Dilemma." *European Journal of International Relations* 12, no. 3 (2006): 341–70.
Mor, Ben D. "Accounts and Impression Management in Public Diplomacy: Israeli Justification of Force during the 2006 Lebanon War." *Global Change, Peace & Security* 21, no. 2 (2009): 219–39.
———. "Credibility Talk in Public Diplomacy." *Review of International Studies* 38, no. 02 (2012): 393–422.
———. "Public Diplomacy in Grand Strategy." *Foreign Policy Analysis* 2, no. 2 (2006): 157–76.
———. "The Rhetoric of Public Diplomacy and Propaganda Wars: A View from Self-Presentation Theory." *European Journal of Political Research* 46, no. 5 (2007): 661–83.
———. "Using Force to Save Face: The Performative Side of War." *Peace & Change* 37, no. 1 (2012): 95–121.
Morgenthau, Hans Joachim. *Politics among Nations: The Struggle for Power and Peace.* New York: Knopf, 1960.
———. *Truth and Power: Essays of a Decade, 1960–1970.* London: Pall Mall, 1970.

Morozov, Evgeny. *The Net Delusion: How Not to Liberate the World.* New York: Penguin, 2011.

National Security Act 1947. July 26, Washington D.C. Public Law 80–253, 61 STAT 495. Accessed March 13, 2013, http://intelligence.senate.gov/nsaact1947.pdf.

National Security Council Report 68, 1950. Accessed 13 March 2013, https://www.mtholyoke.edu/acad/intrel/nsc-68/nsc68-1.htm.

Nayak, Meghana, and Eric Selbin. *Decentering International Relations.* London: Zed Books, 2010.

Negroponte, Nicholas. *Being Digital.* New York: Knopf, 1995.

Nelson, Thomas E., Rosalee A. Clawson, and Zoe M. Oxley. "Media Framing of a Civil Liberties Conflict and Its Effect on Tolerance." *American Political Science Review* (1997): 567–83.

Nettelfield, Lara. *Courting Democracy in Bosnia and Herzegovina: The Hague Tribunal's Impact in a Postwar State.* New York: Cambridge University Press, 2010.

———. "Research and Repercussions of Death Tolls: The Case of the Bosnian Book of the Dead." In *Sex, Drugs, and Body Counts: The Politics of Numbers in Global Crime and Conflict,* edited by Peter Andreas and Kelly M. Greenhill. Ithaca, NY: Cornell University Press, 2010. 159–187.

Newey, Glen. "Philosophy, Politics and Contestability." *Journal of Political Ideologies* 6, no. 3 (2001): 245–61.

Nitze, Paul. "The Development of NSC 68." *International Security* 4, no. 4 (1980): 170–76.

Norris, Christopher. *Derrida.* London: Fontana, 1987.

Norris, Pippa, and Ronald Inglehart. *Cosmopolitan Communications.* Cambridge: Cambridge University Press, 2009.

Nye, Joseph S., Jr. "American and Chinese Power after the Financial Crisis." *The Washington Quarterly,* 33 (2010): 143–53.

———. "The Changing Nature of World Power." *Political Science Quarterly* 105, no. 2 (1990): 177–92.

———. *The Paradox of American Power: Why the World's Only Superpower Can't Go It Alone.* New York: Oxford University Press, 2002.

———. "Public Diplomacy and Soft Power." *The Annals of the American Academy of Political and Social Science* 616, no. 1 (2008): 94–109.

———. "Soft Power." *Foreign Policy* 80 (1990): 153–71.

———. "US Power and Strategy after Iraq." *Foreign Affairs* (2003): 60–73.

O'Hanlon, Michael. "Libya and the Obama Doctrine." *Foreign Policy,* August 31, 2011. Accessed September 1, 2011, http://www.foreignaffairs.com/articles/68237/michael-ohanlon/libya-and-the-obama-doctrine.

———. "Winning Ugly in Libya." *Foreign Policy,* March 30, 2011. Accessed September 1, 2011, http://www.foreignaffairs.com/articles/67684/michael-ohanlon/winning-ugly-in-libya.

O'Loughlin, Ben. "Images as Weapons of War: Representation, Mediation and Interpretation." *Review of International Studies* 37, no. 1 (2010): 71–91.

———. "Small Pivots: Should Local Struggles take on Global Significance?" *Global Policy,* April 29, 2013. http://www.globalpolicyjournal.com/blog/29/04/2013/small-pivots-should-local-struggles-take-global-significance.

Oates, Sarah. 2006. "Through a Lens Darkly? Russian Television and Terrorism Coverage in Comparative Perspective." Paper prepared for The Mass Media in Post-Soviet Russia International Conference, University of Surrey, April 2006.

Obama, Barack. *Inaugural Address.* Washington, DC, January 20, 2009. Accessed April 4, 2013. Available at: www.whitehouse.gov/blog/inaugural-address.

———. "Remarks by the President at the National Defense University," May 23, 2013. Accessed May 23, 2013, http://www.whitehouse.gov/the-press-office/2013/05/23/remarks-president-national-defense-university.

———. "Remarks by the President on a New Beginning." Cairo University, Cairo, Egypt, June 4, 2009. Accessed May 21, 2013, http://www.whitehouse.gov/the-press-office/remarks-president-cairo-university-6-04-09.

———. "Remarks by the President on Securing Our Nation's Cyber Infra-structure." The White House, Office of the Press Secretary, May 29, 2009. Accessed August 29, 2012, http://www.whitehouse.gov/the-press-office/remarks-president-securing-our-nations-cyber-infrastructure.

———. "Renewing American Leadership." *Foreign Affairs* (2007): 2–16.

———. Speech to the National Defense University, Washington, DC, March 28, 2011. Accessed May 1, 2013, http://www.whitehouse.gov/the-press-office/2011/03/28/remarks-president-address-nation-libya.

"Obama Speech Gets Solid Reaction World-Wide." *Wall Street Journal*, June 4, 2009. Accessed September 1, 2012, http://online.wsj.com/article/SB124412266343885095.html.

"Obama: We'll Mull 'Sanctions that Bite' If Iran Nuclear Talks Fail." *Haaretz*, September 25, 2009. Accessed April 4, 2013, http://www.haaretz.com/news/obama-we-ll-mull-sanctions-that-bite-if-iran-nuclear-talks-fail-1.7174.

Office of the Director of National Intelligence. *Iran: Nuclear Intentions and Capabilities, National Intelligence Estimate.* November 2007. Accessed April 4, 2013, http://www.dni.gov/files/documents/Newsroom/Reports%20and%20Pubs/20071203_release.pdf.

Orford, Anne. *Reading Humanitarian Intervention: Human Rights and the Use of Force in International Law.* Vol. 30. Cambridge University Press, 2003.

Organski, Abramo F. K. *World Politics.* New York: Knopf, 1958.

ÓTuathail, Gearóid. "Theorizing Practical Geopolitical Reasoning: The Case of the United States' Response to the War in Bosnia." *Political Geography* 21, no. 5 (2002): 601–28.

Owen, John M., IV. *The Clash of Ideas in World Politics: Transnational Networks, States, and Regime Change, 1510–2010.* Princeton, NJ: Princeton University Press, 2010.

Pamment, James. *New Public Diplomacy in the 21st Century: A Comparative Study of Policy and Practice.* London: Routledge, 2012.

Panke, Diana, and Ulrich Petersohn. "Why International Norms Disappear Some-times." *European Journal of International Relations* 18, no. 4 (2012): 719–42.

Parasiliti, Andrew. "Iran: Diplomacy and Deterrence." *Survival* 51, no. 5 (2009): 5–13.

Pape, Robert A. "Soft Balancing against the United States." *International Security* 30, no. 1 (2005): 7–45.

Paul, Thazha V. "Soft Balancing in the Age of US Primacy." *International Security* 30, no. 1 (2005): 46–71.

Pew Research Center. "Public Wary of Military Intervention in Libya: Broad Concern that U.S. Military Is Overcommitted." March 14, 2011. Accessed May 22, 2013, http://www.people-press.org/2011/03/14/public-wary-of-military-intervention-in-libya/.

Petersen, Thomas. "Testing Visual Signals in Representative Surveys." *International Journal of Public Opinion Research* 17, no. 4 (2005): 456–72.

Pfau, Michael, Michel M. Haigh, Theresa Shannon, Toni Tones, Deborah Mercurio, Raina Williams, Blanca Binstock, "The Influence of Television News Depictions of the Images of War on Viewers." *Journal of Broadcasting & Electronic Media* 52, no. 2 (2008): 303–22.

Porter, Wayne, and Mark Mykleby. *A National Strategic Narrative*. Washington DC: Woodrow Wilson International Center for Scholars, 2011.

Posen, Barry R., and Andrew L. Ross. "Competing Visions for US Grand Strategy." *International Security* 21, no. 3 (1997): 5–53.

Postman, Neil. "The Reformed English Curriculum." In *The Shape of the Future in American Secondary Education*, edited by Alvin C. Eurich. New York: Pitman, 1970. 160–168.

Press, Daryl G. *Calculating Credibility: How Leaders Assess Military Threats*. Ithaca, NY: Cornell University Press, 2005.

Price, Monroe E.. *Media and Sovereignty: The Global Information Revolution and Its Challenge to State Power*. Cambridge, MA: MIT University Press, 2002.

———. "Al-Obedi's Tripoli Surprise and the Packaging of Libya's Future." *Huffington Post*, April 20, 2011. Accessed May 22, 2013, http://www.huffingtonpost.com/monroe-price/strategic-narratives-of-t_b_851701.html.

———. *Fierceness of Competition, Softness of Power: Freedom of Expression in a Time of Strategic Communicators*, forthcoming.

Putnam, Robert D. "Diplomacy and Domestic Politics: The Logic of Two-Level Games." *International Organization* 42 (Summer 1988): 427–60.

Ramo, Joshua Cooper. "The Beijing Consensus." *Foreign Policy Centre*, 2004. Accessed March 13, 2013, http://fpc.org.uk/fsblob/244.pdf.

Ramo, Joshua Cooper. *Brand China*. Foreign Policy Centre, 2007.

Rengger, Nicholas J. *International Relations, Political Theory, and the Problem of Order: Beyond International Relations Theory?* London: Routledge, 2000.

Rice, Susan. "Remarks by Ambassador Susan E. Rice, U.S. Permanent Representative to the United Nations, in an Explanation of Vote on UN Security Council Resolution 1973, March 17, 2011, New York." Accessed September 1, 2011, http://usun.state.gov/briefing/statements/2011/158559.htm.

Richards, Barry. *Emotional Governance: Politics, Media and Terror*. Basingstoke: Palgrave Macmillan, 2007.

Ringmar, Erik. "Inter-Texual Relations: The Quarrel over the Iraq War as a Conflict between Narrative Types." *Cooperation and Conflict* 41, no. 4 (2006): 403–21.

Ringsmose, Jens, & Børgensen, Berit. "Shaping Public Attitudes toward the Deployment of Military Power: NATO, Afghanistan and the Use of Strategic Narratives." *European Security*, 20, no. 4 (2011): 505–28.

Risse, Thomas. "International Norms and Domestic Change: Arguing and Communicative Behavior in the Human Rights Arena." *Politics and Society* 27, no. 4 (1999): 529–59.

———. "'Let's Argue!': Communicative Action in World Politics." *International Organization* 54, no. 1 (2000): 1–39.

Roberts, Geoffrey. "History, Theory and the Narrative Turn in IR." *Review of International Studies* 32, no. 4 (2006): 703–14.

Rogin, Josh. "European Governments 'Completely Puzzled' about U.S. Position on Libya." *Foreign Policy*, March 16, 2011. Accessed August 21, 2011, http://thecable.foreignpolicy.com/posts/2011/03/16/european_governments_completely_puzzled_about_us_position_on_libya.

———. "How Obama Turned on a Dime toward War." *Foreign Policy*, March 18, 2011. Accessed August 21, 2011, http://thecable.foreignpolicy.com/posts/2011/03/18/how_obama_turned_on_a_dime_toward_war.

Rose, Nikolas. "Governing 'Advanced' Liberal Democracies." In *Foucault and Political Reason: Liberalism, Neo-liberalism, and Rationalities of Government*, edited by Andrew Barry, Thomas Osborne, and Nikolas Rose. London: UCL, 1996.

Rose, Nikolas, and Peter Miller. "Political Power beyond the State: Problematics of Government." *British Journal of Sociology* 61 (1992): 271–303.

Roselle, Laura. *Media and the Politics of Failure: Great Powers, Communication Strategies, and Military Defeats.* 2nd ed. New York: Palgrave Macmillan, 2011.

Rosenau, James N. *Distant Proximities: Dynamics beyond Globalization.* Princeton, NJ: Princeton University Press, 2003.

Rotberg, Robert I. "Failed States, Collapsed States, Weak States: Causes and Indicators." In *State Failure and State Weakness in a Time of Terror*, edited by Robert I. Rotberg. Washington, DC: World Peace Foundation, 2003. 1–25.

Rousseau, David L. *Identifying Threats and Threatening Identities: The Social Construction of Realism and Liberalism.* Stanford: Stanford University Press, 2006.

Rousseau, David L., and Rocio Garcia-Retamero. "Identity, Power, and Threat Perception: A Cross-National Experimental Study." *Journal of Conflict Resolution* 51, no. 5 (2007): 744–71.

Rumelt, Richard. *Good Strategy, Bad Strategy: The Difference and Why It Matters.* London: Profile Books, 2011.

Runciman, David. *The Politics of Good Intentions.* Princeton, NJ: Princeton University Press, 2006.

Ryan, Marie-Laure. "On the Theoretical Foundations of Transmedial Narratology." In *Narratology beyond Literary Criticism: Mediality, Disciplinarity*, edited by Jan-Christoph Meister, Tom Kindt, and Wilhelm Schernus. Berlin/New York: De Gruyter, 2005. 1–24.

Sarkozy, Nicolas. "Libya—Paris Summit for the Support of the Libyan People—Statement by Nicolas Sarkozy, President of the Republic." March 19, 2011. *Ambafrance-uk.org.* Accessed May 22, 2013, http://www.ambafrance-uk.org/President-Sarkozy-urges-Gaddafi-to.

Schimmelfennig, Frank. "The Community Trap: Liberal Norms, Rhetorical Action, and the Eastern Enlargement of the European Union." *International Organization* 55, no. 1 (2001): 47–80.

———. *The EU, NATO and the Integration of Europe: Rules and Rhetoric.* Cambridge: Cambridge University Press, 2003.

Schmidt, Vivien A. "Does Discourse Matter in the Politics of Welfare State Adjustment?" *Comparative Political Studies* 35, no. 2 (2002): 168–93.

Schmidt, Vivien A., and Claudio M. Radaelli. "Policy Change and Discourse in Europe: Conceptual and Methodological Issues." *West European Politics* 27, no. 2 (2004): 183–210.

Schudson, Michael. *Watergate in American Memory: How We Remember, Forget, and Reconstruct the Past.* New York: Basic Books, 1992.

Schultz, George P. "Diplomacy in the Information Age." In the *Conference on Virtual Diplomacy*. Washington, DC: U.S. Institute of Peace, April 1, 1997.

Schweller, Randall L., and Xiaoyu Pu. "After Unipolarity: China's Visions of International Order in an Era of US Decline." *International Security* 36, no. 1 (2011): 41–72.

Seib, Philip. *The Al Jazeera Effect: How the New Global Media Are Reshaping World Politics.* Washington, DC: Potomac Books, 2008.

———. *New Media and the New Middle East.* Basingstoke: Palgrave Macmillan, 2007.

———. *Real-Time Diplomacy: Politics and Power in the Social Media Era.* Basingstoke: Palgrave Macmillan, 2012.

———, ed. *Towards a New Public Diplomacy.* Basingstoke: Palgrave, 2009.

———. "Transnational Journalism, Public Diplomacy, and Virtual States." Paper prepared for conference entitled "Journalism in the 21st Century: Between Globalization and National Identity," University of Melbourne, July 16–17, 2009.

Selbin, Eric. *Revolution, Rebellion, Resistance: The Power of Story.* London: Zed Books, 2009.

Sen, Amartya. *Identity and Violence: The Illusion of Destiny.* London: Penguin Books India, 2007.

Shah, Nisha. "Beyond Sovereignty and the State of Nature: Metaphorical Readings of Global Order." In *Metaphors of Globalization*, edited by Markus Kornprobst, Vincent Pouliot, Nisha Shah, and Ruben Zaiotti. Basingstoke: Palgrave Macmillan, 2007.

Sharp, Paul. *Diplomatic Theory of International Relations*. Cambridge: Cambridge University Press, 2009.

———. "Obama, Clinton and the Diplomacy of Change." *The Hague Journal of Diplomacy* 6, no. 3–4 (2011): 393–411.

Shlapentokh, Vladimir. "Perceptions of Foreign Threat to the Regime: From Lenin to Putin." *Communist and Post-Communist Studies* 42, no. 3 (2009): 305–24.

Sikkink, Kathryn. "Beyond the Justice Cascade: How Agentic Constructivism Could Help Explain Change in International Politics." Revised paper from a keynote address, Millennium Annual Conference, October 22, 2011, "Out of the Ivory Tower: Weaving the Theories and Practice of International Relations," London School of Economics, to be presented at the Princeton University IR Colloquium, November 21, 2011.

Simon, Luis. *Geopolitical Change, Grand Strategy and European Security*. Basingstoke: Palgrave Macmillan, 2013.

Simpson, Emile. *War from the Ground Up: Twenty-First-Century Combat as Politics*. London: Hurst, 2012.

Singh, J. P. "The Meta-Power of Interactions: Security and Commerce in Networked Environments." In *The Meta-Power Paradigm: Impacts and Transformation of Agents, Institutions, and Social Systems: Capitalism, State, and Democracy in a Global Context*, edited by Tom R. Burns and Peter M. Hall. New York: Peter Lang, 2012. 469–90.

Skinner, Quentin. *Liberty before Liberalism*. Cambridge: Cambridge University Press, 1998.

Skonieczny, Amy. "Trade Talk: Narratives of US Identity in the Making of Economic Policy." Paper prepared for the Annual Meeting of the American Political Science Association. Toronto, Canada, September 3–6, 2009.

Skuse, Andrew, Marie Gillespie, and Gerry Power, eds. *Drama for Development: Cultural Translation and Social Change*. London: Sage, 2011.

Slaughter, Anne-Marie. "America's Edge-Power in the Networked Century." *Foreign Affairs* 88 (2009): 94.

———. *A New World Order*. Princeton: Princeton University Press, 2005.

Smith, Daniel, W., and Yousif al-Timini. "Iraq TV: Obama in Cairo, Dog Eaten Corpses." *Iraq Slogger*, June 4, 2009. Accessed September 4, 2012, http://iraqslogger .powweb.com/index.php/post/7742?PHPSESSID=86b6121176d9268d5067ebce 23e8a267.

Snyder, Jack. *Myths of Empire: Domestic Politics and International Ambition*. Ithaca, NY: Cornell University Press, 1991.

Sontag, Susan. *Regarding the Pain of Others*. New York: Farrar, Straus and Giroux, 2003.

Steele, Brent J. *Defacing Power: The Aesthetics of Insecurity in Global Politics*. Ann Arbor: University of Michigan Press, 2012.

———. "The Limit(ation)s of International Society?" In *Maritime Piracy and the Construction of Global Governance*, edited by Michael Streutt, Jon D. Carlson, and Mark Nance. Abingdon, UK: Routledge, 2012. 171–191.

Stiegler, Bernard. *For a New Critique of Political Economy*. Cambridge: Polity, 2009.

Strauss, Claudia. "Models and Motives." In *Human Motives and Cultural Models*, edited by Roy G. D'Andrade and Claudia Strauss. Cambridge: Cambridge University Press 1992.

Straw, Jack. "Interview with Foreign Secretary Jack Straw on UK Diplomatic Relations with Iran." UK Foreign and Commonwealth Office, July 4, 2004.

IranWatch.org. Accessed April 5, 2004, http://www.iranwatch.org/government/UK/uk-mfa-strawinterview-070404.htm.

Suganami, Hidemi. "Agents, Structures, Narratives." *European Journal of International Relations* 5, no. 3 (1999): 365–86.

———. "Narratives of War Origins and Endings: A Note on the End of the Cold War." *Millennium* 26 (1997): 631–50.

Tharoor, Shashi. *Pax Indica.* London: Allen Lane, 2012.

Thies, Cameron G. "International Socialization Processes vs. Israeli National Role Conceptions: Can Role Theory Integrate IR Theory and Foreign Policy Analysis?" *Foreign Policy Analysis* 8, no. 1 (2012): 25–46.

———. "Role Theory and Foreign Policy." Working paper, University of Iowa, 2009. *UIowa.edu.* Accessed May 22, 2013, http://myweb.uiowa.edu/bhlai/workshop/role.pdf.

———. "The Roles of Bipolarity: A Role Theoretic Understanding of the Effects of Ideas and Material Factors on the Cold War." *International Studies Perspectives* (2012).

Thompson, Mark. "Delivering Public Value: The BBC and Public Sector Reform." Smith Institute Media Lecture, October 11, 2006. Accessed September 4, 2012, http://www.bbc.co.uk/pressoffice/speeches/stories/thompson_smith.shtml.

Thrift, Nigel. "The Insubstantial Pageant: Producing an Untoward Land." *Cultural Geographies* 19, no. 2 (2012): 141–68.

Tisdall, Simon. "Libya: Reaction: Britain and France Appear Ever More Isolated as World Opinion Turns Hostile: China, Russia, Germany, Brazil Voice Objections NATO Also Divided as Turkey Blocks Agreement." *The Guardian,* March 22, 2011: 6.

Todorov, Tzvetan. *The Poetics of Prose.* Oxford: Blackwell, 1977.

Tomlinson, John. "Global Immediacy." In *Cultural Politics in a Global Age: Uncertainty, Solidarity and Innovation,* edited by David Held and Henrietta L. Moore. Oxford: Oneworld, 2008.

———. *Globalization and Culture.* Chicago: University of Chicago Press, 1999.

Traub, James. "Obama Realism May Not Play Well in Cairo Streets." *New York Times,* May 30, 2009. http://www.nytimes.com/2009/05/31/weekinreview/31traub.html.

Trend. "Iran May Be Willing to Talk on Nuclear Issue, Says EU's Ashton." May 22, 2010. Accessed May 21, 2013, http://en.trend.az/regions/iran/1692278.html.

Turner, Bryan S. "Religious Authority and the New Media." *Theory, Culture & Society* 24, no. 2 (2007): 117–34.

United Nations Security Council. *Resolution 1737,* S/RES/1737, December 23, 2006. Accessed April 4, 2013, http://www.cfr.org/iran/un-security-council-resolution-1737-iran/p12334.

———. "Security Council Demands Iran Suspend Uranium Enrichment by 31 August, or Face Possible Economic Sanctions." SC/8792, 5500th Meeting (AM), July 31, 2006. Accessed May 21, 2013, http://www.un.org/News/Press/docs/2006/sc8792.doc.htm.

———. SC/10200, 6498th Meeting. Accessed September 1, 2011, http://www.un.org/News/Press/docs/2011/sc10200.doc.htm#Resolution.

United States Senate. "A Resolution Strongly Condemning . . . Libya." S.Res.85, 112th Cong. (March 1, 2011). Accessed May 1, 2013, http://thomas.loc.gov/cgi-bin/query/z?c112:S.RES.85.

U.S. Department of State. *The National Security Strategy of the United States of America.* September 2002. Washington, DC: Office of the Executive, 2002. Accessed May 21, 2013, http://www.state.gov/documents/organization/63562.pdf.

———. *The National Security Strategy of the United States of America.* March 2006. Washington, DC: Office of the Executive, 2006. Accessed April 4, 2013, http://www.comw.org/qdr/fulltext/nss2006.pdf.

Van Ham, Peter. *Social Power.* London: Routledge, 2010.

Walker, Stephen G. "Role Theory and Foreign Policy Analysis: An Evaluation." In *Role Theory and Foreign Policy Analysis*, edited by Stephen G. Walker. Durham, NC: Duke University Press. 241–59.

Walt, Stephen M. *Origins of Alliances.* Ithaca, NY: Cornell University Press, 1987.

———. *Taming American Power: The Global Response to U.S. Primacy.* New York: Norton, 2005.

Waltz, Kenneth N. "The Emerging Structure of International Politics." *International Security* 18, no. 2 (1993): 44–79.

———. "Imitations of Multipolarity." In *New World Order: Contrasting Theories*, edited by Birthe Hansen and Bertel Heurlin. Basingstoke: Palgrave, 2000.

———. *Theory of International Politics.* Reading, MA: Addison-Wesley, 1979.

———. "Why Iran Should Get the Bomb: Nuclear Balancing Would Mean Stability." *Foreign Affairs* 91 (2012): 2.

Weber, Cynthia. "Popular Visual Language as Global Communication: The Remediation of United Airlines Flight 93." *Review of International Studies* 34, no. 1 (2008): 137–53.

Weber, Steven, and Bruce W. Jentleson. *The End of Arrogance: America in the Global Competition of Ideas.* Cambridge: Harvard University Press, 2010.

"The Welcome Return of French Diplomacy." *Economist*, March 20, 2011. Accessed September 1, 2011, http://www.economist.com/blogs/newsbook/2011/03/frances_role_libya.

Weldes, Jutta. "Constructing National Interests." *European Journal of International Relations* 2, no. 3 (1996): 275–318.

———. *Constructing National Interests.* Minneapolis, MN: University of Minnesota Press, 1999.

Wendt, Alexander. "Identity and Structural Change in International Politics." In *The Return of Culture and Identity in IR Theory*, edited by Yosef Lapid and Friedrich Kratochwil. Boulder, CO: Lynne Rienner, 1996. 47–64.

———. *Social Theory of International Politics.* Cambridge: Cambridge University Press, 1999.

Wibben, Annick. *Feminist Security Studies: A Narrative Approach.* London: Routledge, 2011.

Williams, Michael J. "(Un)Sustainable Peacebuilding: NATO's Suitability for Post-conflict Reconstruction in Multiactor Environments." *Global Governance: A Review of Multilateralism and International Organizations* 17, no. 1 (2011): 115–34.

Williams, Michael C. "What Is the national interest? The Neoconservative Challenge in IR Theory." *European Journal of International Relations* 11, no. 3 (2005): 307–37.

———. "Words, Images, Enemies: Securitization and International Politics." *International Studies Quarterly* 47, no. 4 (2003): 511–31.

Wittgenstein, Ludwig. *Philosophical Investigations.* Oxford: Blackwell, 2001.

Wittig, Peter. "Explanation of Vote by Ambassador Wittig on the Security Council Resolution on Libya," March 17, 2011, New York. Accessed September 1, 2011, http://www.new-york-un.diplo.de/Vertretung/newyorkvn/en/__pr/Speeches/PM__2011/20110317_20Explanation_20of_20vote_20-_20Libya.html?archive=2984642.

Wohlforth, William C. "The Stability of a Unipolar World." *International Security* 24, no. 1 (1999): 5–41.

Wolfers, Arnold. *Discord and Collaboration: Essays on International Politics.* Baltimore: Johns Hopkins University Press, 1962.

Wolfsfeld, Gadi. *Media and the Path to Peace.* Cambridge: Cambridge University Press, 2004.

Woodley, Daniel. 2013. "Radical Right Discourse Contra State-Based Authoritarian Populism: Neoliberalism, Identity and Exclusion after the Crisis." In *Analysing Fascist Discourse: European Fascism in Talk and Text*, edited by Ruth Wodak and John E. Richardson. New York: Routledge, 2013. 17–41.

Wu, Tim. *The Master Switch: The Rise and Fall of Information Empires*. London: Atlantic Books, 2010.

Yang, Aimei, Anna Klyueva, and Maureen Taylor. "Beyond a Dyadic Approach to Public Diplomacy: Understanding Relationships in a Multipolar World." *Public Relations Review* 38, no. 5 (2012): 652–64.

Zakaria, Fareed. *The Post-American World*. New York: Norton, 2008.

Zarakol, Ayşe. "Ontological (In)Security and State Denial of Historical Crimes: Turkey and Japan." *International Relations* 24, no. 1 (2010): 3–23.

———. *After Defeat: How the East Learned to Live with the West*. Vol. 118. Cambridge: Cambridge University Press, 2010.

Zehfuss, Maja. *Constructivism in International Relations: The Politics of Reality*. Vol. 83. Cambridge: Cambridge University Press, 2002.

Author Index

Michalski, Milena, 22
Miller, Derek B., 7
Miller, Peter, 150
Ministry of Defence, 4, 128
Minow, Martha, 118
Miskimmon, Alister, 4, 7, 8, 18, 72–3,
    77, 81, 170, 179, 181
Mitchell, William John Thomas, 22,
    112
Mitzen, Jennifer, 117–18
Moen, Daryl R., 110
Mor, Ben D., 104, 119–26
Morgenthau, Hans Joachim, 3, 5, 13,
    62–3
Morozov, Evgeny, 108
Mykleby, Mark, 2, 72, 128

National Security Act 1947, 58–9
Nayak, Meghana, 63
Negroponte, Nicholas, 185
Nelson, Michael, 119
Nelson, Thomas E., 7
Nettelfield, Lara, 118–19
Newey, Glen, 17
Nitze, Paul, 66, 109
Norris, Christopher, 17
Norris, Pippa, 157
Nye, Joseph S., 3, 9, 13, 63–4, 89, 101,
    117

O'Loughlin, Ben, 4, 6, 8, 18, 22, 40–3,
    50–1, 62, 120, 125, 135, 151–3,
    155–64, 170, 185
Oates, Sarah, xii, 36
Obama, Barack, 20, 31, 47, 50–3,
    79–89, 113, 135–9, 149, 151,
    157–64, 178, 186
Office of the Director of National
    Intelligence, 131
Oliver, Michael, 137
Olsen, Johan P. 32
Orford, Anne. 73, 178
Organski, Abramo F. K. 1, 60, 64, 66
ÓTuathail, Gearóid. 20
Owen, John M., IV., 1, 68
Oxley, Zoe M., 7

Pamment, James, 4
Panke, Diana, 103
Papacharissi, Zizi, 185
Pape, Robert A., 64
Parasiliti, Andrew, 131, 137
Paterson, William E., 38
Paul, Thazha V., 64

Perlmutter, David, 7
Petersen, Thomas, 7
Petersohn, Ulrich, 103
Peterson, John. 131
Pew Research Center, 84
Pfau, Michael, 7
Porter, Wayne, 2, 72, 128
Posen, Barry R., 64
Postman, Neil, 11
Power, Gerry, 166
Press, Daryl G., 36
Price, Monroe E., 6, 11, 62, 69, 116,
    141, 166
Pu, Xiaoyu, 69
Putnam, Robert D., 8, 61, 153

Radaelli, Claudio M., 114
Ramo, Joshua Cooper, 72
Ranly, Don, 110
Rengger, Nicholas J., 60
Ribes, David, 150
Rice, Susan, 80
Richards, Barry, 112
Ringmar, Erik, 21
Ringsmose, J., 3, 102, 106, 113
Risse, Thomas, 9, 32, 106, 109
Roberts, Geoffrey, 5, 63
Rogin, Josh, 73
Rose, Nikolas, 150
Roselle, Laura, 8, 18, 36–7, 114, 170,
    179, 182
Rosenau, James N., 151
Ross, Andrew L., 64
Rotberg, Robert I., 39–40
Rousseau, David L., 31
Rumelt, Richard, 13
Runciman, David, 62
Russett, Bruce, 36
Ruston, Scott W., 3
Rutigliano, Lou, 157
Ryan, Marie-Laure, 12

Sachsenmaier, Dominic, 68
Sarkozy, Nicolas, 73–5, 84–8
Schimmelfennig, Frank, 7, 10, 134
Schild, Joachim, 38
Schmidt, Vivien A., 114
Schudson, Michael, 34
Schultz, George P., 154, 156, 164, 166
Schweller, Randall L., 69
Seib, Philip, xii, 6, 10–11, 47, 62, 72,
    125
Segerberg, Alexandra, 185
Selbin, Eric, 63

Subject Index

PGMO 06/21/2018